Local Journalism in a Digital World

Journalism

Series Editors: **Sarah Niblock**, Professor and Head of Journalism, Brunel University, UK

Rosalind Coward, Professor of Journalism, University of Roehampton, UK

This series provides journalists, academics and students with a unique practical and critical guide to key areas of contemporary journalism practice for the digital age. Each volume offers a local and global perspective, with digital aspects considered throughout. The first series to really synthesise theory with practice, these books will both demonstrate how real-world journalists navigate and accommodate everyday demands, challenges and opportunities in the industry and teach us how to reflect on this.

Published titles:

Rosalind Coward
SPEAKING PERSONALLY

Murray Dick
SEARCH: THEORY AND PRACTICE IN ONLINE JOURNALISM

Kristy Hess and Lisa Waller
LOCAL JOURNALISM IN A DIGITAL WORLD

David Machin and Lydia Polzer
VISUAL JOURNALSIM

James Rodgers
REPORTING CONFLICT

Local Journalism in a Digital World

Kristy Hess
Senior Lecturer in Communication, Deakin University, Australia

and

Lisa Waller
Senior Lecturer in Communication, Deakin University, Australia

First published 2017 by
PALGRAVE

Palgrave in the UK is an imprint of Macmillan Publishers Limited, registered in England, company number 785998, of 4 Crinan Street, London, N1 9XW.

Palgrave Macmillan in the US is a division of St Martin's Press LLC, 175 Fifth Avenue, New York, NY 10010.

Palgrave is a global imprint of the above companies and is represented throughout the world.

Palgrave® and Macmillan® are registered trademarks in the United States, the United Kingdom, Europe and other countries.

ISBN 978–1–137–50477–7 hardback
ISBN 978–1–137–50476–0 paperback

This book is printed on paper suitable for recycling and made from fully managed and sustained forest sources. Logging, pulping and manufacturing processes are expected to conform to the environmental regulations of the country of origin.

A catalogue record for this book is available from the British Library.

A catalog record for this book is available from the Library of Congress.

Contents

Preface   vi

Acknowledgements   vii

Introduction   1
1 Understanding Local Journalism   12
2 Defining the Local in a 'Geo-social' Context   36
3 Local Media Around the World   59
4 Shaping 'Local' News   84
5 Connectors, Champions and Advocates   111
6 Changing Journalistic Practices   135
7 Subsidize or Commercialize? The Economics
   of Local Journalism   162
Conclusion   188

Endnotes   194

References   195

Index   226

Preface

Journalism and media is undergoing a rapid period of change across the globe. But amidst all of this, one thing stays relatively constant. We base ourselves somewhere in the world, for family, work or social reasons. We develop affinities with some places where we come to consider ourselves 'local', part of a 'community' or feel a 'sense of place'. Sometimes we don't get a choice about where we live or where we travel. Regardless, information about our 'place' in the world is important for us to navigate our day-to-day lives or to fulfil a basic desire to belong somewhere and be connected to others.

As media researchers we have worked as local journalists and experienced the contrasts between a big city metropolitan daily and life in a small newsroom. While the basic principles of journalism don't change from one news environment to another, there can be different news cultures.

In this book we carve out a theoretical and practical space for the local media sector in the digital era. So much attention is often devoted to 'big media' that journalists at the grassroots level should aspire to. But in this topsy-turvy world, we argue that all levels of journalism can learn much from changes occurring in local media and from the practices that make it unique.

Acknowledgements

This book emerged from our simple yet steadfast belief that in a global world, local journalism matters. We would like to thank Lloyd Langman and Nicola Cattini at Palgrave Macmillan for their enthusiasm and guidance from start to finish. We are grateful to Bob Franklin for his encouragement and support; and to Kerry McCallum, Ian Richards and Kathryn Bowd who have contributed so much to our thinking. Our appreciation goes to the reviewers who gave their time to offer feedback and suggestions to ensure the book is interesting and relevant to academics, students and industry practitioners throughout the world.

We are indebted to British media scholar Nick Couldry for his work around media power and practice theory. Our appreciation to Andy Williams and Dave Harte for helpful conversations about hyperlocal news. American academics whose scholarly contributions have influenced our own include Barbie Zelizer, Sue Robinson, Ted Gutsche, Avery Holton, Seth Lewis, John Hatcher, Bill Reader, Jack Rosenberry and Penny Abernathy. In Australia, Michael Meadows, Susan Forde, Jacqui Ewart, Kerry Foxwell-Norton and Brett Hutchins have also influenced our approach to studying journalism and of thinking through the importance of community media and information flows at the local level. To the Edward Wilson Trust, we are thankful for your constant involvement and philanthropic support of local journalism education and research in Australia. It has helped us undertake an extensive literature review of local media throughout the world, with the kind assistance of Monica Andrew.

We are indebted to our wonderful partners, families and friends for their love and cheer, and importantly for their patience.

And finally, we are grateful the universe aligned at the very start of our academic careers. We have worked closely right from the beginning, sharing strength, encouragement, wisdom and friendship in a challenging and exciting academic world. Our journey is only just beginning.

This book is derived, in part, from the following articles published in academic journals and books and extended in this manuscript:

Hess, K. 2013, 'Breaking boundaries: Recasting the small newspaper as geo-social news', *Digital Journalism*, vol. 1, no. 1, pp. 45–60.

Hess, K. 2013, 'Tertius tactics: Mediated social capital as a resource of power for traditional news media', *Communication Theory*, vol. 23, no. 2, pp. 112–130.

Hess, K. & Waller, L. 2014, 'Geo-social journalism: Reorienting the study of small commercial newspapers in a digital environment', *Journalism Practice*, vol. 8, no. 2, pp. 121–136.

Hess, K. & Waller, L. 2014, 'River flows and profit flows: The powerful logic driving local news', *Journalism Studies*. doi: 10.1080/1461670X.2014.981099.

Hess, K. 2015, 'Ritual power: Illuminating the births, deaths and marriages column in news media research', *Journalism: Theory, Practice Criticism*. doi: 10.1177/1464884915570419.

Hess K. & Waller, L. 2016, 'Hyperlocal and community media: A sustainable model', in S. Eldridge and B. Franklin (eds) *Routledge companion to digital journalism studies*, Routledge, London.

Introduction

Being 'connected' is more than a digital phenomenon – it's an age-old and deeply human compulsion. For centuries before the Internet was dreamed about, local news in all its forms – from town crier to newspaper, radio and TV bulletin – played a leading role in satisfying people's need to know and connecting them with other people and social institutions. Action and drama, controversy and revelation, business and pleasure, history and human interest have always been part of the mix. Local news has also been an important sphere of influence as a forum for discussion and debate on matters of public interest and as a check on powerful players in politics, commerce, public life – even the criminal underworld. News outlets have made fortunes from their two key roles in the local marketplace. Firstly, they had a cheap, mass-produced and popular product to sell. Secondly, they provided a valuable service for anyone wanting to make something known – from a birth, marriage or death to available work, a tender for public works or an upcoming concert. For more than 100 years, local news outlets generated 'rivers of gold' and built powerful empires from people's need to buy, sell, announce and find out.

Despite its importance and power in society, local news has mostly been taken for granted – like so many of the major institutions, products and relationships that form the fabric of society. Its existence and its future used to be unquestionable. The local newspaper in particular stood alongside the bank and the post office, housed in prominent buildings on the main streets of cities and towns throughout the world. The local newspaper building was usually a solid edifice in the centre of town – reliable and imposing. A busy place with a public face that trained and employed locals in a range of roles – from advertising sales representative to accounts clerk, reporter or printer. Newspaper premises reflected local news institutions' important position and spoke of their histories. Then the digital revolution came along, rewrote the street map and even put it online. Just like the bank and the post office, local news media have had to renegotiate their position on the high street – in every sense. In the process, local journalism has become more noticeable and arguably more interesting and important to a range of people, including many journalists and journalism scholars who hardly used to acknowledge it, or if they did tended to dismiss it as national and international news's poor relation. It is increasingly recognized for its diversity and its resilience, its value has become more obvious and interesting, and it is being credited as a powerful site for examining the evolution of news more generally.

Changing journalism in a changing world

Local journalism faces many of the same challenges encountered by national and international journalism. It continues to evolve as part of wider structural transformation (still taking shape) of the news media more broadly, which is led by digital change but also other factors. These include the ways people access news, and its relationship to advertising and to sources of news. Chapter 3 provides an overview of local journalism around the world, which illustrates that change has not had the same consequences everywhere. It varies from country to country, place to place and media outlet to media outlet. The change may take different forms but it is profound, and clear trends can be detected across liberal democracies where print is in decline and broadcast news has been transformed by on-demand, multi-channel TV. Digital media more broadly have revolutionized the ways people communicate with one another and access and share information, which has disrupted the traditional business model and triggered a 'crisis' about the future of journalism.

Most of the academic enquiry about the structural transformation of news has been tightly focused at the national and international levels. Notably, there has been relatively little work on conceptualizing local journalism's place in a networked society, or how understanding the 'community ties' thesis that has historically underpinned most scholarship on local news could help 'big' news media to maintain its relevance to society. This is surprising, as despite the media maelstrom, citizens' need for news and information about the people and events in their immediate orbit has remained relatively stable. Enterprising individuals and groups have identified niche opportunities for 'hyperlocal' journalism outlets in places where commercial operations have left town, or now fail to meet news needs. Often aligned with online news start-ups, hyperlocals are devoted to the stories and minutiae of a particular neighbourhood, ZIP code or interest group within a certain geographic area (Picone, 2007, p. 102). These publications have attracted attention within industry and academic circles in recent times, with questions from whether hyperlocal sites can offer a sustainable business model for local journalism and fulfil its public accountability role through to identifying the new skill set required and whether government funding should be part of the mix. At a conceptual level, the hyperlocal turn goes to the very essence of how everyday people, journalism scholars and practitioners understand and position themselves in the social world. It challenges understandings of what journalism and news is and how it should be presented, and reminds us of the dangers in massification of small-time news. Hyperlocal news is sometimes hyped as something new, but arguably much of its appeal and relevance lie in the ways it taps a deep and old news culture.

Understanding 'community ties'

Local news media is identified in much literature as reinforcing our connection to place and to others. Scholarship that examines local news has celebrated its place in facilitating community integration and civic involvement – from thinkers like de Tocqueville to John Dewey and Robert Park (Zelizer & Allan, 2010, p. 70). Park's writings signalled a shift in urban sociology that continues to inspire scholars of local media today. He was aligned with the Chicago School's urban ethnography movement of the 1920s, which placed particular emphasis on the study of marginalized groups. His main interest was the role of the ethnic press in establishing various causes and the sense of intellectual and social liberation that immigrants gained from reading newspapers in their own languages (see, e.g., Park, 1922).

Park's successor, University of Chicago sociologist Morris Janowitz (1967), used content analysis and survey research to explore community integration. Janowitz viewed local newspaper readership as a contributing factor to the integration of people in a community. He argued, 'the community newspaper's emphasis on community routines, low controversy and social ritual are the very characteristics that account for its readership' (Janowitz, 1967, p. 130). Local media scholar Jack Rosenberry (2014) has highlighted that in the United States, one of the deepest parts of research about local journalism extends from the community ties hypothesis that began with Janowitz to include the work of Keith Stamm. These scholars were noteworthy in explaining how local news media could influence the way individuals connected with their communities and could serve as agents for community building. Stamm (1988) suggested that the various kinds of community ties could be distinguished in terms of what the individual is tied to (community as place, process or structure) and the nature of the tie (spatial, cognitive, affective). Stamm encouraged researchers to distinguish and establish the temporal order of relationships between community ties and media use. To do this, he urged scholars to follow new residents to communities, observing the order in which key community ties are constructed in relation to the points at which they begin to attend to local news and information. He contended:

> If there is to be a community, the individual cannot just take; each individual must give something. Such interdependence also applies to newspapers and other 'local' media. Local media benefit when the interdependence of individual and community is strong. But they cannot take such interdependence for granted. They must contribute something to it. (Stamm, 1988, p. 357)

In today's scholarship, news providers that serve small towns and cities are often referred to as 'local' or 'community' media. However, many news outlets have become 'local' in name only (Franklin, 2006), weakening the interdependence Stamm advocated. They have been centralized, amalgamated and the news they offer is produced in far-flung regions. For example, at some Australian regional newspapers, the volume of content produced in the local newsroom has declined significantly. Much of it is now sourced from other mastheads in the same company stable, or produced by their operations in New Zealand, The Philippines and India. Despite this, small news outlets continue to perpetuate the belief that they are 'local' even though about the only local thing about many of them is the place name in the newspaper masthead, and on radio and television the use of the phrase 'local news update'. Chapters 4 and 7 explore how weakening genuine community ties can undermine what it means to be 'local', and why this can have damaging consequences for news outlets' legitimacy and relationships with the societies they serve, and which in turn sustain them.

The world of local news

Some of the key questions for those with an interest in local news concern how the meaning of 'local' might have shifted in a globalized and networked media society, and what opportunities and challenges this could present for journalists, traditional news organizations and hyperlocal start-ups. The chapters that follow critically engage with these themes, and tackle some taken-for-granted terms and concepts, such as 'community', to generate fresh perspectives that can inform both practice and theory.

Local journalism can be understood broadly as both a practice and a product that relates to a specific geographic area and the events and people connected to it. It is a global phenomenon with myriad long and proud histories. It is as important to people living in big cities as it is to those in regional and remote locations. It not only reports on the people of the region and parochial happenings such as council meetings, crimes and festivals; it also interprets national and international events and issues from a local angle. Much 'local' news takes digital forms and can be accessed from anywhere with an Internet connection. 'Local news media' refers to media organizations and outlets that serve people and institutions that have interests in the distinct geographic zone, from audiences to advertisers, public authorities and businesses.

As mentioned previously, it is important to be awake to the truth that in many parts of the world such news media are increasingly 'local' in name only. This is just one of the problems with a broad definition of 'local news'. A generic definition can also disguise the fact that throughout the world journalism is produced, circulated and consumed in culturally specific ways. In the US, Europe and Australia most local news outlets are commercially owned and operated. In China and Vietnam the state controls most media production. In the South Pacific, churches are major players. In African countries community radio is a major source of local news; in the US there are more than 8000 local newspapers. How local news industries are organized and regulated, and the ways they address audiences, cannot be explained simply by the combination of today's technology and the current state of the economy or national political system. The cultural context is paramount. History and geography are also central, both when comparing countries and in understanding how news media within a country position themselves in relation to one another. Understanding the similarities and differences between news systems throughout the world is important; especially as specific physical and social contexts give local news everywhere its distinctive flavours.

Some of the factors that make the study of local journalism so interesting and important include the diversity of news styles and agendas found from place to place, as well as between media forms; and the small media's resilience and ability to maintain traditions in the face of momentous change and disruption, as well as its capacity to experiment and transform. The complex social roles and exercise of media power at the local level have been under-theorized, but can generate rich insights into journalism and society more broadly.

Putting local journalism on the conceptual map

Journalism scholars have contributed much to the critical understanding of key concepts including 'public', 'truth' and 'objectivity'. 'Local' and related ideas such as 'sense of place' and 'community' have not been given the same status or attention, despite their importance to understanding the largest sector of news throughout the world. These taken-for-granted concepts in journalism studies deserve to be properly unpacked to determine their power and limitations, and what theoretical insights can offer to the future of news.

One of the key contentions in the chapters that follow is that place still matters in a digital world. However, in discussions about local news media, place must always be considered in the context of its relationship to wider social space and global information systems. Local journalists of the 21st century must not only specialize in 'place-based' news. They need a clear understanding of how their locality and its people fit in the context of a globalized world because local news outlets not only report the happenings within a discrete geographic area. They also interpret national and international affairs and how these shape economic, political, social and cultural aspects of daily life in local communities. Furthermore, local journalists are increasingly working for news organizations with a global reach. Even bloggers who produce local news rely on search engines such as Google to reach audiences.

We introduce the concept of 'geo-social' news (Hess, 2013a) in Chapter 2 as a way of interpreting a local news outlet's solid link to geographic territory, while acknowledging the wider social space in which it plays a role – both in holding an influential position in certain social flows and movements, and as a node to wider global news media and communication networks.

Rethinking community and the local

'Local' is a concept that connects geography and place with a sense of belonging. To be considered a 'local' implies that our feet are planted firmly on the ground somewhere and that our physical surroundings are deeply and comfortably familiar. We invest in a locality – socially, economically, culturally and psychologically. It is where we feel most like 'a fish in water'. But to be 'local' takes time to develop. It can also be heavily guarded, and this is when binaries sometimes emerge – divisions and tensions that can polarize outsiders and insiders. Concepts related to 'local' such as 'sense of place' and 'community' are often used in scholarship about journalism and allude to similar feelings, but they are much more fluid terms that are not inherently tied to the importance of us 'being' in a place. Sense of place, for example, often implies a deep connection to a physical space – a room in a house, a street, a scenic lookout, but we do not necessarily have to have our feet constantly or firmly planted there. We might also share such sensibilities about more than one place as society becomes increasingly transient.

The notion of 'community' stretches beyond physical territory. It is used to refer to any group of people who congregate around a shared interest or activity, such as communities of Internet users, communities of scholars, communities of vintage car owners. In contrast, local is inherently tied to a place and requires us to be there, or have a symbolic presence in one way or another. When people are torn from their homes, or leave to take up opportunities, negotiating new surroundings and developing a sense of belonging are real challenges. Robert Park's observations almost a century ago remain relevant today: local journalism can still play a key role in assisting newcomers by providing windows on their new domain and offering ways to connect with people and organizations; making their presence known and understood, and also providing opportunities for their voices to be heard. However, there has also been a major change since Park's time: online news outlets make it possible to remain connected to the people and happenings of the 'local' place that has been left behind physically – but not socially.

'Local' and 'community' can be multi-layered. Within a large city, people may further identify themselves by suburb or even neighbourhood (geography), as well as by cultural groups. For example, in Sydney, Australia, people who live in the large municipality of Sutherland, south of the city centre, describe themselves proudly, and are widely recognized, as from 'The Shire'. The dominant demographics and lifestyles associated with this particular local area, centred on its beaches and waterways, have been documented and celebrated in Australian popular culture – from the novel made into a film and television series, *Puberty Blues*, to the reality television series *Sylvania Waters* and *The Shire*. However, The Shire is also a good example of how a strong sense of belonging can create social tensions and 'outsiders', and the local news media's role in this. In the summer of 2005 there was mass racist violence against 'young men of Middle Eastern appearance' on Cronulla

Beach in The Shire. The 'local' antagonists resented the presence of people from a different cultural background, whom they perceived as belonging elsewhere. They resorted to physical attacks in their attempts to expel 'foreigners' from the beach. An inquiry found local Sydney news media played a key role in fanning the conflict (Poynting, 2006).

The smaller the village the more people appear likely to be united through kinship and reciprocity. But in today's world, towns and cities – no matter how small – are part of a globally networked world and feature increasingly transient populations. To describe geographic spaces simply as 'communities' can mislead us into thinking their inhabitants exist together harmoniously for the sake of the collective, and overlooks issues of equality, social class and power.

Democracy and advocacy

Democracy demands that citizens have access to good quality information on which to deliberate and an arena for public discussion to take place. Journalism is not only understood to enable democracy but is also an essential part of it because it *is* the democratic forum for ideas and community debate.

Chapter 1 provides an extended discussion of journalism and democratic theory, so we will not wade into a long discussion of these ideas here. However, there are two points worth making at the outset. The first is that democracy begins at the local level; the second is that in order to deliberate on local issues, citizens require a local public sphere for which local news media are essential. There is much concern that the democratic role of local news is in jeopardy due to the collapse of the advertising business that underwrote accountability journalism. While the emergence of 'news gaps' poses risks, it has also inspired bold new experiments in the funding, creation and delivery of local news. These are discussed in Chapter 7.

Global and national issues are experienced in the local context as well as truly parochial matters such as local government. National policies relating to health, education, housing, immigration, subsidies to agriculture and other industries, and so forth, have real impacts on localities and their residents, who judge the effects of wider policy on local terms and demand space for informed political debate at the community level. Furthermore, many of the voluntary groupings that are central to grassroots democracy are organized on a geographic basis. Take the example of the Country Women's Association of Australia. This national organization, which was formed in 1922, aims to improve social conditions for women and children and make life better for families, especially those living in rural and remote Australia. As the largest women's organization in Australia with more than 1200 branches around the country, it is a powerful lobby. The state chapter in New South Wales has 10,500 members who belong to more than 400 local branches. They campaign on a range of national, state and local issues, such as having 'khaki weed' declared a noxious weed in a specific agricultural area.

Of course there are the more transient groups that often form around locally based issues, especially aspects of the environment, such as saying 'No' to a nuclear dump or to an airport being built. Others form in response to the local impact of global shifts, such as communities welcoming or fearing refugees. The importance of local journalism to grassroots democracy, both as a source of reliable information and a forum for discussion, is relatively uncontroversial and is touched upon throughout the book. However, Chapter 4 moves into different territory. It explores one dimension of local journalism's role in public life that often jars with 'big' journalism's view of the field, where the boundaries are fenced by the ideological force field of 'objectivity'. The key difference is that local journalists and news providers, and especially small newspapers in the United States, have a strong tradition of serving as champions and campaigners for the towns, cities and regions they serve. Advocacy journalism can be understood as a news outlet's ability to campaign or advocate on behalf of a perceived collective on matters of public interest. Chapter 4 draws on examples from a number of countries where local media have successfully campaigned for things such as new hospital equipment, disability services, improvements to roads and schools, and environmental programmes. Mainstream local media outlets have the power to represent community sentiment, which policymakers and other powerful groups understand as public opinion because of their wide reach with mainstream audiences. This power to connect local news audiences with dominant players in society means the practice of advocacy journalism can be understood as a form of power available to established local media organizations, which benefits them at the same time as the interests they serve.

Changing views of local news

In outlining the reasons why small media deserves our attention, Nielsen argues the study of local media is not all that 'sexy' (Nielsen, 2015). In fact, it has been given short shrift in journalism studies until recently. The rise of the 'professional journalist' at the turn of the 20th century rested on the concepts of 'objectivity', 'editorial autonomy' and the 'watchdog' role of the press. This ran counter to local journalism's intimate relationship with community, advocating on its behalf, and the owner-operator model where journalists write news and run the business at the same time. The study of national and international journalism, its values and relationship to political elites became the overwhelming concern. Robert Park's research on community integration was taking place about the same time that the rise of the professional journalist began to dominate 20th-century understandings of journalism. The community ties thesis didn't fit entirely with the Fourth Estate function or social responsibility model of the press. The 'purity' of journalism was paramount and had to be protected from the business end of the game – advertising became a 'dirty word'. Now many local and hyperlocal news ventures have no option but to face the reality of their situation – they need to make money to survive and as small enterprises they must not only write the news, they must sell the news.

New business, social and technological environments for local journalism have demanded significant changes in the everyday practices of news in the past decade or so, just as they have everywhere. However, the news values and routines that determine agendas at the local level have always had a slightly different emphasis. Chapter 5 outlines how local media practices differ from 'big city' journalism, with an accent on the local journalist having to develop expertise on all aspects of the region, rather than specific news beats. It will also discuss the ethical dilemmas that local journalists encounter in their day-to-day practice. These include questions related to the balancing act between the journalist's allegiances as a citizen and their professional responsibilities: how do you face your neighbours when you've written a court story about their daughter? How does an editor deal with being a highly visible member of the community?

Embracing change

Journalists are positioned in society as the people best placed to provide the news, yet the very essence of what a journalist is and does is being challenged in the changing media landscape. The business model that once sustained traditional journalism has broken down as media become increasingly enmeshed in a complex web of global information flows. News providers are working frantically to detangle themselves and find their 'place' in the new media world. This book argues that the key to fresh understandings of journalism and its relationship to society can be found at the local level because it is here that the relationships between journalists and the people and places they report upon and to is arguably closest.

The norms and values that shape our understanding of local news are not set in concrete – they respond, expand and adapt to change. For much of the 20th century political, economic, social and technological contexts were reflected by ideas related to objectivity, political economy, sociology, the pursuit of truth and professionalism. The social world has shifted on its axis, and journalism finds itself on new ground. Now anyone can publish an opinion online, and that opinion can be accessed throughout the world. 'Sharing' is the new economic buzzword and people no longer have to be media professionals to publish stories and images. Methods of gathering, circulating and consuming news have been transformed, and scholars are taking fresh approaches to conceptualizing the roles and practices of digital journalism. The local level is an exciting space for considering the key questions arising about contemporary journalism more broadly because it offers a close-up view – from a different angle.

Some of the new ways of doing journalism and understanding the challenges and opportunities in the 21st century relate to the ideas discussed in this chapter and encountered throughout the book. These include 'community', 'power', 'culture', the business and sustainability of journalism, and rethinking the question of what is news to local audiences.

To serve as a clear signpost directing people to information they might need or want about a specific place presents immense advantages in this media abundant world. It also generates and reinforces issues of power. But local journalism must distinguish itself in this crowded and competitive space, and both practitioners and scholars need to understand its importance to people at every level of society.

1 Understanding Local Journalism

Introduction

Scholars often talk about the value of applying a particular theoretical 'lens' to a research problem because theories provide different ways of looking at and interpreting the world. Theories can be used to generate a range of perspectives on the same issue or social phenomenon, cast them in particular lights and stimulate different arguments, findings and conclusions. Just like the array of camera lenses, wide-angled, telephoto, zoom, macro and so forth, certain theories will suit or equip the enquirer best. A theory might be used because it aligns with the researcher or journalist's own worldview, or because it is the best tool for working on a specific problem or assignment. For example, a journalist who reports on local government might look to democratic theories about the role of the journalist to understand and justify their 'watchdog' role and adversarial interviewing style. Reporters may also find convergence theory helpful for thinking about the way both news producers and audiences influence the way new technologies are used in the co-creation of local content.

Theories reflect different philosophical traditions and concerns about society, so it is important to locate the major concepts related to local journalism and introduce the *media power lens* used throughout this book. This approach draws on democratic, sociological and cultural theories that are helpful for tackling the big questions about local journalism, from its roles in politics, community formation and social change to its various relationships with audiences and how questions of power, place, labour and technology link the local with the world. Viewing local journalism through a lens of media power offers ways of seeing how it serves the best interests of society, and the factors and circumstances under which its considerable influence can also be misdirected. Furthermore, rather than seeing political economy, with its accent on the production of journalism, in conflict with cultural approaches that emphasize the role of the audience, both are understood as part of a necessary and helpful continuum. French sociologist Pierre Bourdieu's tradition of field-based research straddles the divide between political economy and cultural theories. It provides a useful set of concepts for exploring questions of media power as well as the practice of local journalism.

A media power approach can be used to interrogate the relationship between local journalism and digital technologies and the complex power struggles across print and online spaces over the production and circulation of local news, and allow marginalized people's battle to be 'heard' in public debate. While it is crucial to consider business models that help to sustain local journalism, the needs and wants of local audiences and what they do with 'news' are paramount. A media power perspective provides scope to consider how local journalists obtain legitimacy among audiences, play a role in establishing a sense of place and community, hold powerful institutions to account, filter the news and advocate on behalf of their audiences.

The sections that follow explore democratic theories and the Fourth Estate notion of the press, which has become almost axiomatic in discussions of news, public debate and politics. This theory and the debates attached to it are highly relevant in discussions of local media's importance in political participation.

Many of the other concepts introduced here relate to journalism's changing relationship with audiences. Different understandings of 'convergence' and distinguishing between multiplatform journalism practice and the theory can explain the ways in which new technologies not only bring different mediums together but also shape relationships between media audiences, media owners, producers and content. They can also provide a framework for understanding journalism history and changing practices, as well as the emergence of new business models.

Democratic theory

Sociological theory offers numerous pointers to the desirable, as well as the less desirable, roles that journalism can and does play in social life (Zelizer, 2004). Among the most important of these is democratic theory, which acknowledges a close relationship between politics, public life and journalism in liberal democracies. Journalism's democratic roles are often treated as 'normative' concepts because they are concerned with what journalism ought to be doing, rather than what it actually does, which leaves these ideas open to criticism for failing to live up to democratic ideals. At the root of these debates lies a fundamental tension between conceptualizations of journalism as a neutral mediator and as an active participant in public affairs (see e.g. Christians et al., 2009). This section outlines the various streams of democratic theory that relate to local journalism, including the Fourth Estate function of the press, social responsibility model, deliberative democracy, participatory democracy and the radical democratic function of the press.

Journalism as the Fourth Estate

Libertarian theory positions the press as a marketplace of ideas, pursuing profits in a process believed to support democracy (Siebert et al., 1956). Government is seen as the primary, if not the only, threat to press freedom from this perspective. An outgrowth of libertarianism is the 'Fourth Estate' ideal of journalism, which is intertwined with the idea of freedom of the press (Weiss, 2009). It is also commonly referred to as the 'watchdog' role and involves critical scrutiny of the powerful, including government, business and other influential spheres of society.

The term 'Fourth Estate' was attributed to Edmund Burke by the 18th-century public intellectual Thomas Carlyle, who used it in 1841 to refer to reporters in the British House of Commons (McQuail, 2003). It has often been used to characterize the position of the press in the process of government as a source of power equivalent to that of the other branches, especially the judiciary and the upper and lower houses of parliaments. The essential elements of the Fourth Estate concept are autonomy from governments and politicians and a duty to the truth, whatever the consequences, as well as a primary obligation to the public and media audiences (McQuail, 2003). In this theory, the power of the press is understood to reside in its capacity to express and influence public opinion and to keep a watchful eye on governments.

The social responsibility model

The social responsibility model of the press has been one of the more influential contributions to contemporary normative theories of journalism (Hutchins, 1947; see also Weiss, 2009). It places less emphasis on news profits and much more on the need for balanced information where the reporter continues to serve as 'watchdog' and the norm of objectivity is paramount. The concept was first sponsored by Robert Maynard Hutchins (1947), the chairman of a committee that wrote a report advancing the view that the press must make a contribution to the maintenance and development of a free society (see Carper, 1997). It is worth noting that the Hutchins Commission model was proposed by academics and cultural elites, and that none of the Commission's members were journalists. The report was widely criticized by professional journalists and sections of the public who remained suspicious about the motivations and objectives of the press. These critics argued the news media was too powerful. They pointed to its monopolistic tendencies and accused corporate owners of self-interest. Commercialization of the news was also criticized for debasing culture (Pickard, 2015).

Deliberative democracy

Habermas's concept of the public sphere (1989, 1996) underpins the deliberative democracy model. Habermas argued that the public sphere operates as an intermediary system between state and society with an emphasis on the formation of public opinion (1989; see also Kies, 2010 for useful discussion). The public sphere designated an arena in which political participation could be enacted through the medium of talk, and a space in which citizens could deliberate about common affairs to reach consensus about the public good (Fraser, 1990; Habermas et al., 1974). It was considered a realm insulated from the influence of state and commercial interests, in which citizens could debate and deliberate on matters of mutual and general concern to a self-governing community (Howley, 2005, p. 19). However, Habermas argued that the growth of the capitalist economy resulted in a highly commercial press and an uneven distribution of wealth. The press was transformed from a forum for rational-critical debate for private citizens, who assembled to form 'a public', to a privately owned and controlled institution that could be steered by publishers. Habermas (1989) contended this was largely precipitated by the collapse of the barrier between editorial and advertising.

Democratic participatory theory

According to participatory theory, journalists are central to promoting critical involvement of citizens in society. This theory emphasizes diverse viewpoints and active citizen involvement more than the quality of discourse as advocated by Habermas (Benson, 2008). Christians and colleagues (2009) outline the facilitator and radical role of journalism in democratic societies. The role of the facilitator is to deliberate and reflect political order but be accountable to widely shared moral frameworks in the communities they represent. There is now increasing emphasis on the interactional possibilities afforded by new media:

> The focus is not so much on *citizen* engagement but rather *audience* or *user* interaction; instead of theorizing and empirically examining journalism's role for democracy (participation through news), the focus is on participation in news – democracy *in* journalism, rather than *through* it. (Peters & Witschge, 2014, p. 20)

This includes direct participation in the public sphere via social media, email and other digital platforms. In the pre-digital era media forums such as 'letters to the editor' alone fulfilled this function (see Singer, 2010).

Radical democratic role

Under the framework of a radical democratic role, Christians and colleagues (2009) insist on the absolute equality and freedom of all members in a democratic society where the media exists to oppose, contradict or challenge power structures in society. In this way, journalists 'represent' the public by ensuring that 'the voice of the people' is heard through news agendas that reflect popular sentiment and pursue matters of public interest (Birks, 2010). The notion of 'participation' is taken from a mediating role to a more active one when journalists become direct participants, and even advocates, for the communities they serve. At the local level journalists are often active in advocating or championing an issue or cause. Rather than upholding the notion of 'objectivity' they can be partisan, seeking to persuade the people – and powerful interests – to a particular view.

Democratic theory and local journalism

The strong link to 'community' has often led scholars to reach for democratic theory to understand local media's relationship to public life (Hatcher, 2012b). The various strands of democratic theory have arguably been most influential on scholarship about local news, inspired by the work of libertarians such as de Tocqueville's theory of democracy (de Tocqueville, 1945, p. 112): 'The newspaper (brings people) together and the newspaper is still necessary to keep them united'; to scholars who draw on the synergies between Habermas's idea of public sphere and notions of community (see Hatcher, 2012b). In their study on local government communication in the UK, Firmstone and Coleman (2015) examined practices of public engagement as tangible features of local democracy. They argue there are three emerging characteristics of the relationship between news media, citizens and governing institutions: strategies designed by local authorities to engage citizens; heightened opportunities for citizens to use digital media in order to become producers and disseminators of news; and the potential of digital media to allow local government to communicate directly without journalists as intermediaries. However, they found mainstream local news continued to be the most legitimate and trusted way that councils engage with citizens (Firmstone & Coleman, 2015).

Democratic theory has inspired the work of scholars such as Robert Putnam, whose conceptualization of social capital uses local newspaper readership as an indicator of community and political engagement in small cities and towns (Putnam, 2000). There is a rich body of scholarship that recognizes media use as a positive influence on people's involvement in civic affairs (see Shah et al., 2001; Jeffres et al., 2007; Bowd, 2012; Richards, 2013). However, a decline in local newspapers can reduce political activity, regardless of whether other media operate in the locality (Schulhofer-Wohl & Garrido, 2013).

The social responsibility model of the press continues to be particularly influential in journalism education, where the importance of objectivity and balance in all facets of journalism practice is paramount. Nielsen (2015) highlights that local journalists often prefer to see themselves as independent and detached from the community they cover, even if in reality they are highly dependent on it (Nielsen, 2015, p. 11). In his overview of local media, Nielsen (2015) contends that journalists see their most important role as holding power to account and keeping people informed about public affairs as read through the lens of liberal representative democracy (Nielsen, 2015, p. 9). Alongside 'watchdog', terms such as 'guard dog' have also been applied to describe local journalism – the idea that local media serves those in established positions of power most effectively.

Some of the most revered news stories at the local level come from serving the important watchdog role, which is a highly celebrated aspect of news reporting within the wider journalistic field. For example, in 2014 an investigative reporter at the small Oregon news outlet the *Willamette Week* exposed secret deals made by the governor's fiancée, forcing the governor's resignation in 2015. The series of articles won an Investigative Reporters and Editors award, which recognizes outstanding journalism across the US. Investigative reporting takes time and money to produce, which is why other theoretical lenses, such as a political economy approach, are useful for journalism.

Civic republicanism

There is also a vein of literature that advocates for a civic republicanism approach that resonates with the deliberative democracy model. Here the emphasis is on the collective and active involvement of citizens through communication, where individuals can put aside their own interests for the benefit of the common good. Communication scholar James Carey was inspired by republican models, in which the press exists as an instrument that both expresses the interests of the public and helps it form and find its identity (Carey, 1999). He argued the liberal belief in individual rights and freedoms is the 'single most pervasive image and myth of our time' (Carey, 1999, p. 4). He used the example of people's response to a power outage to make apparent that we are truly dependent on others and rely on people's common decency to exist and feel safe. Public journalism scholars, who are particularly active in discussions about local media, also argue for republican, communitarian or deliberative democratic models. We will discuss this in more detail in Chapter 5.

Critiquing democratic theory and local journalism

Often scholars who adopt democratic theory as the lens for studying journalism do so from a positivist political science perspective, where the media is viewed as a neutral channel through which information flows, or exists to serve the interests of the polity ahead of all else. For this reason such research might be accused of functionalism. Habermas's original idea of a single public sphere made the assumption, for example, that individuals could deliberate as if they were social equals. This public sphere model failed to consider that multiple and intersecting publics operate within a culture and did not take into account social inequality (Fraser, 1990; Curran, 2002). In media research, functionalist approaches treat society as an integrated, harmonious and cohesive whole and news media are understood to contribute towards cohesion and integration (Fourie, 2007, pp. 186–187). This perspective has been criticized, firstly, for overlooking the fact that news outlets do not necessarily function identically for all people or groups; secondly, for disregarding conflict and issues of power; and thirdly, for tending not to acknowledge the importance of contexts – social, political and cultural – as influences on all stages of the communication process (Watson & Hill, 2000, p. 149).

The idea that media serve as a powerful channel to instigate change, shape ideas of community and, in the process, generate advantages and inequalities, is a key contention of this book. While democratic theory is useful, it creates some blind spots in scholarly examination about local news media. In the next section, we will shift from the traditional to the most contemporary of theories influencing scholarship on local journalism – the role of convergence in digital times. We will then address the other important scholarly paradigms of political economy and cultural studies before outlining our own approach to local media that emphasizes the place of media power.

Convergence theory

It is important to differentiate 'convergence theory' from the practice of multimedia or 'convergence journalism' – the latter Kolodzy (2013, p. 1) defines as 'providing news to people when, where and how they want it using any communication tools available'. 'Convergent journalism' places emphasis on the multi-skilling of journalists, but 'convergence' is also a key theory in media studies that should not be mistaken for teaching journalists how to multi-task. The theory helps to illuminate the ways in which new technologies bring different mediums together, and how this shapes relationships between media audiences, media owners, producers and content. It provides a framework for linking journalism history to the present and investigating labour relations of emerging business models, through to assisting critical analysis of multimedia newsroom practice. It is especially helpful for thinking about participatory journalism, including how and why traditional news organizations have sought to 'make their peace' with citizen journalism, including blogging, Twitter, podcasting, video-blogging and user-generated footage (Jenkins, 2006, p. 24).

In his seminal book *Convergence Culture* (2006), Henry Jenkins explores how changes in communication and information technology reshape and change everyday life, altering patterns of media production and consumption. Jenkins observes that media convergence operates as a 'top-down' and 'bottom-up' process, recognizing that both media makers and media consumers influence the way new technologies are used. Jenkins conceptualizes convergence as the place where old and new media intermingle and where 'community' and corporate media confront one another. It is a way for exploring how the power of the media producer and the power of the consumer interact in unpredictable ways.

His conceptualization of convergence captures the movement of content across multiple media platforms, the alliances between multiple media industries and the flexibility of media audiences, who will go anywhere in search of the information and experiences they want.

Convergence and journalism

It is worth noting there are different approaches to and understandings of convergence in journalism studies, apart from it being used to describe a theory and a practice. For example, the academic literature from the United States and some parts of Europe focuses on the coming together of previously separate print, broadcast and online news organizations and the resulting converged outputs (see, for example, Aviles & Carvajal, 2008). In the UK, convergence is usually understood as an internal process of integration between online and print or broadcast newsrooms within the same organization. Thurman and Lupton (2008) explain this is largely due to the UK's cross-media ownership laws that do not allow newspaper companies to control radio or television stations. What is common across the international literature is that convergence not only redefines the tasks of journalists; it also re-shapes the business environments of media companies – and audience participation.

Communication companies of the 19th and 20th centuries formed newspaper chains and networks of radio and television stations. These empires were structured so costs, profits and resources were shared, from advertising revenues and telegraph services to buildings, presses and broadcasting equipment, as well as editorial and general staff. Media convergence in the digital age not only offers ways to realize these same kinds of advantages; it can be seen as an expansion and intensification of the same logic, involving the establishment of multimedia newsrooms and integrated news companies. However, Jenkins (2006) argues the greatest change ushered in by convergence is the shift in audience participation towards co-creation. This transformation can be seen through projects such as WBEZ 91.5's Curious City in Chicago, where audience members pose questions about the region and its people and work closely with the programme's professional journalism team to help investigate. Their co-created reports are disseminated via radio, podcasts, a dedicated website, and on Facebook, Twitter and Tumblr. Finnish women's magazine *Olivia* provides a different model, with its MyOwnOlivia project, which uses a point system to reward readers for completing 'challenges', such as pitching story ideas and undertaking research, including finding sources and composing interview questions. The magazine's journalists collaborate closely with contributors, whose points can be cashed in for prizes worth hundreds of euro.

Convergence theory can be used to examine the power dynamics between traditional media and new social media sites (see Hess & Waller, 2011). Journalists, including those at the local level, are able to exploit content from social media – especially YouTube – because they are perceived as being 'free for all' and celebrated for their democratic potential. Consider the rise of UK spinster songstress Susan Boyle, who became a global YouTube sensation after she appeared on the talent show *Britain's Got Talent*. Her first ever television appearance was uploaded by a YouTube user for the world to see. Mainstream media outlets, including local media that served Boyle's hometown, all play a significant role in elevating content from the YouTube archive and amplifying it globally. Meanwhile, scholars such as Robert Gehl (2009) have extended convergence theory to discuss the success of YouTube as an archive produced in a co-creative environment.

Political economy

There has been much hype about how new technologies, and especially social media such as Facebook and Twitter, have made media more open and participatory. As convergence theory highlights, however, the news media is still largely corporatized, commercialized, commodified and concentrated. A political economy approach enables us to examine this in depth and alerts us to the fact that those in control of news media wield a great amount of power. Analysis of these characteristics is important for understanding the production and meanings of local journalism in the digital age.

The study of political economy concerns economics and is grounded in social theory. Wasko (2014) has traced its roots to 18th- and 19th-century thinkers including Karl Marx, Adam Smith and Frederick Engels, through the critical turn of the 20th century, which gave rise to the Frankfurt School in Europe, and an American tradition that critiqued US information systems. Influential thinkers in this tradition include Golding and Murdock (1991) and Robert McChesney (2015), who has long problematized the contradiction between a for-profit, highly concentrated, advertising-saturated corporate media system and the communication requirements of a democratic society. Herman and Chomsky (1998) developed the 'propaganda model', which found US media consistently served the purposes of corporate and state power. Concepts such as the 'propaganda model' belong to what is termed 'critical political economy of communication', which was defined during the radicalism of the 1960s according to Hardy (2014). He says its mission involves taking Marxist thought and democratic politics to generate questions about power in communication and creating conditions for realizing democracy. The fundamental concern of critical political economists is with the allocation of resources within capitalist societies, and finding ways to make these allocations more just:

> Through studies of ownership and control, political economists document and analyse relations of power, class systems and other structural inequalities. Critical political economists analyse contradictions and suggest strategies for resistance and intervention using methods drawn from history, economics, sociology and political science. (Wasko, 2014, p. 260)

Academic scholarship tends to focus on media ownership issues involving global enterprises (think Rupert Murdoch and News Corporation), but local media proprietors wield a great deal of power in their communities. The former owner of one Australian regional newspaper – a multimillionaire businessman and active community member – provides an extraordinary example of news media owners using their influence to support personal political views or business agendas. Take this extract from the Australian online news site *Crikey* about the late proprietor's influence on journalism practice at the everyday level:

> On early Tuesday morning, a liquid gas tanker flipped on its side on the busy Riddoch Highway, just near Mt Gambier's airport. Although the driver emerged unharmed, the road took at least five hours to clear with the help of a crane, and the truck sustained $150,000 worth of damage. Pretty big Mt Gambier news and yet there wasn't a sniff of the story in the local paper *The Border Watch* nor on local *WIN TV*. But it's clear that local news outlets couldn't have missed the story – Crikey hears that several journalists were on the scene, not to mention the fact that a major road was blocked. So what's going on? It's perhaps not surprising that the story didn't get a run in *The Border Watch*. Mt Gambier's local – and only – paper is owned by the Scott Group, the company of South Australian trucking magnate Allan Scott. The tanker which overturned was a Scott truck. (Nethercote, 2006)

There are also examples of local media proprietors *not* interfering in coverage of unflattering news about them. In December 2015 the *Las Vegas Review-Journal* investigated and exposed the secret identity of its new owners (Bustillos, 2016). Within a few weeks the interim editor of the newspaper developed a new set of 13 editorial guidelines for covering the paper's ownership, including that the family of owners would receive no special treatment. Through a political economy lens, that story might illustrate how unusual (hence, newsworthy) it is for a news organization to 'go against' its owners' wishes.

The critical political economy approach to understanding journalism includes theoretical discussion as well as different levels of analysis – from studies of specific news outlets to single corporations and national and global news media systems. Historical analysis is seen as crucial for documenting change as well as continuity. For example, Nord (1915) takes a political economy approach to analysing the relationship between cities and urban newspapers in the US and Britain during the Victorian era:

> The modern daily newspaper was born in the 1870s in the industrial cities of the American Midwest: Detroit, Cleveland, St Louis and Chicago. These newspapers were the first genuinely urban mass media in America. They recognized that the rise of the modern city had changed the nature of community life. This realization was partly cultural, but it was fundamentally political and economic. As business firms themselves, newspapers were direct contributors to the growth of commerce and manufacturing in mid-nineteenth-century cities; they were also ardent advocates of private enterprise. (Nord, 2015, p. 74)

Media and labour is another key theme, as questions about the conditions in which news is produced and class issues are key theoretical foundations for the political economy approach and essential for assessing media power. Analysts have engaged with transformations in work practices and arrangements, including de-professionalism and professional–amateur hybridizations. Scholars including Deuze (2007b, 2011) have also addressed patterns of paid, unpaid and precarious labour in journalism.

Much research in this tradition has been concerned with news as a commodity that is produced and distributed by profit-seeking organizations, or, in other words, the business of journalism. Critical political economists argue that in recent decades the commodification of news has intensified across traditional media, and expanded significantly into new, converged digital media. This is discussed in detail in Chapter 7. Analysis of news as a business has involved, but is not limited to, the themes discussed below.

Concentration

Political economy acknowledges that the capitalist system places a high value on competition in the marketplace. However, through studies of the actual levels of competition, or the lack of competition where a handful of conglomerates dominate, especially in the local media sector, this approach often challenges the myth of a competitive media market and also investigates the consequences of this for democracy and society. In the UK the BBC faced a challenge concerning the production and future of regional news (Baines, 2013). In 2008, the BBC argued there was 'nobody who can be satisfied with the quality of local news in most parts of the UK' (Lyons, 2008, as cited in Fenton et al., 2010). BBC management viewed the gap as a public service issue and posted a £68 million initiative to introduce local video to online news sites. The BBC Trust rejected the proposal, mainly on the grounds that an expansion of BBC local was a threat to commercial media services, especially newspapers (Lyons, 2008).

Commercialization/commodification

News and information services are understood as commercial products that are bought and sold. Critical political economists are interested in related issues, such as the intensification of commercial messages for consumers and privatization of media outlets occurring throughout the world.

In China, regulatory and government policy still determines the extent to which commercial forces are able to shape the sector. However, the past few years have witnessed the gradual introduction of the dual forces of commercialization and competition. Television is popular, with 400 million Chinese households and 93 per cent of the population having access to a television set (Patton, 2015). The choice and range of channels appear diverse, with 2000 available at different locations – a small number at the national level, others at the regional level and many more targeted only at individual cities or small local areas. Beneath the surface, the situation is less positive, with many channels losing money, lacking focus and offering poor production quality. At a local level, the number of channels has fallen by 30 per cent over the past four years, primarily through mergers but also closures (Patton, 2015). Public channels are facing financial pressures because of their small scale and lack of access to advertising. Many are reinventing themselves, such as Chaoyang TV in Beijing, which focuses on local information and issues and has streamlined its operations. Patton (2015) warns the future of many of these local channels is in jeopardy if the current trend of commercialization and financial accountability continues.

Diversification

Opening new lines of business and conglomerating a wide range of activities can provide potential for news media businesses to work together to more effectively market products, or create synergies to maximize profit and decrease risk. The Gannett Company in the US reported revenues of $727 million for 2014. At the time it owned news media including USA TODAY, as well as local newspapers in 92 markets across the nation, from the *Detroit Free Press* to *The Des Moines Register* and the *Great Falls Tribune* to name just a few (see Gannett.com for a full listing). Gannett also had more than 20 local television stations with various NBC, CBS and ABC affiliates owned in different states, as well as major stakes in employment and car market online sites. In 2015 Gannett split into two independent publicly traded companies, one focused on its newspapers and publishing, which kept the Gannett name, and one on broadcasting and digital, named TEGNA. According to USA TODAY, the split finalized a strategy to protect the organization's broadcasting and digital businesses from the decline in print advertising revenues (Yu, 2015).

Horizontal/vertical integration

The Gannett/TEGNA organization also provides an example of strategies for streamlining costs and boosting profits including adding companies in the same line of business (horizontal integration). At the time of the split in 2015 Gannett said it planned to push its community newspapers to work more closely together and share resources and stories under a new structure called USA TODAY Media Network. New distribution technologies and deregulated markets also provide opportunities for vertical integration, such as acquiring companies in the same supply chain or those that are involved in different stages of the news production process. Gannett also adopted this approach by expanding its local publishing business through the acquisition of the remaining 59.4 per cent stake in the Texas-New Mexico Newspapers Partnership that it did not previously own. It also made a deal with Digital First Media, which added 11 newspapers in three states, lifting its editorial workforce to more than 4000 in the US and the UK (Yu, 2015).

The political economy approach has a strong focus on news media production, whereas the cultural studies approach, which is discussed in the next section, shifts the focus of attention from media production to consumption and locates power and agency over meaning-making with news audiences and more recently digital co-producers (Jenkins, 2006).

Cultural studies approach

The cultural approach in media studies is an amalgam of theoretical strands emanating from the US and the UK. Turner (2003) traces the first major coalescence to the Birmingham group in the UK in the early 1970s. In journalism studies, scholars have tended to look to the US tradition. The cultural approach in news media studies was inspired largely by American communication scholar James Carey, who argued for the role of news as a symbolic system that helped make meaning in culture. Carey was influenced by John Dewey's view that the problems of communication are linked to problems of community, to problems surrounding the kinds of communities we create and in which we live (Carey, 1989, p. 15). Carey identified two theories of communication. In the 'transmission' model, 'messages are transmitted and distributed in space for the control of distance and people' (Carey, 1989, p. 4). He contrasted the transmission model with the 'ritual' view, which he said was the older understanding:

> In a ritual definition, communication is linked to terms such as 'sharing', 'participation', 'association', 'fellowship', and the possession of a 'common faith'. This definition exploits the ancient identity and common roots of the term 'commonness', 'communion', 'community' and 'communication'. (Carey, 1989, p. 7)

Carey observed that when we think about society, and the role of journalism, we are 'almost always coerced by our traditions' into seeing it in terms of a political order or alternatively, an economic order. He reminds us that 'life is more than power and trade' and well before local news migrated to digital platforms, he cautioned scholars against taking the narrow view:

> ...because we have looked at each new advance in communication technology as an opportunity for politics and economics...we have rarely seen these advances as opportunities to expand people's powers to learn and exchange ideas and experience. (Carey, 1989, p. 7)

The cultural view of journalism's power to create and maintain community has been a key idea in much of the scholarship about journalism at the community level.

Benedict Anderson's concept of 'imagined communities' is another important idea for understanding media power at the local level. Anderson (1983) argued that as society has become so large, diverse and complex it is impossible for people to know everyone and everything that goes on. The media therefore plays a central role in community and identity formation through the creation of what he termed 'imagined communities'. Hess also draws on cultural studies to argue that local journalists obtain and reinforce power partly because they can generate 'bonding' social capital in society, instilling or being seen as central to ideas of community, and as a way of people being able to connect to a locale where they may feel a sense of place (Hess, 2013b, 2015a).

The cultural analysis of journalism has flourished for as long as it has been a target of intellectual endeavour, and Zelizer (2004) has provided a comprehensive assessment of its body of scholarship and the tensions and debates that have surrounded it for almost as long. She has observed that cultural enquiry in journalism is critical, saying it 'travels the uneven road of reading journalism against its own grain, while giving that grain extended attention' (p. 176). In a departure from other approaches, it encourages us to look toward audiences to locate journalism's workable dimensions. Zelizer (2004) has acknowledged this can conflict with the 'firm assumption' in journalism practice and much scholarship that journalism takes place in the newsroom. However, she observes this tension can be productive and cultural enquiry has generated:

> a fruitful line of scholarship that links the untidy and textured *materiel* of journalism ... with the larger world in which journalism takes shape. (Zelizer, 2004, p. 175)

The cultural approach's accent on meaning-making as a primary activity of journalism explicitly challenges two aspects of its enquiry: the normative biases of much existing journalism research and the professional notions of journalists themselves (Zelizer, 2004). Bill Reader encourages scholars to draw from the 'critical cultural well' in research about journalism at the local level. He argues that the cultural studies approach is ripe for new research in this field, even though it challenges many of the traditions of 20th-century professionalism and science (Reader, 2012). As he points out, the goal of cultural studies is not about 'testing hypothesis and finding answers, but rather about discovering new and more interesting questions' (Reader, 2012, p. 109).

Mythical divide between political economy and cultural studies

Political economy scholars have at times been accused of both a preoccupation with the formal properties of news organizations and neglect of the impact of journalism on everyday interaction and relations (see Bourdieu, 1977; Cottle, 2003; Couldry, 2003a; Zelizer, 2004; Fenton, 2006). The role and motivations of the audience and what they consider to be 'news' have traditionally been the domain of cultural studies, which 'reminds political economy scholars that the substance of its work, the analysis of communication, is rooted in the needs, goals, conflicts, failures and accomplishments of ordinary people attempting to make sense of their lives' (Fenton, 2006, p. 8). Much has been made of how new technologies, including the Internet, smart devices and pure players including YouTube have given audiences new and considerable power, and how this can change mainstream journalism, especially by making it a more collaborative practice (Phillips, 2015).

Scholars argue that the differences between political economy and culturalist approaches tend to be oversimplified and that such a divide is indeed a 'mythical' one (Fenton, 2006; Hesmondhalgh, 2007). Tuchman (2002, p. 90) argues political economy and cultural approaches should be seen as different aspects of news production, conceptualizing journalism as 'a product as well as a productive process'. Nick Couldry is one of many media and communication scholars who argue that we cannot study media in isolation, as if they are a detachable part of the wider social process (see, e.g. Couldry, 2004, 2012; Zelizer, 2004; Fenton, 2006; Moores, 2012). Fenton, for example, has argued the need for a more holistic approach to media studies that combines political economy and cultural approaches. She contends:

> The struggle over meaning takes place between the process of production and the act of reception – both of which are determined by their place in wider social, political economy and cultural context and both of which are subject to constraints. Choices made by audiences must be looked at within the social context of their daily life and the content itself must be interpreted according to the social and political circumstances of its production. (Fenton, 2006, p. 25)

In the search for a holistic approach to news production – one that factors in the needs, wants and practices of audiences as well as the commercial and cultural aspects of journalism practice – we have sought inspiration from scholarship on media power, in particular the work of Nick Couldry and Pierre Bourdieu.

Media power and the myth of the mediated centre

Different theoretical approaches to understanding journalism provide a range of ways for thinking about media power. For example, democratic theories emphasize journalists' claims to objective truth and their power to hold other powerful institutions up to public scrutiny, including parliaments, courts of law and big businesses. Critical political economy scholars argue that to understand the journalist's role in society it is essential to understand relationships between media power and state power, as well as journalism's relationships with other economic sectors. Political economists also discuss news in relation to the public sphere, public citizenship and democracy. Cultural studies approaches are much more concerned with the relationship between journalists and audiences, place the accent on news as part of everyday life and increasingly explore the ways new technologies might enable more meaningful citizen participation in the activities of journalism.

Some scholars who work in Pierre Bourdieu's field-based tradition argue that journalism's ability to represent reality is its greatest source of power to shape the wider social space. In *An introduction to reflexive sociology* (1992), Bourdieu used the term 'meta-capital' to describe the concentration of different types of capital (power) in the state, giving it power to decide what counts as capital in specific fields. Couldry (2003) argued the media's power can be theorized the same way:

> Just as the state's influence on cultural capital and prestige ... is not confined to specific fields but radiates outward into social space generally, so the media's meta-capital may affect social space through the general circulation of media representations. (Couldry, 2003b, p. 668)

Couldry (2003) uses the example of cooking to illustrate this point. TV has not only created a gallery of celebrity chefs and television cooking programmes that have a major impact on society's relationship to food; the media can be understood to have changed people's viewing and reading habits, the way we shop, cook, eat, even holiday and spend our leisure time. Internationally syndicated cooking programmes, cookbook publishing and the plethora of websites and blogs devoted to gastronomy through to what gets stocked in supermarkets can all be understood as mediated. Furthermore, Couldry contends that the media has *more power* than the gourmet field to decide who will be the celebrity chefs, what the star ingredients will be and what will be successful across multiple platforms, from TV series to books, DVDs, websites and merchandise.

Bourdieu suggests there can be 'no symbolic power without the symbolism of power' (1991, p. 75), which he describes as:

> A power of constituting the given through utterances, of making people see and believe, of confirming or transforming the vision of the world and thus the world itself, an almost magical power which enables one to obtain the equivalent of what it obtained through force. (Bourdieu, 1991, p. 170)

The media, imbued with symbolic power, is perceived as having a privileged relationship with, or even seen to stand in for, society's centre, which Couldry conceptualizes as the 'myth of the mediated centre'[1] (Couldry, 2003a, p. 45). While much of Couldry's scholarship seeks to unmask this symbolic power – or media power – in order to challenge it, he argues it is not to deny 'that for particular purposes in particular struggles, both within and beyond media institutions, the "myth" has a strategic use' (Couldry, 2003, p. 47).

We examine positive use of the 'myth' in Chapter 4, where ideas of community are discussed in relation to traditions and rituals as sources of news. The role of local media as central to the social in the 'communities' they serve is a key focus of this book, but it should always be examined in the context of power dynamics and issues of inequalities it might present. For example, forms of local journalism are increasingly dependent on powerful commercial information channels such as Google and Facebook to reach and engage with audiences. However, these are not neutral players in the media world (Picard, 2015). Viewing this relationship through a media power lens provides a way of seeing that as dominant media change and evolve, so too does the relationship with local media forms. Media power might become less visible and more fluid as old structures collapse, giving rise to the digital dynasty's new media empires and moguls. Picard (2015) has advised that studies about the use of social media should therefore be viewed through a critical lens. He goes further to argue that all forms of information technology should be studied in terms of power relationships rather than with the naïve perception that the Internet is about widespread democratization (Picard, 2015). Local newspapers and websites that belong to big media corporations are most obviously connected to powerful information nodes and flows through their own networks, as well as via platforms such as Twitter, Google and Facebook. Stories deemed to be important are picked up more quickly and given traction in other media owned by the same parent company, and further afield.

Bourdieu and the journalistic field

Our approach to researching local journalism and media power finds great benefit in utilizing and extending the conceptual toolkit of Pierre Bourdieu (1930–2002). In *On television* (1998), Bourdieu's main focus was describing the inner workings of the journalism field and what separates it from other fields, but he also examined the effects journalism has on other social spaces, especially politics. This short book is a provocative commentary on how television has changed French political culture, rather than a scholarly work, and went to the top of the bestseller list in France when it was first published there in 1996. It offers critical insights on the limits of contemporary journalism, but we must look elsewhere in Bourdieu's writings for a robust framework for exploring the field of local journalism because the news media was not a key focus for this French anthropologist and sociologist. Many journalism scholars use his major concepts of field, capital and habitus because they provide a helpful framework for explaining and understanding the way journalism operates as a professional field to create its own rules and its own pressures, and how it changes and evolves over time (see, for example, Benson & Neveu, 2005; Schultz, 2007). Bourdieu can also be drawn upon to shed light on the way the journalism field interacts with other professional fields to shape the wider social space. His work can be employed in empirical studies to analyse how the journalism field reproduces itself, and also how it can be transformed by pressures from inside and outside. In her study of 'the journalistic gut feeling' in Danish newsrooms, Schultz (2007) observes that 'field theory has its strength in taking into consideration the relations between the newsroom and the journalism field, and between the journalism field and the field of power' (Schultz, 2007, p. 192).

Bourdieu's 'field theory' is used throughout this book to interrogate how local media generates power and how this can be used for the benefit of the profession and society. Other journalism academics find it a useful set of concepts for improving individual journalism practice. As Phillips argues:

> What is important for practising journalists is to be able to survey the field and to see where light has been thrown onto the practices that are too easily taken for granted and how the insights of academic researchers can be used to make more 'reflexive' practitioners capable of examining and improving what they do. (Phillips, 2015, p. 2)

Bourdieu's approach strived to overcome some of the dichotomies in other social theories (such as structure and agency, mind and body) and placed great emphasis on reflexivity (Bourdieu & Wacquant, 1992). There is no point outside the social space we inhabit from which we can gain a neutral, disinterested perspective, and so Bourdieu acknowledged that he operated within what he analysed – he was both an analyst and an actor in the fields he entered (Bourdieu & Wacquant, 1992). Developing a reflexive practice is considered an important attribute for professional journalists (Burns, 2012).

Field

Bourdieu did not develop his concept of 'field' as a grand theory, but as a suite of tools, including capital and habitus, for interpreting practical problems through empirical studies (Bourdieu, 1992, p. 232). He defined social arenas such as politics, health, education, journalism, science and economics as fields (Bourdieu, 1977). Within and across these fields human action is organized around relations of power. People negotiate and compete for resources, and the position of each agent in the field results from interaction between the specific rules of the field, the agent's habitus and the capital they possess.

In Bourdieu's theory, capital takes a number of forms. It can be economic, social, cultural and/or symbolic. Most fields are subordinate to the wider field of power. Bourdieu compared these dynamic fields with physical force fields, in which the actions of social agents produce reactions (Webb et al., 2002). The concept of field can be used to explain differentials in power between people in a particular field, and also between fields. It can also be used to study how people resist power and domination. Bourdieu suggested fields are structured around the opposition between the 'heteronomous' pole representing external forces (primarily economic and political) and the 'autonomous' pole (Bourdieu, 1984, 2005b). Within the small commercial newspaper field, those driven purely by the desire to increase dividends for shareholders or advertising revenue lie at the heteronomous pole (such as general managers and advertising representatives), whereas those such as journalists with a desire to maintain their cultural position and influence lie closer to the autonomous pole (see Phillips, 2010, p. 89).

Habitus

People often experience power differently depending on what field they are in, as well as their position in the field, so context and environment of the field are key influences on what Bourdieu termed 'habitus'. The concept of habitus captures the 'permanent internalization of the social order in the human body' (Eriksen & Nielsen, 2001, p. 130). It is the almost unconscious knowledge and skill an actor possesses – the feeling of being a fish in water, metaphorically speaking – or knowing what makes a place or a social system tick; when behaving in a certain way is second nature. The habitus or 'rules of the game' establish what Bourdieu called a 'logics of practice', which lays down what rationalities will guide decisions for those in a particular field (Bourdieu, 1989).

Neveu has emphasized the importance of habitus to the operation of fields:

> A social space comes to work as a field when the institutions and characters who enter it are trapped in its stakes, values, debates, when one cannot succeed in it without a minimum of practical or reflexive knowledge of its internal rules and logics. (Neveu, 2007, p. 338)

Habitus is created through social processes. It is not fixed or permanent and can change in response to transformations in a field, or over a long time. This idea is extended in Chapter 2 to explore the notion of 'local habitus' – what makes a place, and the people within it, tick, and what this means for local news organizations, journalists and audiences navigating changes wrought by digitization.

Capital

Bourdieu argued that individuals and organizations compete, consciously or unconsciously, to valorize those forms of capital they possess (Benson, 2004). The forms of capital are equally important in Bourdieu's scheme and can be accumulated and transferred. Bourdieu used capital as a metaphor to examine the notion of power, qualifications, status, social connections and assets (Fine, 2001, p. 57), and suggested that power and dominance derive not only from possession of material goods but also from possession of cultural and social resources and social recognition (Grenfell 2008, p. 88). Bourdieu contended that cultural capital remains on the side of the 'purest' journalists of the press, and they are the ones who launch the critical debates that others pick up:

> As Einsteinian physics tells us, the more energy a body has, the more it distorts the space around it and a very powerful agent within a field can distort the whole space, cause the whole space to be organised in relation to itself. (Bourdieu, 2005a, p. 43)

For Bourdieu (2006), capital is the expression that general power takes in specific forms. The various types of capital can exist in three forms that can be understood as 'continuous with each other … as moments of one thing rather than three different varieties of the thing' (R. Moore, 2008, p. 105). It can be objectified (things invested with capital, such as books), habitus (knowledge of the rules of the game) or embodied (in the attributes of a person).

Summary

The aim of this chapter has been to introduce and align the theoretical strands that are woven through the rest of the book. The central idea is that viewing local journalism through a lens of media power offers ways of seeing how journalism contributes to serving the best interests of society, and the factors and circumstances under which its considerable influence can also be misdirected. The media power lens draws on democratic, sociological and cultural theories that are helpful for tackling the big questions about local journalism, from its roles in politics, community formation and social change to its various relationships with audiences and how questions of power, place, labour and technology link the local with the world. Rather than seeing political economy, with its accent on the production of journalism, in conflict with cultural approaches that emphasize the role of the audience, we argue both are part of a necessary and helpful continuum. Bourdieu's tradition of field-based research straddles the divide between political economy and cultural studies. It offers a robust framework for explaining and understanding the way journalism creates its own rules, pressures and value, and how it changes and evolves over time. It can also be used to shed light on the way journalism shapes the wider social space.

The chapter began with democratic theories and the Fourth Estate notion of the press, how this idea has become almost axiomatic in discussions of news, public debate and politics, and has been widely criticized. When we turn our attention to the role of local media in public life and the consequences for healthy political discussion and participation, this theory and the debates attached to it become highly relevant.

Many of the concepts introduced here relate to journalism's changing relationship with audiences. For example, we have explored different understandings of 'convergence', distinguishing between multiplatform journalism practice and the theory, which explains the ways in which new technologies not only bring different mediums together but also shape relationships between media audiences, media owners, producers and content. We have argued that convergence can also provide a framework for understanding the history of journalism and investigating how the 'work' of journalism is changing, as well as examining the emergence of new business models which will be discussed in Chapter 7.

2 Defining the Local in a 'Geo-social' Context

Introduction

'Local' is a slippery concept that means different things to different people depending on their place in the world, and has received little attention in scholarship about journalism. This chapter addresses that gap through its examination of the theoretical and conceptual challenges local media present. Some of the questions addressed here include:

- How can we understand local media in the digital age?
- What does it mean to be local anyway?
- How do notions of 'community' fit into this picture and what motivates people to engage with local news?

These questions will be approached from a practical angle in the chapters that follow. However, in order to really engage with them it is helpful to draw on scholarly debates about place, space, social space and information flows. We also make use of Bourdieu's theoretical toolkit, outlined in the previous chapter – especially his concept of 'habitus' – to explore what it means to be local and the importance of local 'know-how' to the future of news. Theoretical exploration has great value because it helps us think deeply by seeking out the 'why'. It can also illuminate the unknown, things we may not have thought about, and open up new insights. Let's begin the theoretical discussion of local media by constructing a metaphor. Metaphors can be useful for shaping philosophical convictions (Barnes, 1991) and will help us to get a handle on important conceptual ideas that relate to local news.

In many children's nurseries or play settings there is a popular toy known as a shape ball. Here curious toddlers pick up a variety of shapes and try to match them to contours cut out around the ball. The sections that follow outline five concepts: geo-social, local, local habitus, community and sense of place. We have refined the geo-social framework

(Hess, 2013a; Hess & Waller, 2014) so that it serves as a permeable shell or shape ball that concepts such as 'the local', 'community' and 'sense of place' can be pushed or pulled through. This is necessary because in discussions about local media, too often local and community are positioned as something tangible, synonymous with a town or city – and serve as the structure in which journalism is examined. Webb et al. (2002) observe that one of the enduring beliefs in most societies is that 'community' in both local and national contexts has a real existence, saying it is treated as 'an identity as tangible as the continents and as natural as the Amazon forest or the Rhine river'. We join the chorus of scholars who argue that the concept of community is not natural or inevitable. It is constructed by a series of discourses about society.

The shape ball metaphor helps us to forge a better understanding of 'local' and 'community' in relation to journalism. Positioning these key ideas as elements within a geo-social model provides a much more robust and steady framework for understanding and unpacking the key threads that make local media unique. So let's explore the overarching structure that shapes our understanding of local journalism – that of 'geo-social' news.

The geo-social model

'Geo-social' is a concept that emphasizes a local news outlet's solid link to geographic territory, while acknowledging the wider social space in which it plays a role – both in holding an influential position in certain social flows and movements and as a node to wider global news media and communication networks (Hess, 2013a). On more partial terms, geo-social is a useful concept because we cannot assume that a local news outlet is entirely produced or serves only audiences within a given geographic area. An American may be living in Christchurch, New Zealand, but regularly visit a local online news site in Duluth, Minnesota, because of their continuing connection or affinity with that area in the US. Their 'news' needs might differ from a 'born and bred' local resident who continues to reside in Duluth and we will unpack the idea of what makes news in Chapter 4. In this chapter we will draw on empirical data and exemplars to show how the geo-social approach provides a framework for understanding the ways in which local media organizations operate in relation to national and international news circuits and economic and political spheres, as well as traditional and digital formats.

While we acknowledge the wider social flows and movements in which local media are a part, we stress the need to give credence to geography at a time when much social theory has tended to downplay the importance of location and instead emphasize time-space compression (Harvey, 1989) – the geographic stretching of human relationships, where modernity tears 'space' from 'place' and where people are no longer together to engage in face-to-face interaction in one 'locale'. Meyrowitz (1985), for example, suggests that electronic media alters our 'situational geography' by undermining 'the traditional relationship between physical setting and social situation' (1985, pp. 6–7). Understanding the news outlet of the 21st century in all its forms requires reconceptualizing the boundaries to incorporate its connections to geography, space and sense of place.

Putting the 'geo' in geo-social

David Morley suggests that in a modern media world geography is not dead and he makes reference to the long history, from the Greeks to the Romans, of 'imaginary geographies' in which the members of a society locate themselves at the centre of the universe, at a spatial periphery of which they picture a world of threatening monsters and grotesques (Morley, 2000, p. 141). Small newspapers have traditionally constructed geographic boundaries from which they draw their news and information and frame the local in the context of the global. These geographic boundaries are evident by mapping a newspaper's circulation footprint: where a newspaper is distributed and sold and advertisers and readers are attracted.

The content of local news continues to relate to the happenings within a particular geographic location, or those connected in some way to it. This is especially true of local newspapers that often have strong historical ties to specific geographic areas and are distinguishable by the titles of their mastheads, which pay homage to the geographical locations in which they serve. A snapshot of such newspapers may include, for example *The Basingstoke Gazette, Essex Country Standard, Cornish and Devon Post* in the UK; the *Duluth News Tribune, Crookston Daily Times* and *St Paul Pioneer Press* in the US state of Minnesota; and the *Fort Saskatchewan Record* and *Lac La Biche Post* in Alberta, Canada. The number of these newspapers across the Western world is arguably in the thousands. To illustrate this, the online home pages of these 10 newspapers on 28 March 2015 all featured stories relevant to the geographic area represented in their mastheads as the top five articles. The home page of the *Fort Saskatchewan Record,* a small commercial newspaper in Alberta, Canada, for example, included reports on the city council approving a $1.2m debt to upgrade sewers, a vandalism spree in a residential area, new equipment for a high school's woodwork workshop and a local politician fighting to have daylight saving laws changed (see www.fortsaskatchewanrecord.com). The importance of geography also stretches to include local radio and television broadcasts, where reporters often equate 'locally significant' news to happenings that relate to a clearly defined geographic area. In Australia, for example, the idea of what constitutes 'local content' on commercial television is determined via licensing agreements that revolve around a series of zones designated on a geographic map.

Geography is also reflected in a set of journalistic news values recognized as perhaps the strongest expressions of how journalists shape the news across mainstream and local media outlets. 'Proximity', or events which are geographically close to readers, is considered among a series of important news factors, which overlap and are shared across news organizations (Galtunge & Ruge, 1981). Shoemaker et al. (2007) suggest that proximity has both physical and psychological aspects, which is a helpful insight for understanding small commercial newspaper practices in the local-global nexus. It can also be useful for conceptualizing the news media's role and readers' connection to place, which we discuss later in this chapter.

Research on newspapers highlights a continuing synergy between geography and news in a changing media landscape. In their review of the literature on 'community' newspapers, Lowrey et al. (2008) found that 40 per cent of studies focus on the relationship between the news media and a small town or neighbourhood. Thomas (2006) argues that newspapers that reflect people's local city/town/village are still the most appealing in Wales, while Mersey's survey in Maricopa County Arizona (2009) suggests a geographic connection remains important to local newspapers. Her study found that geography continued to matter to citizens and to journalism, and respondents were more attached to their geographic communities than those online. She argues this reinforces 'the importance of journalists covering geography in the first place' and indicates the challenge to local newspapers in light of dwindling circulation figures is to remain geographically relevant (Mersey, 2009, p. 357).

Interviews with journalists in Australia point to an increasing emphasis on geography in online news. An editor working for a large media company in one of its regional newsrooms said sub-editors were being encouraged to ensure names of towns and cities were included in head-lines to make stories easier to find on the Internet:

> I have to fix up headlines to make them 'Google worthy' – if there is a fire in a small town and the headline in the print edition says 'HOUSE FIRE KILLS TWO PEOPLE' I now make sure I get the name of the town in the headline that appears online. People seem to be more likely to 'google' a place name...if you type into Google the words 'HOUSE FIRE', you might get 100,000 different things pop up but if you are more specific in your headline you have got more chance of people finding their way to [the newspaper's] website.

While the relationship to geography is a distinctive characteristic of small commercial newspapers, it becomes increasingly important to understand the role such outlets play in a local-global context and for this it is worthwhile engaging with the scholarship on 'flows', 'spaces' and 'places'. These concepts are important to the idea of geo-social news as they allow us to acknowledge the connection a small newspaper has to a geographic territory while also considering the degree of openness and boundlessness of the social space in which a newspaper operates.

The social dimension of geo-social

As news outlets are able to publish 24 hours a day, the Internet has to some extent eliminated geographical boundaries to competition and advertising (Sparks, 2000). Since Marshall McLuhan's (1967) global vil-lage (see especially McLuhan & Powers, 1989; McLuhan et al., 2001) and Baudrillard's contention that 'henceforth it is the map that pre-cedes the territory' (1983, p. 2), much academic attention has focused on the order of movement and communication across flows and spaces (Castells, 2010) or 'time-space compression' (Harvey, 1989). Simply put, such scholarship highlights how technologies from transport to email, Internet and media broadcasting have created a geographical stretching of social relations (Massey, 1994). Manuel Castells in his conception of a *network society* suggests communication space *is* society. To him, mod-ern cities are constructed around a 'space of flows' where geographic locations can be seen to be part of a local-global network defined by important information and interaction (Castells, 2010). Castells consid-ers 'space of flows' a spatial logic that determines the expressions of society (Hutchins, 2004, see also Moores, 2005) and is associated with functionality, power, politics and wealth. He writes:

> The 'space of flows' is the material support of simultaneous social practices communicated at a distance [without geographical conti-guity]. This involves the production, transmission and processing of flows of information. It also relies on the development of localities as nodes of these communication networks and the connectivity of activities located in these nodes by fast transportation networks oper-ated by information flows. (Castells, 2010, p. xxxii)

A limitation to the space of flows in discussions about local news is that while Castells sees the media as playing an increasingly important role in all social action he does not consider this to be one of power (see Couldry & Curran, 2003, p. 3). As highlighted in the previous chapter, there must be scope to acknowledge that local media serve as a power-ful node in information networks and also represent a form of symbolic power in given social spaces – for example, constructing and reinforcing ideas of 'community' and the 'local' and serving as the centre of social activity, which we shall discuss soon.

The viability of small news outlets is in part due to the fact that they act as mediators and interpreters of global networks of power and flows (Hutchins, 2004). Within a newsroom, professionals are needed to sift and edit state, national and global news to localize stories, explain their relevance to readers and to make sense of the cascading streams of news that flow ceaselessly. The concepts of *proximity* and *scope* (Shoemaker et al., 2007) are useful here for understanding how this works. Proximity is a characteristic of an event tied to physical referents, whereas scope is the aspect that represents journalists' judgement of an event's psycho-logical closeness to the audience and helps to explain the subsequent angle new outlets give to certain events and information.

Unlike geographic closeness, which is fixed, journalists can enhance an event's psychological closeness and overcome the negative force of long physical distance by emphasizing or interpreting the local angle on state, national or international issues. One example of this is coverage of the Eyjafjallajokull volcanic eruption in 2010 by the small Australian commercial newspaper the *Warrnambool Standard*. It highlights how proximity and scope can work together in placing the global in context of the local. The newspaper published articles about one of its journal-ists being stuck in Ireland surrounded by ash in the wake of the erup-tion (Alexander, 2010) and also ran stories discussing the importance of the region's own volcanic history to tourism and whether the region's only dormant volcano could erupt again in the future (Collins, 2010). Two years later, the newspaper reported that a puff of Icelandic ash had made its way to Warrnambool when two Icelanders visited the city with a container of ash to show at a Rotarian conference.

The Internet has transformed the work process of local news outlets, which have become globally connected and internally networked organizations (Castells, 2010). This presents significant advantages as the power of network flows becomes increasingly important (Lim, 2003). Fairfax Digital Media, which owns national newspapers and radio stations and is one of the largest owners of small commercial newspaper publications in Australia, provides a good example. According to the editor of one small newspaper within this network, being part of Fairfax Media with its local/global connections has particular advantages for smaller publications. He says:

> The digital network that we are part of is a national network. If we put up a 'must have' news story on our website…it will be picked up by the national network and then that's when it might go international in the blink of an eye. That's how news traffic flow works. Within minutes you've got attention from around the world. It really is incredible to watch.

Small news outlets are not only filtering information from global and national network flows; they also send out, through their internally linked news networks, information that has value in a global context. The editor quoted above helps to crystallize the advantages of this:

> In the digital space, an international audience doesn't care about where the story breaks and they don't have to live in our town to get access to the newspaper and that story – if it's 'click bait', that is, if the story is sexy enough it doesn't matter where the story originates from, proximity is not important to international news sites if there are other news values, particularly if it is novel or unusual.

The editor's reference to 'click bait' highlights the importance of news values much broader than proximity and scope when news travels from the local to the global. He gave the example of a story the newspaper published about a live shark being dumped on the front doorstep of the newspaper office. He said within minutes the story was picked up by the Fairfax network and disseminated to news websites across the country, attracting interest from national television, radio and international news providers, including the BBC and the *China Daily*, all of which focused on the unusual nature of the story (BBC News, 2009; China Daily, 2009). Most importantly, the editor said the story translated to unprecedented interest in the newspaper's own website from audiences across the globe.

Unpacking the local in a geo-social context

We now turn our attention to the term 'local' because while it is used widely in both journalism practice and theory, there has been surprisingly little analysis of what it means to journalism studies. As Pauly and Eckert (2002) contend:

> Scholars, for their part, have thoroughly studied other keywords that journalism uses to describe itself, most notably *independence, objectivity,* and *public,* but *the local* has escaped similar scrutiny. (Pauly & Eckert 2002, p. 311, emphasis ours)

In this section we examine 'local' carefully, highlighting the problems associated with using it to *describe* small news outlets in the 21st century, but emphasizing its *meaning and value* for such media as they seek to remain relevant. Franklin (2006) has suggested that direct reference to the town or city in a newspaper's masthead may be one of the few remaining local features of the paper, an argument that also has relevance to local television and radio across the globe.

Franklin points to ownership of local press ceasing to be local, newspaper offices moving from the town centre as part of cost-saving measures, production shifting to centralized locations, and the fact that journalists are less likely to be 'local' and spend their entire working life on a particular paper (Franklin, 2006, p. xxi). The same applies to discussions about commercial local radio and television, with newsreaders often reading from teleprompters in studios far removed from the regions they are perceived as serving. Franklin associates 'local' news media with geographic territory, or physical location in some shape or form. This is also the case in wider journalism studies and industry circles, where 'local' is synonymous with news and information that serves a well-defined physical area – most notably small towns, cities and shires, or, as its digital subsidiary 'hyperlocal' implies, a neighbourhood or street. Under the geo-social framework, we need to examine the meanings we give to geographic territory – as we will demonstrate, the local is much more than a descriptor of physical space alone.

Theoretical perspectives on 'local'

Pauly and Eckert (2002) suggest 'local' is a myth invoked to signify our sense of connectedness. Kaniss (1991) claims the news media produce local identity as much as they produce news. In this way the media can be seen as constructing *the idea* of local where news exists not only to provide information for and about a well-defined locality, but also to define local identity. Cheng's (2005) review of the term 'local' in media literature found it was generally associated with geographic territory, but there was also a strong view of 'local' as people oriented; that is, referring to people rather than geographic territory. As part of our research on what it means to be local we asked people living in a regional area of Australia for their understandings. Their responses support the idea that 'local' has a strong people-oriented dimension and is associated with a continuing and prolonged connection with a place. Take this focus group discussion, for example:

> Participant: You're a local if you've lived here a long time.
> Interviewer: What would you consider a long time?
> Participant: At least a few years, if not a decade or more.

And this from a journalist at one of the newspapers in the area:

> I've only been here a few weeks and I don't think I'll ever be considered a local. To be a local you have to be born and bred here.

In contrast, readers often described people who had lived in the area but relocated elsewhere as 'former locals'. This focus group comment from a female newspaper reader illustrates this:

> My son [now lives in a big capital city] ... I suppose you would call him a former local. He reads the paper online all the time.

And this from another reader:

> My cousin is a former local who reads it online everyday from Darwin [in Australia's Northern Territory]. She's lived there for 10 years but she reads this local paper to see what's happening, to stay in touch.

These 'former locals' still read the 'local' newspaper online. Later in this chapter we argue their 'sense of place' means they feel a need to stay connected to the events, issues and people of the area and the local media is a key resource for maintaining that relationship and view of themselves.

Local: practical and embodied

We have established the important link between the local and a physical site, but it also has a strong association with the body. The word 'local' derives from the Latin *locas* (place) and was first used in late 14th-century medicine to describe any ailment that was confined to a specific part of the body. Revisiting this age-old link is theoretically useful as we argue that our attachment to localities, the feeling of being 'local', is practical and embodied and that this directly relates to how we produce and consume news. Scholars including Moores (2012) and Couldry (2000) highlight the power of 'place', but the need for examination of 'the local' has tended to be overlooked. While Tuan (1977) does not discuss the 'local' specifically, he argues that the 'know-how' required to get around in urban spaces and to feel at home in everyday physical environments is practical, embodied and involves a combination of bodily senses (Tuan, 1977; see also Moores (2012) on this important subject).

Tuan argues that for people to form a lasting attachment to a location, to know a place, there must be repetition and return. This may involve everyday movements that swing back and forth 'like a pendulum' (Tuan, 1977, p. 180) – they take time. This kind of repetitive behaviour relates to the habit of reading the local newspaper. Take this comment from a 65-year-old reader of a daily newspaper and focus group participant, which captures how embodied the practice of reading the local news can become for some citizens:

> If I don't read the paper in the morning I feel like my arm's been cut off. It's just what I do, If I don't, I feel cut off from everything that's happening locally.

Not only does this woman express a reliance on the newspaper in quite dramatic physical terms; her comment reveals a belief that this daily ritual connects her with a social and physical environment. Tuan (1977) contends that this kind of embodied knowledge and practice takes time to develop, but that it shapes people to a significant degree, and can be expressed physically as well as psychologically:

> Abstract knowledge about a place can be acquired in short order if one is diligent ... but the 'feel' of a place takes longer to acquire – it is made up of experiences, mostly fleeting and undramatic, repeated day after day and over the span of years. It is a unique blend of sights, sounds and smells, a unique harmony of natural and artificial rhythms such as times of sunrise and sunset, of work and play. The feel of a place is registered in one's muscles and bones. A sailor has a recognisable style of walking because his posture is adapted to the plunging deck of a boat in high sea ... it takes time. It is a subconscious kind of knowing. (Tuan, 1977, pp. 183–184)

Local habitus

The concept of embodied knowledge shares synergies with Bourdieu's idea of *habitus*, which we first introduced in Chapter 1. Possessing habitus is feeling like 'a fish in water' in a given social situation, and it has been a useful concept through which to examine class divisions and battles for power and dominance in social space (Grenfell, 2008). Bourdieu described habitus as 'the practical sense, or if you prefer, what sports players call a feel for the game' (Bourdieu, 1990, p. 61).

Habitus forms part of Bourdieu's suite of theoretical tools. It is intertwined with his concepts of *field* and *capital*, and together they are useful for interpreting the social world (Bourdieu, 1990). We are not the first people concerned with understanding 'local habitus', but we are in regard to media. Savage et al. (2005) have used the term to unpack the relationship between place, class and habitus in a 'working class' village in the UK. Inglis (2008) also refers to the idea of 'local habitus' in discussing Ireland's 'place' in a globalized world. He says local habitus is evident among those who have lived in a village/town for a long time. He refers to the practices that are a product of this habitus:

> ... locals engaging in the gossip and conversations that are central to community survival, knowledge necessary to be able to decipher new information about what has happened to whom, where, where when and why, they are able to engage in the nuanced game of conversational give and take, they show the necessary deference and reverence, shock, display and despair when the latest news is discussed,

names mentioned and events recalled. Those who are new to the area see that it is based on a language they do not know how to speak, a habitus in which they have not been socialized. (Inglis, 2008, p. 203)

A reader from a small country town interviewed as part of our research said he had only moved to the region 12 months earlier:

I started reading the paper to see what all the locals are up to ... I hope to become a local eventually, but it takes time.

This man's comment gives expression to the idea that it's a gradual process to acquire this 'language', or 'local habitus'. He said reading the local newspaper regularly was his way of getting to know the area, to engage with what was going on and learn about local people, places, issues and events. This brings us to the next section, which positions reading the local newspaper as a place-constituting activity. This is followed by a discussion of how journalists and news organizations can utilize 'local habitus' in their professional practice.

Local habitus, news habits and journalism practice

Participants in Hess's 2013 study of regional newspapers in the Australian state of Victoria often closely associated the practice of reading a newspaper with the idea of being a 'local', especially those who had family connections or had lived for a long time in the town or city the small newspaper served. For example, a reader who participated in a focus group said:

If you live here and you consider yourself a local you tend to read the local paper. I do, my parents do ...

The editor of a daily newspaper offered another insight, which points to the importance of local media to individuals' view of themselves as citizens connected to society: 'if you read it, you see yourself as part of something bigger, of belonging'.

The editor described reading the local newspaper as a practice created by one's experience of a place – in this instance a town or city. His idea of it being a practice that involves seeing yourself as part of 'something bigger' relates to Bourdieu's thinking about the interplay of field, habitus and capital (Bourdieu, 1990). It can be interpreted as the development of local knowledge through reading the newspaper helping to construct a degree of social order. This order can be used to build or maintain an identity or social position as a 'local'. This generates forms of capital that can be beneficial, an idea the following sections explore.

The concept of local habitus is important to discussions about local news because of its value for media workers. In the interviews for this chapter, journalists and others working for small newspapers, from advertising, editorial and management, all highlighted the value of 'local knowledge' to their media-related practices. Some news workers described local knowledge as 'a feel for a place', 'knowing what makes the town tick' often put into practice by knowing automatically who to go to and where to go for news and information, along with the 'history of the place'.

Knowing how to spell and pronounce names of streets and people are obvious manifestations of local habitus, but they do not encapsulate the concept in its entirety. To illustrate this, there were four journalists of different ages interviewed for this chapter who were 'born and bred' in the regions where they worked. They all described themselves as locals. None of them had studied journalism at university and all indicated that one of the main reasons they had been recruited to the industry was because of their understanding of the area in which they worked – its natural, social and cultural dimensions. They considered this an advantage in their day-to-day journalism practice. As a reporter at a country newspaper said:

> Local knowledge is everything ... understanding the area and how it works and the people. You can't do your job properly if you don't have it.

Local habitus can translate into what Bourdieu terms 'cultural capital' (Bourdieu, 1986). This concept helps us to understand the power of social skills and assets that promote social mobility and success, such as education, tastes, material belongings and credentials. Bourdieu identifies three kinds of cultural capital: embodied, objectified and institutional. 'Objectified' refers to things we possess that confer status – in journalism this could be a particularly impressive contact book. The four 'home-grown' journalists suggested that the possession of local knowledge (embodied cultural capital) was often more beneficial than a university degree in journalism (what Bourdieu described as a form of 'institutional' cultural capital). A journalist at the daily newspaper said:

> In gathering local knowledge it's about understanding demographics of the region, like here it's a very conservative largely Catholic

community and a slowly ageing population. You have to know things like where the local school is, the name of the principal ... and the people. It's not just that, you have to know how a place works, what makes it tick. That's not the sort of thing you come away with from a university.

Local habitus and journalists' credibility

One veteran reporter said possessing local knowledge helped to generate an element of 'trust' among sources of news, which might be best understood as what Bourdieu (1986) refers to as 'symbolic capital' in terms of credibility or reputation:

> Building up that rapport with people is almost the foundation of what you do as a journalist in a regional area and you don't realise that when you first start out, unless you're a pretty smart cat. But it's the most important thing you have and local knowledge is essential to that. After 35 years in the job I say that with some authority. If you're a local, or you've been around a long time in the job people tend to trust you more implicitly with information.

Conversely, a lack of 'practical know-how' about a place may be seen to impact on a journalist's reputation (another form of symbolic capital in Bourdieu's terms) in the localities where they play a role. Where journalists appeared to lack local habitus, their reputation among readers and sources did not appear as strong. Said one reader:

> I remember once when I was a kid and there was a new journalist reporting on TV. She pronounced [name of a town wrong] and I remember everyone was talking about it the next day and saying 'what an idiot'.

These participants' experiences and observations provide some evidence that journalists' 'local' status, the depth and quality of their knowledge of the environmental, social and economic features of the place and embodied social capital have important economic and cultural value for the news outlets they represent. It goes to the trustworthiness and legitimacy of the news they produce, affecting reporters' sources and readers' decisions about providing news and buying it. We will return to this important theme towards the end of the chapter.

Resourcing geo-social news production and the impact on local knowledge

Chapter 7 discusses the business models of local news. In the discussion about the viability of local media, however, it is important to consider the significance of investing in local knowledge and what happens if this resource is depleted in a local newsroom setting. Local knowledge and social connections take time to form, but small newspapers throughout the Western world are renowned for high staff turnover as many young reporters use such publications as stepping stones to careers in metropolitan news (Franklin, 2006). The ability to build local knowledge can also be impeded by staff cutbacks and the depletion of editorial resources. As a 23-year-old journalist said:

> Resources and time to do things has got less and less over the past four years. My boss is less willing to let me travel distances to meet people and get that local knowledge, less willing to do stories that require time. There is a shrinking of resources and in any way you can cut costs and anything superfluous to that, anything that sits outside budget is not considered worth it.

One editor interviewed for this chapter said while coverage of local news was what made the business model for small commercial newspapers competitive in the wider news marketplace, his company's persistence in cutting resources made it difficult to chase and cover the news and for new reporters to develop local knowledge:

> Editorial staff are doing more with the same resources. Is that the right thing? Probably not, from an editorial perspective. One of the tools that's being used to get business 'under control' has been to get journalists to take annual leave ... you end up with a skeleton staff covering day-to-day issues. The business model and the bottom line I feel are more important to the company.

And this from a younger journalist:

> You get local knowledge by getting out and meeting people, seeing how things work, getting a feel for the area. But there's no time, there's no resources. You have to just keep churning out copy.

Resourcing and changes to the large media company's business model had also impacted on the geographic stretching of news production practices (Hess & Waller, 2014). At the time of writing, journalists at all the newspapers where interviews were conducted for this chapter had been informed that jobs would be lost and all sub-editing would be outsourced, or moved to a metropolitan or larger regional area. Some journalists argued the shift towards centralizing production practices devalued the importance of local knowledge. A veteran journalist at the daily newspaper encapsulates this sentiment:

> I think the big fear is, that if there are central subbing nodes, then you miss that local knowledge. It's things like spelling street names, people's names, you don't want to get basic stuff like that wrong ... you would start losing credibility with people. That's the sort of knowledge that subs who don't know the area might not have, but it's what a newspaper should just know.

A veteran sub-editor highlighted the increasing importance of local knowledge in a geo-social news framework:

> I actually don't think it matters where subs are located, but they have to [know this area]. They need to know the issues, the background to the issues, the people and proper spelling of people's names. You can't be a sub-editor without knowing your community, without having seen it, lived it. We had a story and the journalist had the river flowing the wrong way! That was simply ignorance of the local community from not having lived here for long.

The reference to the direction of river flow highlights the subtle dispositions that emerge from one's local habitus. Another experienced journalist, meanwhile, said a failure to recognize the value of this for local news outlets would eventually take its toll:

> I think this will impact on readers in a very big way if you've got people producing a paper without an understanding of that geographic area. The effect will be subtle and immeasurable on a pie graph or a budget for some time, but this disillusionment is a very dangerous thing to happen to a paper. It loses its credibility.

Community

The concept of 'the local' is often considered synonymous with 'community' in conversations about the media. The two tend to go hand in hand when scholars examine journalism beyond the walls of 'big' media. 'Community' has long been a dominant frame of reference for newspapers that serve small towns and cities (see Lauterer, 2006; Reader & Hatcher, 2012). Like the local, it is an idea that fits within the geo-social shape ball. It conjures notions of familiarity, shared interests and collectivity. Aristotle, for example, described community as composed of politically engaged citizens who contribute to the construction of a government that seeks a 'good life for all' (Hatcher, 2012b, p. 131). The importance of localness and the value of community have capti-vated scholars for centuries, but these are feelings that are not easily measurable or replicated by us all. Classic urban sociological theories, for example, have sought to understand human relationships and their value to society – from the individual to the collective – and to pinpoint the social glue that binds people together in a given place. There has been a particular emphasis on 'community' and its symbiotic relation-ship to traditional, small-scale societies. For example, French sociologist Émile Durkheim (1912) sought to unravel differences between mechani-cal solidarity (social integration stemming from common values) and organic solidarity (cooperation based on the need for one another's ser-vices). Tonnies (1957) distinguished between *Gemeinschaft* – 'a lasting and genuine form of living together' – and *Gesellschaft* – the arrange-ment where individuals engage in artificial relations for their own ends, such as the market, trade association or state.

The smaller the village the more people appear likely to be united through kinship and reciprocity. But in today's modern world, towns and cities – no matter how small – are part of a globally networked world and feature increasingly transient populations. To describe geo-graphic spaces simply as 'communities' can mislead us into thinking their inhabitants exist together harmoniously for the sake of the collec-tive and overlooks issues of equality, social class and power.

The notion of community is particularly dominant in discourses of rural areas (Rose, 1996; Herbert-Cheshire & Higgins, 2004; Bowd, 2010). Bowd highlights how early theorists of community, such as Wirth (1938), Simmel (1955) and Redfield (1955), tended to associate small-town and rural life with close and long-lasting relationships and view city/metropolitan life as impersonal and anonymous, which fits with popular understandings of community (see Bowd, 2010, p. 27).

For many scholars, however, the fact that individuals may engage in similar communication channels or reside in one geographic space does not necessarily make them part of the same community. Foster (1996) suggests that although communication serves as the basis of community, it should not be equated with it. In other words, we can communicate with another person without considering them to be a member of our own community. Lee and Newby argue that just because people live close to one another does not necessarily mean that they have much to do with each other:

> There may be little interaction between neighbours. Rather it is the nature of the relationships between people and the social networks of which they are a part that is often seen as one of the more significant aspects of 'community'. (Lee & Newby, 1983, p. 57)

Bourdieu contends that socially distanced people find nothing 'more intolerable' than physical proximity (1999, p. 128) yet there are people of different class and cultural backgrounds who may all reside in the same small town or city that a small newspaper serves. There is also considerable slippage in the use of the term 'community'. Hillary (1955) identified 16 different concepts of community from 94 different definitions. The idea of 'community' can be considered a place, value or common purpose.

On its own, 'community' serves as a weak theoretical foundation for building our understanding of local media. The rise of new technologies has seen the term 'community media' now transcend geographic spaces to be used interchangeably with alternative, independent, underground and radical media, particularly public broadcasting, blogging and Internet sites (Couldry & Dreher, 2007; Howley, 2010; Ndlela, 2010; Forde, 2011). There also remains some confusion over whether community media is not-for-profit or commercial in nature (see Forde, 2011). Howley (2010) defines community media as an alternative to profit-oriented media, catering for the wide range of tastes and interests of ethnic, racial and cultural minorities who are often ignored, silenced or otherwise misrepresented by mainstream media:

> This rather generic definition ... accommodates a diverse set of initiatives, community radio, participatory video, independent publishing, and online communication to name but a few. (Howley, 2010, p. 2)

Forde suggests alternative and community media resonates with the unrepresented, working outside established societal power structures, dedicated to the role of journalism in democracy and occupying a place in the media-scape as 'an endangered species' (Forde, 2011, p. 53). It cannot be said that local news providers work outside established societal power structures – the geo-social concept highlights how intertwined they are with global information flows and movements. Commercial local news outlets are often owned by media conglomerates and rely on powerful players such as Google to disseminate information and engage with audiences.

Community and symbolic power

The geo-social framework serves as a theoretical shell that helps to show where 'community' and 'local' fit and can be used to help understand small news media with geographic relevance which stretches beyond physical spaces into digital networks. It emphasizes that community is a powerful *idea*, rather than a tangible reality. Chapter 1 discussed the value of viewing local news through a media power lens. There is a rich vein of literature that discusses the media's ability to shape and define reality as a potent form of social power (Hall, 1973; Couldry, 2003b; cf. Entman, 2010). It is here that the small news outlet's connection with 'community' is perhaps best understood. Anderson (1983), for example, argues that society has become so large and complex that people can no longer be personally familiar with it, so instead they rely on the news media as their window on the world. Mersey (2010) contends that within boundaries of community, feelings of emotional safety, a sense of acceptance and willingness to make a personal investment can develop (Mersey, 2010, p. 63). Michael Schudson says that news media carry a great deal of symbolic freight in regional identity, 'more than they know'. They help to 'establish in the imagination of people a psychologically potent entity – "a community" that can be located nowhere on the ground' (Schudson, 1995, p. 95). Shaun Moores (2000) follows Anderson to argue that community might be best understood as a 'fictional reality' – communities appear to have an objective existence but are actually products of the imagination (Moores, 2000, p. 39).

The dark side of community

In any discussion of community, issues of power must be examined. 'Community' can have a dark side – it is not all about shared interests and collectiveness. 'Community' is a constructed notion that creates advantages and inequalities and generates boundaries between insiders and outsiders. Recent research shows how local radio, for example, can at times create 'polarizing' views (Ewart, 2014, p. 804). In all forms of community media, journalists play important gatekeeping roles in deciding what news and information is considered of value or interest to the community in question. Hess (2015a) highlights how the news media's ability to generate a sense of community can restrict 'outsiders'. She provides examples where minority groups are under-represented in Australia's country newspapers and discusses how this can contribute to social exclusion. For example, while a cultural minority group might consider itself to be 'local' to a particular area, at times it might not be given a voice by local media representing it. The very idea of 'local' and 'community' can also generate feelings of being 'out of place' for those who might live in a particular location but do not feel as connected or share the same sensibilities as others. We must be careful to acknowledge, therefore, that generating feelings of 'community' among audiences, especially in times of crisis such as terrorist attacks, can result in exclusion as well as inclusion. In a complex, globalized world, a retreat into 'communities' can be a refusal to engage or connect with difference and complexity. Deuze (2007b) argues contemporary society is anything but solid or socially cohesive. He says under conditions of worldwide migration (of capital and labour), global conflict and environmental apprehension most people experience a growing precariousness in everyday life: 'As a response, citizens increasingly retreat into hyperlocal enclaves (suburban ghettos or guarded-gate communities) or global personal spaces such as Facebook' (Deuze, 2007b, p. 671).

People involved in all forms of community journalism are constantly negotiating what it means to be part of the community – not only bringing community into existence, but also questioning and contesting how it happens and the shapes it takes. At the other end of the spectrum, we must also provide scope to acknowledge those individuals who actively resist involvement in a geographic 'community', even if they are 'local'. An example of this might be criminal gangs or secret societies that communicate 'in house'. They resist the cultural norms and conventions that come with the desire to be part of a geographic community, including engagement with news. Some research indicates when criminals are 'named and shamed' in local media for misdemeanours, they wear the coverage like a badge of honour (see Hess & Waller, 2013), refusing to conform to wider 'community' expectations. We will discuss this in more detail in Chapter 5.

Place and sense of place

We have spent much time discussing the connection of local and community to local news media. The geo-social model also directs us to consider the motivations of those who do not consider themselves local or

part of a community but engage in some way with local news. For this
we draw on notions of 'sense of place'.

The term 'geo-social' is used in the field of information technology to
describe mobile locatable services for identifying users, or connecting
and coordinating them with local places and events that match their
interests, based on their geographic location (Gupta et.al., 2007; Vicente
et al., 2011). Whereas such applications for smart devices including
phones and tablets emphasize 'user location', we suggest 'sense of place'
helps to conceptualize individuals' physical, psychological and/or social
connections to particular geographic spaces without assuming they are
located within such physical spaces.

Local media outlets, from newspapers to hyperlocal sites, generate a 'sense of place' among readers as they bring together historical, regional, national and international perspectives and thereby
'place' readers in the context of the world (Buchanan, 2009, p. 64).
Importantly, 'sense of place' also offers scope to consider the more
individualistic motivations and choices of those who read small newspapers. Buchanan defines 'sense of place' as one's identification with a
place engendered by living in it (Buchanan, 2009, p. 66). However, she
also acknowledges that one's sense of place can have social, emotional
or economic foundations. This ranges from one's social ties, family
'roots' and nostalgic connections, to those who view sense of place as
a means to an end such as goods, services and opportunities. (Eyles,
1985; Butz & Eyles, 1997). As an Australian small newspaper editor
commented:

> Who is our audience? It's a difficult question really and we are still
> guessing. There are the usual suspects – the people who live here,
> but ... increasingly there are many more readers who don't live here,
> but they either most certainly once lived here, they still know some-
> one who lives here ... or they want to come and live or work here.

Not only can a geo-social news outlet be considered as 'placing' readers and their locality in the context of the world, it also acknowledges
that connection or identification varies from individual to individual.
Readers do not necessarily need to reside within the 'place' to be motivated to read such publications. Importantly, a 'sense of place' differs
from the more collective, cohesive notion of 'community' and does not
assume that individuals have shared values, points of view or common
interests merely because they reside in a particular geographic space or

have some connection to it. As Massey reinforces, 'place' and 'community' are rarely coterminous:

> ...[there] has been a persistent identification of 'place' with 'community'. Yet this is a misidentification. One the one hand, communities can exist without being in the same place – from networks of friends with like interests, to major religious, ethnic or political communities. On the other hand, the instances of places housing single 'communities' in the sense of coherent social groups are probably and, I would argue, have for long been quite rare. Moreover, even where they do exist this in no way implies a single sense of place. For people occupy different positions within any community. (Massey, 1994, p. 153)

It is helpful to distinguish between the physical and psychological elements of proximity as a news value for journalism (Shoemaker et al., 2007), particularly in deciphering information in a local/global context. It is also useful for understanding local news outlets and 'sense of place'. Physically speaking, content continues to concern people and events with a connection to a particular geographic location. The psychological element of proximity, or scope, is useful in highlighting the news media's communicative and symbolic role in shaping a sense of place for its audiences in a local/global context. It also acknowledges that people have their own social and psychological reasonings for developing an affinity or connection with geographic territory and others within these spaces without considering themselves as part of a geographically centred 'community'.

Summary

This chapter began by making the theoretical concepts underpinning local news appear as simple as child's play. We constructed the conceptual shape ball of geo-social news and studied the 'shapes' that fit within, from local to community and sense of place. Studying 'the local' as a discrete and key concept in journalism studies – rather than as a mere descriptor of the physical territory journalists serve – is important in understanding what really makes local news media 'tick'. We have shown that what we term 'local habitus' is a valuable resource for journalists and their media organizations. In the near future, digital transformation may mean that most 'local' news is delivered through a multimedia application on a smart device. Given the enduring news value of 'proximity' – in both its physical and psychological dimensions – the news people choose to access may very well reflect their 'sense of place' and/or where they consider themselves a 'local', or part of a 'community' regardless of where they are physically located. Local habitus is therefore vital for the successful production and consumption of local news and needs to be considered in the social, cultural, economic and political interests of society. It means media companies with local ambitions need representatives on the ground, in powerful and visible sites such as town halls, courts, schools and sports fields, as well as coffee shops, pubs and people's homes.

The concept of 'geo-social' news not only acknowledges geography as an important characteristic of local journalism; it points to the importance of the wider social spaces in which a small news outlet operates and the constellation of social relations in which individuals come to identify with a place. It does not mean that local journalists do not play a powerful role in constructing the idea of 'community' and 'local' – geo-social news can, for example, instil a sense of 'local' identity – but it does not immediately designate people as part of a 'community' and avoids using such terms to describe and define geographic space. Most importantly, it provides greater scope to understand local news in the local-global nexus and the increasing emphasis on flows and nodes of information, as well as the changing nature of audiences and advertisers.

3 Local Media Around the World

Introduction

In this chapter we embark on a world tour to understand how local media is studied and practised across the globe. Our journey comes in difficult and changing times, not only in terms of the media landscape, but also from a geo-political standpoint. Issues including terrorism, climate change, increasing numbers of refugees and rapid technological advances increasingly dominate news headlines. Furthermore, as American community journalism scholar Bill Reader reminds us (2014), although local journalism is a global phenomenon, we should not assume the practices and roles of community-focused news media are the same across diverse societies and cultures. Each locality is unique in some way, depending on geographic, political, social and/or cultural influences. For example, the political climate has a major impact on the ways local journalism is practised in different countries – from the strict state control of communist nations like China and Vietnam to the celebrated Fourth Estate function of the 'free' press in the United States. Media companies in many parts of the world are making rapid advancements in digital news and experimenting with other new technologies. At the same time, developing nations battle to bridge the digital divide and continue to rely heavily on 20th-century mediums like community radio for their cost effectiveness and ability to target niche audiences across different dialects and literacy capabilities (see especially areas such as Africa and parts of Asia). The digital revolution continues to cause upheaval as the traditional business model that once supported local news crumbles. Thousands of newspapers, radio and television stations that once dominated the landscape have suffered, and many have been forced to restructure and even close their doors.

What is certain is that no matter where you stand in the world, local journalism matters to people. A review of the literature, from the Americas to Africa, Asia, Europe, the Middle East, United Kingdom and Oceania, reveals a consistent theme of celebrating the news media's role in connecting people and fostering a sense of community and local identity. Some argue it is this very aspect that is key to its economic survival (Abernathy, 2014). Other common themes to emerge include changes to local journalism practice, advocacy and political campaigning, the role of audiences in producing news, increasing 'news gaps' at the local level and the binary between local versus non-local.

This chapter is not an exhaustive review of the scholarly research. We are monolingual researchers, so our focus is limited to the literature written in English. There is certainly much more scholarship in a range of other languages.

North America

A number of important themes dominate discussion and research on local journalism in North America. Across the US and Canada local media outlets are closing or reducing the amount of local news they produce. These closures and the creation of news gaps are a major cause of concern because without adequate resources journalism cannot expose new information, affect public policy or keep local governments honest.

Canada

Canada is a large country with a relatively small media market. Goldstein (2015) notes that lack of scale, a split of audiences by language and the dominance of national newspapers over local have combined to make the country's local newspapers especially vulnerable to a challenging market. He has made the grim prediction that by 2025 Canada will have few, if any, printed daily newspapers, and that there might not be any local broadcast stations either. 'It should be obvious that both of those potential developments pose serious issues for the future of local journalism' (Goldstein, 2015, p. 2). These shrinking newsrooms mean media outlets are increasingly in the hands of fewer proprietors, prompting some politicians to cite concerns for democracy (The Guardian, 2016). There is concern a dramatic slump in oil prices has affected the appetite of advertisers. There have been calls for the government to reinstate its role as the industry's largest advertiser and create tax incentives for local coverage.

Since the early 2000s local television reporting in Canada has been gradually 'fading to grey'. The Canadian Broadcasting Corporation cut back its local news from an hour to half an hour across the country in 2000. According to the Canadian Association of Journalists, this contraction had a much greater impact on people living outside large metropolitan areas, because in cities such as Montreal and Toronto people have access to an array of local news sources (www.caj.ca). More recently, a study commissioned by watchdog group Friends of Canadian Broadcasting has warned that, without intervention, half of Canada's small- and medium-market commercial television stations could be gone by 2020, and with it 910 jobs (Lu, 2016).

The United States

In the US, the local journalism sector is dominated by non-daily newspapers, local radio and niche magazines. American scholars can be credited with developing the concept of 'community journalism' (see Lauterer, 2006; Reader & Hatcher, 2012; Robinson, 2014). Lauterer (2006) explains that 'community' journalism was a choice phrase adopted by US researchers in the 1960s to replace 'hometown newspaper' (see also Byerly, 1961) – especially those serving small towns and cities. The United States was also first to advocate and explore the 'public journalism' movement in the early 1990s – the practice where journalists bring together people to discuss civic affairs and shape the news agenda, which is most prevalent at the local level (see, for example, Rosenberry, 2012).

The United States is also the birthplace of the Internet. During the past decade alone, US entrepreneurs have driven large-scale digital innovation – think Google and Facebook. Developed by a university graduate Mark Zuckerberg, Facebook has more than a billion users worldwide and has become a key source of news for people, and for journalists, including those working at the local level. It comes as no surprise that there has been strong emphasis in US scholarship on the future business model and sustainability of local news in such tumultuous times.

The local newspaper business has been a tale of mixed fortunes in recent times. There are approximately 9000 newspapers in the US, 85 per cent of which are small-circulation weeklies. On one hand, about 1500 large local daily newspapers (with strong historical ties to the towns and cities they serve) have been hit hard as advertisers and audiences now have a plethora of ways to communicate with one another. On the other hand, the non-daily press proved especially resilient to the 2008 recession, as well as to competition and cuts experienced among the 'national' and 'metropolitan' news media. The 2014 National Newspaper Association survey of community newspaper readers found two-thirds of residents in small towns across the US still depend on their local community newspaper for news and information (www.nnaweb.org). The survey also found that trust in local newspapers remained high, and the 'pass along' rate, which refers to sharing copies of these newspapers, is also strong. The report's authors note that a striking finding from the survey was that nearly one-third of households still did not have Internet access at home.

Despite this, the US has witnessed the rise of some of the biggest local media online start-up ventures in the world, from Patch (which at its peak operated more than 900 local and hyperlocal news sites in 23 US states) to Next Door (a private social networking service for neighbourhoods). Innovative start-ups like these have struggled to maintain intensity in the marketplace.

Journalism academic and former *Wall Street Journal* executive, Penny Abernathy, has a strong interest in the future business model of local newspapers. She argues good journalism alone is not sufficient to save newspapers (Abernathy, 2014) and the link to community is essential as they build loyalty first among readers who then attract advertisers who want to reach them.

TV is by far the most popular medium for Americans but the US is also home to more than 10,000 commercial radio stations (BBC– United States of America Country Profile). The Pew Research Centre provides a regular, timely snapshot of the state of local media in the US. A recent study highlights that local TV continues to capture broadcast viewers while digital non-profit journalism can provide a second tier of news. The research centre conducted a study on local news ecosystems across three disparate metropolitan areas in the US in 2015. It found nearly 90 per cent of residents follow local news closely and about half do so very closely. About two-thirds of the residents in each city discuss local news (Pew Research Centre, 2015). Meanwhile, research in 2013 found that the news programmes Americans watched on local TV networks had changed significantly, with much more coverage of sport, the weather, traffic reports and breaking news (Pew Research Centre, 2013).

American scholars and industry are protective of local media's valuable Fourth Estate function. Freedom of expression is guaranteed by the Constitution and the watchdog role of the press has come to be celebrated by journalists working in democracies right across the globe. Abernathy (2014) cites several studies and reports that outline the importance of community newspapers as being central to democratic life at a time when larger publications pull back circulation and coverage from outlying communities (Abernathy, 2014; see also Downie Jr. &

Schudson, 2009 on this important topic). Cass (2005) examined four weekly newspapers in Mississippi and found a common characteristic was their ability to supply constant criticism on local governance in the areas they cover, providing a watchful eye on municipal officials.

Local media's relationship to sense of community and the ways in which local journalism is practised also serves as a key area of interest. Paek et al. (2005) argue local print news readership in the US is an essential constituent of communal solidarity. Readership increases the likelihood of community participation in public debate, both at the individual level and in terms of social interaction.

United Kingdom

Our journey around the world takes us to the United Kingdom next. Its media landscape is large and complex and ranks second globally to the US (Bromley, 2009). Possibly the largest media-related issue facing the British government and regulators is whether to continue the BBC as a publicly funded entity beyond 2016 when its charter is due for review (Bromley, 2009). The future of local news has become a key policy issue as stakeholders seek innovative ways of providing support for news providers – or the possibility of drawing on resources from the BBC to help cover local news. Like in the US, business models and sustainability of local media have become a key focus of academic scholarship. Fenton and colleagues (2010) highlight that commercial success in local and regional news now appears increasingly to depend on scale. They argue that since the 1990s (following successive relaxation of ownership rules in the Broadcasting Act of 1996 and the 2003 Communications Act) there has been rapid consolidation of the newspaper industry into a handful of regionally based monopolies (see below), resulting in larger companies serving bigger regions. They argue the result will be news with less and less relevance for local people.

Some of the latest research on local media in the United Kingdom focuses on the emerging hyperlocal sector, with scholars mapping the rise of Internet start-ups across the country in the face of widespread decline of traditional news outlets. Much of this stems from Cardiff's Centre for Community Journalism in Wales, where researchers have developed an overview of the state of the hyperlocal sector across the United Kingdom (Williams et al., 2014; Radcliffe, 2015). A report in 2015 revealed there were more than 400 active hyperlocal websites in the UK, compared with just over 100 local newspapers. Key findings include the revelation that one in 10 people use local community websites at least weekly; functional information about community events, services and local weather are the most popular types of content with hyperlocal audiences; and just 13 per cent of hyperlocal websites generate an income of more than £500 per month (Radcliffe, 2015). Townend (2015) studies the policy climate and has argued local news outlets in the UK would benefit from tax relief (such as gift aid) and eligibility for certain kinds of philanthropic funding (see also Fenton et al., 2010).

The declining quality of British journalism at the local level is an important concern for a number of British scholars. Wahl-Jorgensen (2005) warns that in the UK a market logic works against the right to communicate. In this view the increasing dominance of resource-poor, chain-owned weekly newspapers has encouraged the rise of an anti-political journalism. Wahl-Jorgensen argues that journalism produced 'on-the-cheap', as practised in local papers, becomes a journalism of consensus; one which has the power to enhance community solidarity but cannot question the status quo. O'Neill and O'Connor (2008) point to a study of 2979 sampled news stories in four West Yorkshire papers during one month, representing the three main proprietors of local newspapers in the UK. It revealed a relatively narrow range of routine sources, as well as the troubling finding that 76 per cent of articles cited only a single source. The analysis indicates that journalists are relying less on their readers for news, and that stories of little consequence are being elevated to significant positions or used to fill pages at the expense of more important news. We will discuss this in more detail in the next chapter, but these trends indicate poor journalistic standards and may be exacerbating declining local newspaper sales (see also Franklin, 2006).

Ireland

Ireland has a large number of local weekly newspapers, with most counties and large towns having two or more newspapers, but Felle (2013) has questioned whether they can survive. Ireland's Celtic Tiger economy from the mid-1990s to mid-2000s saw new colour printing techniques and the sale of a number of newspaper titles and companies for multi-million euro figures. In 2007 when the economy collapsed, circulation and advertising revenue went into a downward spiral. Newspaper sales were hardest hit in the commuter belt around Dublin, but Felle also notes that non-metropolitan local newspapers lost on average 5 per cent circulation per year between 2007 and 2012: 'If current circulation trends – roughly 5 per cent declines per year – continue, local weeklies have about a decade left before they will become extinct' (Felle, 2013).

A content analysis of community news sites affiliated with Irish newspapers shows story selection reflects classic community news values and fulfils roles and functions similar to those documented in historical research about community press and social organization in the US (Rosenberry, 2014). This illustrates the potential for Irish local media sites to be important agents in the construction of community identity, and could hold the key to the sector's survival.

Apart from newspapers and their online editions, Ireland has a large number of regional and local radio stations, as well as commercial and public television. Community radio is a relative newcomer to the scene. There were pirate stations as early as the 1980s, but legal community radio did not emerge until an Irish Radio and Television Commission pilot project established 11 stations in 1994 (Gaynor & O'Brien, 2010).

Africa

Across Africa, the role and place of community radio tends to dominate scholarly discussion of local news, especially in isolated areas and among marginalized communities. Academics have been particularly interested in examining the evolution of community radio in post-apartheid South Africa. When Nelson Mandela was elected president in 1994 under the banner of 'The Rainbow Nation', community radio began to flourish and reflect the country's diverse cultures and communities (Odine, 2013). A three-tier broadcasting system replaced the monopoly of the South African Broadcasting Corporation (Olorunnisola, 2002) which had restricted media diversity. While there are some reservations about the quality and value of the sector today (P. Moore, 2008; Kruger, 2011), many researchers contend community radio in Africa offers the most promise as the medium is pervasive, local, extensive, flexible, readily understood, portable and speedy. It has often been examined and celebrated as an instrument for mobilizing and engaging communities (Olorunnisola, 2002; P. Moore, 2008; Mhlanga, 2009; Bosch, 2010; Gatua et al., 2010). Odine (2013) emphasizes the use of community radio to promote culture, with South Africa now home to more than 200 community radio stations broadcasting cultural programmes in 11 languages.

Madamombe (2005) of the Africa Renewal project online highlights that while transmitters may reach only a few miles, community radio stations across Africa provide isolated communities with opportunities to voice their concerns, from gender relations to combating HIV-AIDS: 'They share farming tips and income generation ideas and explore ways to improve education'. Gatua and colleagues (2010) argue radio constitutes an obvious starting point to build inclusion in community, national and global information flows. They suggest community radio also serves as an ideal representative forum for liberation and empowerment in developing countries.

This optimism exists despite a relatively grim picture of the broader local media landscape, especially in South Africa where print and broadcast media are concentrated in metropolitan areas (Kruger, 2012). However, there are an estimated 500 community newspapers across the country (www.fcjonline.co.za). The media landscape is complicated by the 'township' and 'settlement' organization of South Africa, in which townships often lack the economic base to support strong local newspapers (although many are supported by governmental diversity grants). A survey conducted in 2004 found about 80 small community print projects were a shadow of their former selves and were struggling to survive (Hadland & Thorne, 2004). In many areas there are no local media at all. Harber (2011) highlights the absence of local media in Diepsloot, a community of about 200,000 people north of Johannesburg, South Africa. This gap means that rumours abound, local authorities and politicians cannot be held to account and there are fewer legitimate channels for the expression of views outside of public protest, which so often turn to violence.

Kruger's (2011) study of local news on community radio found just 14 per cent of news items in bulletins on community stations were local and generated independently. The rest of the news was obtained from online sites, an issue highlighted by local media scholars throughout the world. P. Moore (2008) contends that, increasingly, community broadcasting in South Africa is failing the people by being too closely associated with norms and practices that have shifted the emphasis from community to business practices, political intervention and censorship. Mhiripiri (2011) also laments that neighbouring Zimbabwe has not seen expansion in community radio stations characteristic of the region in the 1990s.

Local media, social media and activism

When it comes to journalism practice, scholars studying the African local media landscape have explored the rise of digital journalism and social media, especially in regards to activism at the local level. Some researchers have examined the role of social media (Stassen, 2010), and how ICT usage influences newsroom culture among community radio journalists (Nassanga et al., 2013). Bosch (2010) highlights that local activists are increasingly using mobile and online social networking to promote events and causes and reach their constituencies. Chiumbu and Ligaga (2013) analyse the role of new media technologies in transforming radio practices in South Africa. Their study found ICTs expand spaces for public debate and discussion and transform radio publics, but they also acknowledge the realities of the digital divide in South Africa.

News and humanitarian aid

Business models have also captured the attention of African scholars, with some pointing to the role of non-government organizations in the support of community media in Africa. Brisset-Foucault (2011) argues NGOs have penetrated local media and modified the rules of the game in terms of access to resources and protection from repression, and also in terms of professionalism. Conrad (2014) warns the benefits of community radio (meaningful engagement and freedom from political and economic influence) are often not realized because external donors' interests heavily influence the sector.

Kivikuru's (2013) study of Congolese women in refugee camps in Rwanda highlights the importance of 'place' and its relationship to local news. The study found refugee women did not appear to be interested in wider mediated communication as daily concerns fill their lives in the 'non-place' where they find themselves. As a result, the article advocates the need to establish 'small media' or community media in the camps and the possibility of changing the principles of the United Nations (UN) communication policies to better address the needs of refugees.

Asia

Intense periods of modernization and its relationship to news, identity formation and communicating across a range of dialects are some of the themes tackled in scholarship about local media across Asia. Other important topics relate to issues of development journalism and the tightening/easing of government media restrictions – from China's great Internet firewall, to analysing local media in Indonesia after the fall of the Suharto regime. This section provides an overview of local journalism in a selection of Asian countries.

China

China is well known for its strict media regulation – freedom of the press enjoyed in Western nations is not extended to journalists working in the world's most populous country. According to the World Press Freedom index (2015), China is ranked 176 of 179, just ahead of the Syrian Arab Republic, Turkmenistan and the Democratic People's Republic of Korea. Amid its rise to global economic superpower, the Chinese government has grappled with ways to control information in digital space, and has managed to keep a much tighter hold of the reins than other countries. Local news providers in China often have no way of getting first-hand information about the central government or ministries, and must depend on the government-controlled wire news service Xinhau and websites of authorities for information (see Zhang, 2014). While many local news services have been centralized or merged in other parts of the world, the opposite is true in China. Government obstacles prevent the expansion of local media with other media sources. Local government officials consider the local news media their own channel to the people, and they fear media that cross regional boundaries can no longer be controlled by them and may become critical of their operations (Scotton & Hatchen, 2010).

A 2011 survey convened by UNESCO, which polled 115 media professionals in China, highlighted the need to increase locally produced content and found quality was compromised due to inadequate staffing and other resources. The findings portrayed a working environment where small media outlets had to fulfil obligations towards local authorities and faced mounting commercial pressure. Despite rapid modernization in some densely populated regions, scholars have raised serious concerns about information gaps in China. Jiang and Huang (2013) examine media in less developed areas where television signals and Internet access are not available. They conceptualize the rise of what they term 'grey zones' – the phenomenon where people come to know about issues happening in the nation and around the world but ignore local and community affairs. It refers to a shortage of local information through which an individual can generate ideas and identify him/herself in society. Jiang and Huang (2013) contend that while China ranks first in the world in terms of Internet users, communication can be understood as a three-dimensional concept where 'grey zones' influence people's lives, self-development and social development. They argue local media is essential to rebuilding and cleaning up communication grey zones.

As in other parts of the world, China's local news providers are recognized for their role in generating a strong sense of identity and community among users, despite the intense government influence. Lu and Chu (2012) highlight that China's integration into the global economic system has created three dimensions of cultural citizenship identity (cosmopolitan, national and local). They argue there is an especially strong connection between local media use and local identity. Other scholars have singled out the role of broadcast television in generating trans-local belonging – the capacity to identify with more than one place in a global world (see Sun, 2012). The Provincial China Project (based in Australia) has focused on examining the process and consequences of economic reforms and social change at provincial and local levels in China, including the role of media (Sun, 2012). These scholars remind us that globalization is experienced locally, and it is through local media practices and experiences that the idea of globalization has significance. Song and Chang (2013) examine the news and the local production of the global in China. Using data collected from five Chinese regional newspapers in 1989 and 2009, their study indicates that China's integration into the world's capitalist economy has widened the global landscape for the local media, but not necessarily provided greater latitude to negotiate the terrain (see also Sun, 2012).

US community journalism scholar Jock Lauterer has offered a different perspective through his writings on China's new and burgeoning 'community newspaper' sector. His blog, *Blue Highways Journal,* notes there are thousands of cities in China without a local newspaper, and enterprising Chinese publishers are realizing the opportunities and creating hyperlocal start-ups.

Lauterer recounts meeting an entrepreneurial editor, Li Guo Chen, who runs eight hyperlocal start-ups in the southern province of Gangzhou (Lauterer, 2014). At a visit to one of Li's offices, Lauterer met a group of readers, one of whom said the best thing about the new community newspaper was that citizens could constructively criticize the government: 'The party newspaper – it's a mouthpiece, and we don't care about it. But we like this newspaper because it talks about us. We read every page' (Lauterer, 2014).

A local academic confirmed this for Lauterer, saying that in the more progressive and liberal southern province of Guangdong local government was not offended when the online newspaper was critical. Lauterer's blog has documented further evidence of this more relaxed attitude at other hyperlocal start-ups he visited in China's south. He observes that under the Chinese system, the local bureaucracy has few avenues of communication with citizens, and there is now a realization that the community newspaper can serve as a conduit for collecting public opinion. (Lauterer, 2014)

Japan and Korea

Researchers studying local journalism in Japan, South Korea and North Korea have emphasized its importance for bringing people together and generating feelings of belonging. For example, Jiang and Huang (2013) focused on the ways local news media can unite people in times of disaster. They documented how, in the wake of a devastating earthquake in 1995, Kobe City was rebuilt with the help of Radio FMY, which aimed to unite the community and dispel prejudice by providing a voice for people of all ages, abilities and cultures influenced by the disaster. Jung and colleagues (2013) drew on neighbourhood storytelling networks including interpersonal, organizational and community media connectedness to discuss civic participation in the aftermath of the Great East Japan Earthquake in 2011. They argued the neighbourhood storytelling network was important, especially for certain age groups while the Internet also provided a conduit for civic engagement in disaster situations. Japan's regional and local newspaper sector accounts for almost 50 per cent of newspaper circulation across the country, of which some publications have been established since the early 1800s. The Japan Local Newspaper Association represents about 40 local newspapers. Its key objective is to contribute to local culture and it has helped pursue development of local governance, economics and culture for local areas (see Rausch, 2012 for a full account of local media in Japan).

North Korea has the highest government media regulation in the world, according to the Press Freedom Index. While this hampers investigative reporting, Kang (2013) found the use of local media contributed to the development of neighbourhood belonging, collective efficacy and volunteering behaviours.

Indonesia

Like other Asian countries, the role of local media in times of disaster is also highlighted in Indonesian scholarship. For example, the Aceh Nias Reconstruction Radio Network (ARRNet) testifies how community media contributed to rehabilitation and reconstruction of shattered communities in the aftermath of the 2004 Indian Ocean Tsunami (UNESCO, 2011 as cited in Jiang & Huang, 2013).

Scholars who examine Indonesia's local media sector also focus on the problems and prospects of the centralization of radio and television broadcasting in the post-Suharto era (Gazali, 2002). Hollander and colleagues (2008) have outlined the ways in which efforts aimed at democratizing the media system and empowering communities in Indonesia occurred in three discursive periods – the 1998 'Revolution Movement', the 'Reform Era' follow-up, and the 2002 Broadcasting Act. They argued the result of the changing winds so far had been the liberalization of the market in line with global media trends. However, they said the government has tried to frustrate the prospects of community media and its development remains stagnant.

Indonesia's television industry is dominated by five large media corporations, all based in the capital Jakarta, according to Armando (2014). This does not leave much growing space for television stations at a local level, which would be needed to strengthen Indonesia's democratization. Scholars in Indonesia have also highlighted the corruptive practice of 'envelope journalism' and explored how it affects the quality of news at the local level. Here, journalists accept bribes to report favourably about private individuals, companies and state officials. 'Envelope journalism' poses one of the most serious threats to free and independent reporting in the country (DW, 2012).

Thailand and Malaysia

Community radio can serve as an important national resource, giving local voices access to media and providing an alternative to mainstream broadcasters, according to Magpanthong and McDaniel (2011). This resonates with some of the scholarly work in South Africa around this important medium. Magpanthong and McDaniel (2011) examined the status of community radio in two contrasting settings: Thailand where community stations number in the thousands, and Malaysia where community radio has so far not been allowed. Although Thailand's community broadcasters launched their operations without formal authorization, successive governments have not taken action to force their general closure. However, steps to create a legal status for them have moved at a sluggish pace. In Malaysia, authorization for community radio stations seems never to have been seriously considered even though public groups have expressed enthusiasm for the idea. In both nations, political considerations have been major factors governing the slow development of policies for community radio.

Sahid Ullah (2014) laments the increasing influence of Western journalistic practices that ignore the South-East Asian context and the importance of local knowledge.

Development journalism – India, Bangladesh, Nepal and Sri Lanka

Across Asia, studies that examine local media and the value of development journalism are more pronounced than arguably anywhere else in the world. 'Development journalism' describes the role of media in serving the best interests of a nation, often by working with government or making a conscious effort not to incite conflict and to emphasize harmony, especially in religiously diverse nations such as Indonesia. Again, it is community radio that is seen as a beacon of light in assisting national prosperity.

Community radio in India has been recognized for helping to revitalize agricultural and rural development. Das's (2010) study demonstrates the linkages between rural radio, agriculture and rural development and argues that if used with other strategies, community radio can play an effective role in instigating social change.

Chandrasekhar (2010) also highlights community radio's important role in developing stronger and more prosperous societies at the local level. The Indian government has spent millions of rupees in the name of rural development to address issues of poverty, illiteracy and unemployment, but it is not getting desired results, according to Khan (2010). This study identifies a communication gap between government policies and the public as a major issue, and suggests local community media be promoted to enhance community development. Khan suggests community radio is ideal because it covers a wide area, diverse audiences (see also Sharma, 2011) and is most cost-effective.

The power of community radio has been recognized in Bangladesh, where radio broadcasting more broadly is a government monopoly used for propaganda. Ullah and Chowdhury (2006) contend community radio is a tool for social change and allows true participatory communication necessary for sustainable development.

Community radio has also been the focus of a study in western Nepal, celebrated for its ability to provide access to information for the marginalized section of the population and give a voice to the voiceless (Banjade, 2007).

In Sri Lanka, Tacchi and Grubb (2007) examine the social, cultural, political and symbolic behaviours that shape communication. They highlight the role of the e-tuktuk as an interesting example of community media that uses radio and mobile technologies to reach out to remote villages. The e-tuktuk is a mobile information centre located within a three-wheeled auto rickshaw.

South America

Social and cultural development via media – especially at the community level, is a key area of interest in South American scholarship. Local and social media have been analysed for their part in political uprisings from the Zapatista movement in southern Mexico in 1994 (Rodríguez et al., 2014), to the Bolivarian Revolution in Venezuela (Artz, 2012) and the role of community radio through internal civil conflict in Columbia (Murillo, 2003). Rodríguez (2005) argues that social media movements are hybridizing, recycling and adapting media technologies. This research explores how in Mexico (home to more than 12 million people from almost 60 different ethnic groups) Indigenous radio has developed under the auspices of a government organization charged with making policy for these populations. This has created a hybrid model for radio, combining public, state and local community media characteristics. Rodríguez argues such a medium has subtly contributed to the transformation of the dominant symbolic order and has strengthened socio-cultural cohesion among ethnic groups.

Rural community radio created in El Salvador at the end of the long civil war in the early 1990s facilitated growth of civil society, according to Agosta (2007). This study found marginalized groups such as *camesinos*, women and rural small businesses were strengthened because radio helped them to bring their views and issues to the forefront and also introduced them to national debates. Filho (2009) contends Brazil's community media sector (especially radio and television) gains legitimacy through its contribution to development, its local situation and relevance to society at large. Meanwhile, Podber (2012) joins the chorus of international scholars who argue that while many take for granted the explosion of new communication technologies such as Twitter and Facebook, 'old-fashioned' mediums such as radio continue to serve people throughout the world (especially among poorer populations) and remains essential. He argues that although radio predates social media by nearly a century, it continues to connect people to one another and to their local communities.

Middle East

Contemporary scholarship on news media in the Middle East has been dominated in recent years by the Arab Spring – the revolutionary wave of democratic uprisings ignited by social media that spread across the

Arab world in 2011. There are few studies available in English that specifically examine the role of local journalism; however, a recent survey by the Northwestern University in Qatar examining attitudes and behaviours towards media shows a dramatic 'return to the local' (see Paul, 2015 for an overview of this study). A lead researcher on the project, Robb Barton Wood, said the results suggested a move away from a 'pan-Arab' perception of the media (content that looks at the region as a whole and promotes regional identity) and a shift towards a more local or national relationship with news. The survey found a higher use of regional languages as opposed to English, with more than 90 per cent of respondents following all media in Arabic.

Wood said positive assessments of people's own national and local media had increased:

> Some might say that seems to suggest that there is some sort of embrace, whether there is national, cultural or local pride. But you see that sort of 'return' in this very tumultuous period to their own national and local culture. (in Paul, 2015)

Algan (2005) has studied the role of Turkish local radio in the construction of a youth community, while Lev-On (2012) analyses how community members evacuated from their homes use media, especially the Internet, to keep in touch. Lev-On highlights the importance of small media with limited and local reach as predominantly meeting such people's needs, overshadowing mass media usage. The study also found correlations among various media usages and between the use of small media and the user's sense of community.

In research on Israeli journalists, Tsfati and Liveo (2008) found those who perceived there to be strong media influence in the regions where they worked were often new journalists employed by local media outlets.

In terms of infrastructure and technology, the media environment for Palestinians in the Occupied Territories developed extensively between the first and second Intifadas (Bishara, 2010). For decades, Palestinians assembled their media world out of other states' news coverage and a diverse collection of small and large media. The research highlights how during the first Intifada Palestinians relied on local communication like graffiti to evade Israeli restrictions. During the Oslo period, the Palestinian Authority (PA) established official Palestinian broadcast media, while Palestinian entrepreneurs opened broadcasting stations and Internet news sites. During the second Intifada Palestinian news media were hampered by continued PA restrictions and intensified

Israeli violence. Small and new media enabled networks of care and connection, but were not widely effective tools for political organizing.

Some studies of foreign news coverage in the Middle East acknowledge the importance of local knowledge. For example, Murrell (2015) explores how Western news teams recruit 'fixers' to help them undertake their work. Fixers are often local journalists with excellent contacts and local knowledge, as well as language and interpreting skills.

Oceania

We now venture to the Pacific, where many of the world's oldest cultures are part of the world's newest nation states. While there are striking differences in climate, land mass, languages, politics and culture, these countries share histories of colonization by various European powers, including the British, French and Dutch. Many of them still have ties to foreign powers, including the US. Across this vast region, local journalism plays important roles in identity and community building and maintenance. We begin with the largest nation, Australia.

Australia

Australia's local media reflects the vast and diverse terrain it covers. There are some stark contrasts between its commercially owned and operated newspapers, television and radio, its public broadcasters and the vibrant not-for-profit 'community' sector, which has been of more interest to scholars than mainstream local news until relatively recently. The national public broadcaster the Australian Broadcasting Corporation (ABC) provides local news across regional Australia via radio, television and the Internet. However, in recent years its budget has been cut and there are ongoing political and public discussions about how best to fund it, and what its remit should be (Hess et al., 2014). As we've seen in other places on our world tour, shrinking budgets for public broadcasting and takeovers and closures in the commercial media sector are global trends. Australia's local and regional media are not exempt. Many local TV newsrooms in regional areas are being downgraded or closed, with local bulletins produced in major centres and beamed into parts of the country that once had their own half hour of dedicated news featuring local people, places, issues and events (Waller & Hess, 2015). Local newspapers and commercial radio stations in regional Australia are experiencing cuts and closures too – with some being abandoned and others shedding staff and centralizing their production in order to remain profitable and stay in business (Hess & Waller, 2016b). Many of the 300 or more local newspapers across the country are falling into the hands of two major media enterprises – Fairfax and News Corporation.

Van Vuuren (2007) cites a 2005 News Corporation study of 6,500 people that found two-thirds of Australians considered their community newspapers to be the medium of most relevance to them (p. 96).

Community broadcasting

Australia was one of the first countries in the world to introduce not-for-profit community broadcasting (see Forde et al., 2009) and community radio is arguably most closely associated with the community journalism tag. These outfits broadcast in remote and rural places, as well as suburban and urban areas. Rather than being positioned as a medium for 'development journalism' as in Asia, the emphasis is on providing a voice for the under-represented or marginalized groups and challenging government policy rather than working alongside it.

Australian community broadcasting distinguishes itself from other media by actively promoting access and participation in the processes of media operations, administration and production. It is volunteer driven, with more than 20,000 volunteer broadcasters and support staff helping to deliver media 'for the people by the people' (www.cbf.com.au). The McNair Ingenuity research study of community radio found that 64 per cent of non-metropolitan listeners in 2010 and 66 per cent in 2008 nominated local news and information as a reason for listening to community radio (McNair Ingenuity Research, 2008, as cited in Bowd, 2010). However, the 2012 Finkelstein inquiry into Australia's news media expressed some concern that community radio services related mostly to localized communities and had little capacity for regular coverage of local news (Finkelstein & Ricketson, 2012).

There are debates as to whether community stations should stress localness and service the 'geographic' population, or emphasize participation and provide a platform for under-represented voices, views and cultural products (Gordon, 2009, p. 62). It can be argued that while these tensions and debates exist, community broadcasting in Australia is engaged with the issues and strives to provide a wide range of services and cater to diverse audience needs (Jolly, 2014). One of community broadcasting's recognized strengths lies in its delivery of radio and television programming for specific cultural and ethnic groups throughout the land (see for example Misajon & Khoo, 2008). It is a significant resource for people from non-English speaking backgrounds, as they have few media alternatives, and these broadcasts support language and cultural maintenance.

Journalism, 'community' and research

Research on local journalism in Australia strongly reflects the sector's emphasis on its role in community building and community maintenance. For example, Hanusch's 2015 survey of local journalists found advocating, or being a forum for the community, was considered as highly important by Australian journalists working in local mainstream media. The study concludes that:

> Overall, the results reinforce the vast amount of literature in that local journalists express a desire to play a role in their community, to focus on news relevant to it, provide a forum for the community and to advocate for the community. (Hanusch, 2015, p. 829; see also Bowd, 2009; Richards, 2013)

The not-for-profit community sector has been the subject of considerable investigation, especially in Queensland where academics at Griffith University have conducted major national qualitative audience studies of Australian community broadcasting to explore the role being played by community journalism (Foxwell et al., 2008; Meadows et al., 2009). They found about four million listeners in an average week tune into community radio stations around Australia, primarily to hear local news and information, which they argue provides evidence of a failure by mainstream journalism to meet their diverse needs. Forde (2011) argues that the community broadcasting sector is worthy of close investigation because it is one of the few areas of the Australian media landscape that continues to grow.

Aotearoa New Zealand

Journalism in Aotearoa New Zealand has an unusually high level of exposure to globalization, as virtually all of its newspapers, magazines and more than half of its broadcast news outlets have passed into foreign hands in the past 40 years (Lealand & Hollings, 2012). Matheson (2007) says the exceptions are the state-owned broadcasters, Television New Zealand and the Dunedin newspaper, *The Otago Daily Times*. This means there are very few operators with 'immediate political interests in this country' (Matheson, 2007, p. 30). At the most local level, the Australian media giant Fairfax owns 66 community newspapers.

It is interesting to note that journalism scholars in Aotearoa New Zealand have not focused their attention on the study of 'local' news *per se*. Perhaps this is due to this globalized media market being so highly localized. For example, we note that there is no fully national newspaper, with even the country's largest circulation daily, the *NZ Herald*, essentially geared to a parochial Auckland audience. The great majority of TV news journalism remains locally generated and is very popular, according to Lealand and Hollings' (2012) overview of New Zealand journalism – as is local radio.

An important theme emerging from the literature concerns New Zealand's changing demographics, which has a major impact on all aspects of society at the local level. There are concerns over a lack of cultural diversity in local mainstream newsrooms, and the impact of this on the representation of the country's Maori, Pasifika and Asian populations. Robie (2009) notes that for more than two decades, diversity has been a growing mantra for the New Zealand news media. Initially, the concept of biculturalism/partnership with Maori was pre-eminent in the debate, but as the nation's Pasifika and ethnic media have flourished and matured and demographics have rapidly changed, multiculturalism has become increasingly important and challenging. Projected demographics by Statistics New Zealand indicate that the country's Asian population will almost double by 2026. The Pasifika and Maori populations are also expected to grow by 59 and 29 per cent respectively. Robie (2009) argues that the steady expansion of Maori, Pasifika and ethnic media in Aotearoa New Zealand has implications for the media industry and journalism education.

South Pacific

The South Pacific spans 30 million square miles of ocean containing a large number of scattered island groups. There is an array of cultures, economies and political regimes and a combined population of approximately eight million. Political formations across the three zones of Melanesia, Polynesia and Micronesia are just as diverse, with strong influences from their different colonial histories. National entities vary from independent states to overseas territories of France and the US. These differences, plus big variations in population, income, education and communications infrastructure make it impossible to generalize about the South Pacific. Given this, it is not surprising that journalism research has a strong focus on specific places, people and contexts, from Hayes' (2010) detailed study of emerging Oceanic philosophy in Tuvaluan journalism, to Bala-Ndi's (2013) research on public interest journalism in New Caledonia.

Key issues of concern in practice and scholarship include the impact on news of geographic distance, internal strife and state control. There is also a focus on the chronic problems of poor working conditions and lack of training for journalists. Small media markets, diversity of languages and people, and low literacy levels have impacted on media development and practices in the region, according to Papoutsaki and Harris (2008). Most local news media in the South Pacific Islands is either owned by the government, the church or multi-national corporations, so the role of local independent 'grassroots' outlets becomes more critical in providing balance in the overall role of media practice in Pacific Island nations.

Faith-based broadcasters comprise half of all community radio stations in the region (Austin, 2014). Eggins (2008) explores the link between community development and church-based radio broadcasting in Papua New Guinea while Austin (2014) investigates why their position in the media environment is so contentious. She observes that for secular media practitioners, Pacific faith-based media are seen to interject foreign voices and capital into island communities. For the international development sector, partnership with faith-based organizations around development agendas brings fears that aid funds will be used for evangelism. Austin (2014) says they have achieved levels of sustainability that have thus far eluded secular community media through application of culturally appropriate and self-defined development pathways.

Publishing a daily newspaper is not viable for many Pacific nations and news originating from industrialized nations still dominates television and newspapers. Scholars including Robie (2004) focus on the importance of strengthening media at the local level to maintain diversity of opinion, develop distinctive local voices and determine professional codes. The establishment of regional news services, including Pacnews in 1999 and online information services offered by Pacific Media Watch and the Pacific Islands News Association, have assisted regular exchanges of local news (Papoutsaki & Harris, 2008).

When the Pacific Islands are discussed in the international media, 'coups, conflicts and human rights' seem to be the dominant themes (Robie, 2013). Some scholars have examined how this can result in stereotyping, and the negative effects that can result from this representation

(Fry, 1997; Iroga, 2008). There is also research that examines the specific roles journalism plays in South Pacific politics, where local concerns can become entangled with regional events. For example, Matbob and Papoutsaki (2008) explore how the independence struggle in Indonesian-ruled West Papua is represented through the Papua New Guinea media. In contrast, Iroga (2008) takes a peace journalism approach in an analysis of the role of news media in helping to establish peace in Solomon Islands in the wake of divisive ethnic conflict from 1998 to 2003.

External influences, especially from Pacific neighbours New Zealand and Australia, have a strong presence in journalism education and training, and also in terms of practice. Local journalism in the region is generally projected as embracing Western news values with the ideal of 'objectivity' and 'factual' reporting being paramount. However, Robie (2008) argues that while this may well be partially true of the mainstream media in the two largest nations, Fiji and Papua New Guinea, in many respects Pacific media has more in common with other developing nations such as Indonesia and the Philippines. Some argue that a unique style of Pacific journalism is emerging (Layton, 1995; Singh & Prakash, 2008), while others emphasize that Pacific Islands journalism research needs more islander perspectives (Papoutsaki & Harris, 2008; Bala-Ndi, 2013; Robie, 2013).

Europe

We have left a region of many island nations in a vast ocean in the Global South to finish our tour on a continent with many countries, media and political systems and languages in the Global North. For example, some European nations, like Germany, have a media market characterized by very strong local and regional newspapers and public service broadcasters with a strong regional orientation, while others have much more nationally oriented news systems dominated by media based in the capital (Nielsen, 2015, p. 6).

While sophisticated studies of local news exist in Europe, they are typically confined to a single nation. Powers and colleagues (2015) argue this precludes analysis of how cross-national variations in market structures, political systems and professional histories shape the development of local news systems. In spite of this, media are generally understood as a powerful means of creating closer ties between citizens throughout Europe, and local and regional news media are recognized as particularly effective in reflecting its numerous identities and cultural diversity.

At the national level, a rich tapestry of history, politics, issues and identity is evident in each country's news ecology and style of journalism practice. This is reflected in a wealth of research on local media in specific regions. Scandinavian studies in particular celebrate the importance of local journalism to local communities (see for example, Moring, 2000; Hatcher & Haavik, 2014).

As is the case throughout the globe, the impact of digitization on local news is discussed from many angles, but particularly through the decline of print and rise of online news – changing the work of journalists in Europe (see for example, Hille & Bakker, 2014), and audience expectations and participation. For example, Costera Meijer (2010) explores the kinds of social roles Dutch audiences want their local media to perform and concludes they have to supply more nuanced stories about local residents and the places they live.

Academics who are interested in questions about the production and reception of news use a variety of research methods, from comparative surveys (Weaver & Willnat, 2012) to detailed ethnographic studies of individual newsrooms (Hermans et al., 2014) and the media-related practices of everyday citizens (Kotilainen & Rantala, 2009). There is also a strong focus on the collapse of traditional business models and the consequences for the news industry and public life (see, for example, Björkroth & Grönlund, 2014; Sjøvaag, 2014). Media policy and regulation is also an important topic, especially in discussions of not-for-profit community media (Bergés, 2012).

Two broad currents emerge from our review of the literature on local journalism across Europe. There is a strong focus on innovation and experimentation in Northern and Western European research, while media independence, freedom, diversity and equality are key topics in the countries of Central and Eastern Europe that are transitioning to democracy. Examples include Erzikova and Lowrey's (2014) examination of explicit and implicit pressures exerted on news organizations by a regional government in Russia in 2009 and 2010. The study revealed techniques used by the authorities to divert the media from scrutinizing the government and concluded it had the effect of homogenizing the content of regional newspapers since the government becomes the main source of information. Radojković (2009) considers why civil society media is not growing in Serbia and argues the process of transition to democracy provides an opportunity to establish a 'third media sector'. However, it has been unsuccessful because most local media organizations restructuring from government monopoly have chosen the commercial privatization option. The range of perspectives at the local level in Central Europe are emphasized in Voltmer and Wasserman's (2014) investigation of Polish and Bulgarian journalists' understandings of press freedom. They found many Polish journalists feel that they have to fulfil a particular mission in the young Polish democracy – an attitude that is virtually absent in interviews with their Bulgarian counterparts.

Innovation and experimentation

In Northern and Western Europe, which have strong and sophisticated democratic governments, there is a distinctive interest in media innovation and experimentation at the local level, and especially the emergence of hyperlocal start-ups. For example, Smyrnaios and colleagues (2015) observe there has been a proliferation of independent news sites in France during the last few years. They say that since 2010 this 'new wave' has been sweeping across French cities and rural areas where local journalist start-ups are challenging established monopolies. These news websites cherish their independence from local political and economic elites: 'They try to innovate journalistically; they engage in intense relations with their public, with whom they share geographical proximity but also often sociological and political closeness' (Smyrnaios et al., 2015, p. 165). Hyperlocal journalism is thriving in Belgium, where Paulussen and D'heer (2013) explore the case of a regional newspaper experimenting with citizen journalism and user-generated content for hyperlocal news coverage. The findings suggest that the local newspaper uses citizen volunteers as a means to outsource the 'soft', 'good' and 'small' news coverage of local community life, while preserving the 'hard' and 'bad' news as the exclusive domain of professional journalists. Researchers in Western Europe are also interested in transitions to multiplatform journalism. For example, Aviles and Carvajal (2008) have analysed change in journalistic practice and newsroom workflow at two Spanish multimedia groups. The results suggest the emergence of two different models of newsroom convergence: the integrated model and the cross-media model, each with a different production system, newsroom organization, degree of journalists' multi-skilling and business strategy.

Summary

The key aim of this chapter has been to raise awareness of the commonalities and differences in the practice and study of local journalism throughout the world. A number of synergies have emerged, especially the intimate relationship between local news and notions of 'community', as well as a discernible pattern of impacts of digitization on journalists, audiences, and the 'business' of local news. In some parts of the world community radio is the dominant source of local news. It is also worth noting that weekly newspapers remain significant players throughout rural UK, Ireland, South Africa and other parts of the world, with many of them remaining independent of the conglomeration trends among the 'small daily' and 'big weekly' sectors of the industry. In some Western nations where local newspapers are disappearing, online hyperlocal publications are starting up and filling news gaps.

Taking an international perspective emphasizes that 'local journalism' changes according to the people – their cultures, histories, economics, languages, politics and polices – and geography of the region. Furthermore, within the places we have profiled here, local journalism is not static – the various histories discussed briefly show that flows of people, technologies, finance and political events can alter the local context dramatically, changing news agendas as well as the way news is produced and used.

This is why we advocate a critical-cultural approach, which emphasizes the importance of *context* in any study of local news. The concept of 'geo-social' journalism used throughout the book concerns specific social networks and places that are loosely bound by some geographic connection, and is used to explore how news outlets and audiences connect in the digital era. The associated idea of 'sense of place' is also important because in an increasingly transient world people may have a dual sense of place, or affinity with a particular 'local' area (as Chinese researchers remind us). They may seek out news and information that helps them feel connected with a place where they no longer live or work but they are attached to in some way. They may also seek out information to help their day-to-day lives in the 'local' area where their feet are planted. The point is, as important as 'local' is to understanding the future of news media, we must never lose sight of its place in a globalized world.

4 Shaping 'Local' News

Introduction

Local news outlets are sometimes referred to as the 'parish pump' because they are concerned with matters of importance for small communities, reporting everything from the local football scores to details about a volunteer group's annual general meeting (see Lauterer, 2006; Hirst, 2011). It can be a somewhat disparaging descriptor for news that focuses on the local scale as it is considered synonymous with being parochial, close-minded, insular and narrow. Local journalism does engage more often with information about people's everyday lives than with unearthing corruption in the city hall. For this reason, we might argue this type of journalism has lacked appeal in wider academic scholarship because it is viewed as mundane or just not 'sexy' (Nielsen, 2015). Its relationship to the everyday, however, is what makes local news an extraordinary barometer for gauging the types of news and information important to audiences, and for providing a unique picture of how news is generated and produced.

As this chapter shows, it is the social institutions, personalities and events at the most local level that affect people's lives most directly. Local journalism is far from being myopic. When a major international event or crisis occurs, it is through the familiar that people can relate to an issue far beyond their everyday world. Local journalists play a crucial role in interpreting 'big issues' – from global warming to terrorism – through the experiences of those with a geo-social connection to the locality they serve. For example, in the wake of the November 2015 terrorist attacks in Paris, the front pages of many local newspapers around the world featured the colours of the French flag. They also included stories about how the mass violence affected their own regions thousands of kilometres away. Journalists went in search of 'locals' who might be holidaying in Paris, and focused on whether security would be enhanced at local airports and transport links.

Local journalism relies on many of the same news values, routines and sources found in national and international editorial departments, but a different accent is placed on some of these, and it is these distinctions that give local journalism its special flavour. This chapter explores where local news comes from, how local journalists decide what makes news and the types of local information that matter to audiences.

What is (local) news?

Burns explains that while the word news describes 'the things journalists write about' it has been in use for at least 500 years – 'well before newspapers were around' (Burns, 2002, pp. 49–51). Discussions about 'what is news' often focus on information produced by journalists who work for news organizations, especially large media outlets (see Mencher, 2010). Today's editors overseeing newsrooms still apply 19th-century concepts of news and define their news menu as 'a mixture of information, entertainment and public service', according to Mencher (2010, p. 55). He suggests editors tend to agree with the idea that news is 'anything that interests a large part of the community and has never been brought to its attention before' (p. 56). The way we understand local journalism tends to depend on the way big media is studied (Franklin, 2008), how newsroom routines, pressures, journalistic norms and conventions influence the news. In the sections that follow we will challenge and refine some of the dominant cultural codes and conventions that influence the way journalists decide what is news for local audiences, from the powerful notion of objectivity to Galtung and Ruge's well-known study on news values. We will then examine the key sources of information (individuals and events) that journalists rely upon for information and the issues this presents. We conclude by highlighting the need to examine the role of everyday people as both sources of news and as barometers of what makes good journalism in the communities they serve.

Beyond the 'myth' of objectivity

There is a rich vein of literature that highlights how journalists depend on a set of collective cultural codes to assist them in gathering and producing news (cf. Hall, 1973; Tuchman, 1978; Galtung & Ruge, 1981). One of the key concepts influencing the journalistic field is the notion of 'objectivity'. Objectivity stems from democratic theory – especially the social responsibility model and Fourth Estate function of the press outlined in Chapter 1. Objectivity emphasizes the importance of journalists as neutral bystanders in the interests of serving the public good. It assumes the journalist exists above or 'outside' society rather than being embedded within it (Bollinger, 1991; Cottle, 2003). As Bollinger states, objectivity means the journalist:

> lives (figuratively) outside society. Beyond normal conventions and who is therefore better able to see and expose its shortcomings. (Bollinger, 1991, p. 55)

Schudson views 'objectivity' as a norm that has existed in the journalism academy since the 1920s, a period which saw the rise of the industrialized model of news and the 'professional' journalist. It has been used to protect journalists from criticism, embarrassment and lawsuits, and endowed the occupation with an identity journalists can count as worthy (Schudson, 2001, p. 165). Objectivity has since become an institutionalized hallmark of reportorial excellence (see Durham, 1998, for a more complete discussion), and the 'cement' of good journalism (Maras, 2013, p. 1). Journalists claim the existence of an objective and ultimate truth 'out there' that ought to be mirrored and not created, invested or altered in any way; where the observer and the observed are seen as two distinct categories (Bagdikian, 1997; Hanitzsch, 2007). Objectivity is often articulated in a cluster of terms such as 'impartiality, neutrality, accuracy, fairness, honesty, commitment to the truth, depersonalisation and balance … reporting the news without bias or slant' (Maras, 2013, p. 8).

We begin this chapter by challenging the tenet of objectivity, arguing that while it is a 'taken for granted' assumption of journalistic practice across the Western world, it can be suffocating to local journalism practice and prevent the sector from reaching its full potential. From a cultural studies perspective, objectivity can be understood as journalistic *doxa* (Schultz, 2007; Waisbord, 2013) – a Bourdiesian concept used to explain the 'ordinary acceptance of the usual order which goes without saying and therefore usually goes unsaid' (Bourdieu, 1984, p. 424). Schultz (2007) argues journalistic *doxa* pertains to the 'gut feeling' that comes from determining the set of news values that shape a story (see also Waisbord, 2013). We are not the first to challenge the notion of objectivity, especially in discussions about local journalism (see especially Glasser & Craft, 1998; Christians, 1999; Bowd, 2007). It has been described as a myth (Harding, 1991) with critics arguing that news is constructed rather than providing a direct snapshot of reality (Sigelman, 1973; Shoemaker & Reece, 2014). Fowler offers a political economy view:

> News is not a natural phenomenon emerging straight from reality, but a product. It is produced by an industry, shaped by the bureaucratic and economic structure of that industry, by the relations between media and other industries and most importantly by relations with government and other political organizations. (Fowler, 1991, p. 222)

The term 'objectivity' is widely considered to be problematic in discussing local media (Cass, 1999; Bowd, 2009, 2007; Christians et al., 2009). For example, in highlighting the difference between Pacific Islander media and Western 'free press', Cass (1999) suggests local media is a participant in society rather than an observer and journalists act according to the effects their stories may have on society. Lowrey and colleagues (2008, p. 275) describe local journalism as more 'intimate, caring, and personal; it reflects the community and tells its stories and it embraces a leadership role'. Many other scholars highlight the close relationship community newspapers have with their readers (Killenberg & Dardenne 1997; Lauterer, 2006; Meadows et al., 2009). Bowd (2003) lists several factors that contribute to this close relationship and give community newspapers a privileged position when it comes to understanding readers' interests and concerns. One factor is journalists' level of community involvement: the journalists are part of the same community as the readers and are involved in the same groups and share the same facilities. A second factor 'derives from the notion of accountability', as local journalists 'may have more of a sense of being answerable to an audience than metropolitan journalists because they are more accessible' (Bowd, 2003, p. 120; see also Ewart & Massey, 2005).

Drawing on Carey's ritualistic view of journalism, public journalism scholar Clifford Christians argues that rather than disconnecting from 'community' mainstream media should embrace it. Carey argues:

> The conventions of objective reporting were developed as part of an essentially utilitarian-capitalist-scientific orientation towards events.... Yet despite their obsolescence, we continue to live with these conventions as if a silent conspiracy has been undertaken between government, the reporter and the audience to keep the house locked up tight even though all the windows have been blown out. (Carey, 1997a, p. 141)

Christians (1999) argues truth telling in journalism should be located in a moral sphere. He contends a truthful account places emphasis on context and draws on Rorty (1979) to highlight journalists playing a role in determining 'what is better for us to believe rather than the accurate representation of reality' (Rorty, 1979, p. 10). Debunking the myth of objectivity enables local journalists to more fully appreciate and embrace their roles as key connectors and drivers of news and community issues. Local journalists can play a powerful part in seeking to resolve conflict, bring people together, perform boundary work and uphold expected social and moral values. In doing so, we must also recognize the news media's ability to construct reality and the power and inequalities that arise from this. As we argue throughout this book, local journalists contextualize stories for audiences and provide leadership in times of crisis. Dispelling the myth of objectivity does not mean journalists cannot be ethical, fair and balanced in their reporting, providing they strive, or are at least perceived, to always put community interests ahead of their own.

Rethinking news values for local journalism

News values give reporters and editors a set of rules – often intangible, informal, almost unconscious elements – by which to work, from which to plan and execute the content of a publication or a broadcast. News values are recognized, both in practice and in theory, for their importance in shaping journalism and how it represents the world, and have long been criticized in journalism scholarship (see Molotch & Lester, 1974; Tuchman, 1978; Schultz, 2007). Research on news values dates back to 1965, when Norwegian social scientists Johan Galtung and Mari Homboe Ruge published an article in the *Journal of International Peace Studies*. Entitled 'Structuring and Selecting News', they began by analysing the output of a group of newspapers in their homeland, Norway, and identified 11 common values. They then went on to create a system for prioritizing news. As Brighton and Foy (2007) observe, this was groundbreaking research and all scholarship on news values that has followed has been built on those initial findings.

Our concern is to emphasize that the set of values applied by different news media – from local, regional, national and international to print, television, radio and online – are as varied as the media themselves (Brighton & Foy, 2007, p. 6). However, these sometimes subtle but important differences are often overlooked in discussions about journalism. For example, Noelle Neumann (1993) says there is a set of assumptions that *all* news people have about criteria for acceptance of stories by audiences. Evensen lists these as conflict, consequence, prominence, timeliness, proximity and human interest (Evensen, 2008). The suite of 11 values outlined by Galtung and Ruge (1965) are arguably the most well known in journalism circles to the point that their association to news is almost as generic as 'Hoover is to vacuum cleaner' (Waterson, 1998 as cited in Harcup & O'Neill, 2001). They are: frequency, threshold (amount or size of people affected), clarity, cultural proximity, consonance, unexpectedness, continuity, composition, actions of elite, personification and negativity. Harcup and O'Neill (2001) critique this widely renowned news inventory to suggest there are 10 contemporary key news values influencing journalism: the power elite, celebrity, entertainment, surprise, bad news (conflict or tragedy), good news, magnitude, relevance, follow-up, and news agenda (stories constructed by news outlets to advocate a cause or interest).

In assessing the scholarly literature on news values we contend the following are most applicable to understanding how local journalism differs from other news forms:

- Proximity and scope
- Timeliness
- Conflict and conflict resolution
- Narrative appeal
- Actions of elites and prominent individuals
- Human interest
- The unusual and unexpected
- Advocacy

Some of these news values often work in tandem, but the outlines that follow provide a guide for understanding how news is generated at the local level.

Proximity and scope

The most prominent news value for local journalism is arguably 'proximity'. This relates to information and events that are geographically or physically close to audiences (Mencher, 2010) and we outlined this news value in much broader detail in Chapter 2. Here we also introduced the concept of scope (Shoemaker et.al., 2007) to understand the role of local media in contextualizing state, national or international issues for local audiences as part of their role in information flows and movements. Proximity and scope as news values for local media resonate with the work of Lang and Lang (1981) who distinguish between low threshold issues and high threshold issues covered by local news media. Low threshold issues are those that people experience personally in their everyday lives, often within a local area, whereas high threshold issues are those of which they have no first-hand experience, so what they know comes to them indirectly through 'large media'.

The news value of scope comes into play especially when local media cover high threshold issues. Consider a natural disaster like the devastating earthquake that destroyed parts of Nepal in early 2015. Local journalists around the globe (aside from those closest to the disaster) largely rely on big news outlets, politicians and aid organizations to relay information about the disaster. It is the role of local media to then contextualize the story for local audiences, bringing it as 'close to home' as possible. They might search their networks for any local residents who may be holidaying in the destination, or helping out with relief efforts, to 'localize' the global catastrophe. Events such as this have the news value of magnitude (Harcup and O'Neill, 2001) and local journalists often seek emotional and psychological connections to the story in the absence of proximity. When a missile shot down a Malaysian airlines plane flying over the Ukraine in 2014, killing almost 300 people, it became a global media event. The tragedy affected countries across the globe. None of the victims were from Bunbury, Australia, but the local newspaper ran a story about a mother who felt so disturbed by the tragedy that she placed a bunch of flowers and balloons on the beach in a tribute to victims. The woman related the crash to the loss of her own son and wanted people to think inwards, about how lucky they were to be a part of the Bunbury community and to appreciate their lives. In this way, readers could relate to the tragedy on an emotional level, bringing the events 'closer to home' (Miller, 2014). Of course when disaster/tragedy strikes on a local journalist's 'home patch' there is a much more significant role to play – a point we shall return to later in this chapter.

Timeliness

Timeliness is an important news value but as Galtung and Ruge (1965) outline, what is timely depends on individual news production schedules. This warrants some explanation in the field of local journalism, where timeliness is relevant but on a different scale to the fast-paced world of global, digital news. There is great emphasis on the speed at which news and information can be transmitted, yet despite the plethora of communication technology local news outlets are less likely to operate on a 24-hour cycle because of internal resource restrictions. From a political economy perspective, there often isn't the time or funds to produce and upload content as it happens around the clock in local communities. A weekly newspaper in South Africa may consider an event timely if it occurs within a seven-day period between its publication dates, whereas a local radio station may only feature news and events happening on the day a broadcast goes to air. Some hyperlocals and bloggers of local news might focus on events that are happening on a monthly basis. Their aim is to ensure community members are informed and can plan for upcoming events and happenings, or to investigate key issues. *The Saddleworth Independent*, in the UK, for example, is a free hyperlocal tabloid publication produced monthly. It has attracted 20,000 readers in the south Pennine area, is profitable and has won several editorial awards. A competitive news outlet publishing in the same area has also opted to reduce frequency from once a week to once a month, highlighting a reverse trend in the idea of what is considered 'timely' news in the digital environment.

Conflict and conflict resolution

Reporting debates and disagreements are fixtures of all news sites, regardless of whether they feature national or local news. Mencher (2010, p. 12) highlights how conflict is not limited to 'warfare in the Middle East' or running gun battles between Mexican drug lords, but rather intense and bitter battles are fought over ideas, politics, legal issues and the like.

Stories that seek to promote resolution to conflict should also be considered important for local news outlets. An unfortunate by-product of 'objectivity' is that journalists are bystanders to debates. Saleem and Hanan (2014, p. 181) say the result is that the news media 'just works as a mirror in a conflict when it is only concerned with transmitting actual facts to people without taking any position'. Journalists can also be 'escalation agents', playing a role in generating conflict rather than resolving it. This is most likely when news media 'initiate tensions' and 'sensationalize events' (Saleem & Hanan, 2014, p. 181). In discussing the role of the news media in debates about abortion, Ferree argues journalists play the role of *tertius gaudens* – the third who benefits from the conflict of others by creating a polarized pseudo dialogue of drama to sell newspapers (Ferree, 2002, p. 264). Journalists can also be 'de-escalation agents' in a conflict (Saleem & Hanan, 2014).

Public journalism scholar Davis Merritt (1995) suggests news media provide a unique opportunity to recognize, maintain and create spaces where public questions and conflict can be discussed and potentially resolved. He highlights that such a concept 'causes discomfort among traditionalists who contend that journalists who create such forums are intruding, abandoning appropriate detachment' (Merritt, 1995, p. 11). The idea that journalists can consciously and deliberately bring people together given their unique position in information flows and connections sits uncomfortably with the mainstream ideal of journalism as guided by professional ideals of objective and detached reporting (Waisbord, 2009). We will pay much greater attention to such practices in the next chapter.

Narrative appeal

Good news and bad news are two distinct news values, according to Harcup and O'Neill (2001). Local news outlets are often credited with promoting 'good news' stories, which are also called 'soft news' because they are more likely to focus on positive achievements, events and the lives of people within their communities. Journalists rely on their sense of whether a story has narrative appeal when determining news, regardless of whether it is a good or bad news story. Journalists are storytellers. They look for information that resonates with audiences. To create exchange value out of information, local journalists often employ disjointed narratives and archetypes that are familiar to audiences. This is especially so when reporting 'soft news' that is considered *infotainment* and does not have a high priority in the traditional news values scale. It encompasses such fields as entertainment, sport, lifestyle, human interest, celebrity and the arts (Bainbridge et al., 2008).

Traditional themes are often used in news stories that share similar characteristics to oral literature, myth, traditional tales, ballads, literature, family histories and other forms of cultural narrative (Andersen et al., 1994, p. 58). Propp (1975) is well known in media studies for identifying recurrent patterns, set characters and plot actions. The main characters often include the villain, the donor, the helper, the princess, the dispatcher, the hero and the false hero. Booker (2004), in a more contemporary approach to story development, outlines seven basic plots that are structural transformations of ancient tales – overcoming the monster, rags to riches, the quest, voyage and return, rebirth, comedy and tragedy. An edition of the *Wimmera Mail Times*, in Australia, for example, features a sports story about a coach who must overcome injury to lead his side to glory with the headline 'Overcoming Demons'.

Carroll (2001) identifies and explores key stories or archetypes at the source of Western culture – the virtuous whore, the troubled hero, salvation by a god, soulmate love, the mother, the value of work, fate, the origin of evil, and self-sacrifice. Let's consider an edition of a local Canadian newspaper, the *Beacon Herald* in the province of Ontario. The stories all fit neatly into classical narratives, many which can be labelled 'soft news stories'. The edition leads with a story about a teenager who had her 'birthday wishes come true' by meeting a famous musician – in a classic Cinderella-type tale. There is an article glorifying the role of 'donors' who visit the local blood bank and an article about the public being called upon to help solve an 'evil' crime.

Actions of elites and prominent individuals

The actions of elites have always been understood as having high news value (Galtung & Ruge, 1981; Harcup & O'Neill, 2001). In a local media context there are tiers of elite sources, which we will discuss in detail shortly. In wider journalism scholarship, elite sources of news are understood as those that represent recognized power structures in society – on a global level it might be presidents and prime ministers, on a local level, the mayor of a town, local government officers, the courts and the police. The actions of both types of global and elite sources can influence local news. For example, prime ministers become the focus of local news when they embark on a tour of regional and country areas as part of a political campaign. There are also people known as social elites in given communities, those with extensive history, family connections and economic interests in a town. Their actions can determine whether an issue or event will become news. For example, a well-known individual such as a school teacher who is caught drink driving might be more likely to be reported in the media than an 'ordinary' individual.

Human interest

Human interest has powerful news value because it personalizes, dramatizes and emotionalizes the news (Beyer & Figenschou, 2014, p. 1946). Graber (1988, p. 212) describes the 'desire to learn about the personal lives' of other people as 'one of the most potent incentives for following the news'. Price and colleagues (1997, p. 484) observe, 'it is widely assumed that audiences are naturally interested in learning about other people'. Presenting a complex, or 'dry' issue through a human interest angle can provide a way for journalists to pique audience interest (Beyer

& Figenschou, 2014). Often the human interest story is selected in tandem with its narrative appeal, another news value discussed earlier.

Stories about people are universal and appeal at all levels of news, but they are particularly powerful at the local level where individuals are more likely to know others in a given space. Social pages are a regular feature of local newspapers, where journalists and photographers do the rounds of cafés or exhibition openings, taking snap shots of everyday people to include in the next edition. Some audience members interviewed in our studies have highlighted that seeing stories or faces of people they know made them feel more connected to community. One Australian newspaper editor made the directive to journalists to ensure they had 100 different faces each week appear in the newspaper (conversation with author, 2014), such was the appeal of social photos and stories about people for his community.

Finding a local human interest angle also offers ways for 'localizing' national and international issues. For example, profiling a refugee family who have moved into the area provides opportunities to discuss their reasons for fleeing their homeland, as well as national politics and policy on refugees. When a new tax is announced, or a national welfare scheme launched, local radio and TV journalists often profile local people affected by the announcement to link the nationwide change to the local area and explore its impacts.

The unusual and unexpected

In a geo-social framework we can understand how local stories that are perceived as novel or unusual are quick to attract the attention of larger media outlets in global information flows and systems. Harcup and O'Neill (2001) list this news value as 'surprise' while Galtung and Ruge (1981) label it as the 'unexpected'. Happenings that are local and unusual often defy the news value of proximity in the wider journalistic field and quickly become global sensations. For example, in Scotland, *The Courier's* regional edition serving Angus and the Mearns district broke a story about thieving birds stealing underwear and socks from skinny dippers to make nests. The story featured on *The Courier's* online site and within hours was picked up by news outlets across the globe, such as the *UK Express* and *New York Daily News* (New York Daily News, 2015). Meanwhile, a story that appeared in *Patch's* Rancho Santa Margarita site in the US also attracted global attention for its novelty factor. Patch reporter Paige Austin wrote that a woman celebrating her wedding anniversary on a boat was 'attacked' by a dolphin, which broke both her ankles after jumping onboard the vessel (Rancho Santa Margarita Patch, 2015). The geo-social model outlined in Chapter 2 provides scope to understand how the story was picked up by dozens of news outlets, including the *Indian Country Today* media network, *Marine News* online, *Naples Daily* news, *The Guardian*, *The Australian* and *Sky News*. Here the location of the story is insignificant and its unusualness breaks geographic boundaries in journalism.

Advocacy

Advocacy was first proposed as a news value by Harcup and O'Neill (2001) in their critique of Galtung and Ruge's iconic list. They took a political economy view of media to argue that the personal interests of a media proprietor such as Rupert Murdoch can shape the news. We take the concept of 'advocacy' in a different direction in our understanding of local news values. We use it to consider how local journalists identify issues they can put on the public agenda, promoting and/or campaigning for a particular outcome on behalf of their audiences. When this news value comes into play, local news outlets determine what is in the interests of the community and demand change or action, using their power and connections to achieve a common objective. This is referred to as advocacy journalism and theorized as linking social capital (Hess, 2013b, 2015a) or boosterism (Gutsche, 2015), and will be discussed in more detail in the next chapter.

Sources of news

A fundamental tenet of journalism is that journalists cannot simply make up news but instead must rely on what they have been told by somebody holding a perceived level of authority (Hanitzsch, 2007). Modern news is unimaginable without news sources. As Carlson and Franklin (2011) underline, within all but the most trivial news stories information arrives linked to the individuals and institutions providing it. While sources are of huge importance to journalists, we should never lose sight of the value of media power to individuals and institutions. When an event occurs, when an issue is raised, sources have a goal of bringing forward one dominant meaning from among the possible interpretations. For corporate, government and special interest sectors, the ultimate objective is to protect and strengthen their social position and power through interpretations that support the meanings they prefer (Berkowitz & TerKeurst, 1999). We will discuss public relations as a source of news later in this section.

One of the first 'rules of the game' for local journalists is that there is nothing more valuable than their contact book – it is a prized possession. Award-winning Australian newspaper journalist Andrew Rule, who began his career on local newspapers, describes his leather bound address book as his 'bible'. He says not only will social connections benefit a newspaper, but also a journalist's career:

> ... when somebody asks you (for a contact) you say 'no problem, got it boss'... you're the smart guy, suddenly you're the one who got the story and the others didn't, you're the one who gets the pay rise, you're the one who gets the better job next time.

Six of the best

The size and scope of the traditional contact book has changed dramatically, with reporters now able to access and find people via Twitter, Facebook, their own personal blogs, email and telephone. So whose names and numbers do local journalists seek out most? Just like large mainstream media, there are some key sources of news, but some are more integral to the local media scene than others. We outline six main sources of local news: elites and prominent individuals; events (planned); crisis/disaster; news media and social media; traditions and rituals; and everyday people.

It is important to note that while the Internet has been heralded for its democratic potential, its impact on journalists' ability to find new and different sources has been mixed. New technologies might allow everyday people a greater ability to circulate messages and share information with news outlets, but journalists often find themselves even more entrenched with tried and true sourcing practices to meet the unceasing demand for content (Carlson & Franklin, 2011, p 8).

Elites and prominent individuals

To be a news source is to have the power to speak publicly and in the end the question of power remains integral to studying news sources (Carlson and Franklin, 2011). Official figures, such as politicians and spokespeople for public services, are often described as 'routine sources', or 'go-to' people because they can be relied upon to provide information journalists want quickly, and often in a format that suits the news, such as the ability to talk in 'grabs' suitable for radio and television. Having 'go-to' sources saves journalists the time and effort involved in conducting primary research and seeking out a diversity of people and documents.

Elite sources often have symbolic and physical resources, including the backing of powerful institutions, communicative know-how and PR services, that allow them to schedule events, issue handouts, initiate and maintain media contacts, establish rapport and make themselves constantly and instantly available when journalists need them (Gans, 1979). In his critical discussion of the relationship between journalists and their elite sources, Gans (2011, p. 4) has accused some journalists of being stenographers for public officials.

We argue there are three tiers of elite sources for local news: the power elite, agents of the power elite and prominent individuals/local identities (those who possess degrees of symbolic capital).

The power elite

Elite sources situated or aligned with the field of power (especially in political circles) are arguably the most influential. Zvi Reich (2015) observes that sources who receive regular news access are strategically positioned as 'primary definers' of social reality (Hall et al., 1978; see also Tuchman, 1978; Berkowitz, 2008), which in turn reflects on their public image as 'legitimate bearers of facts' (Berkowitz, 2008, p. 110), bestowing a 'patina of truth' to their points of view (Koch 1991, p. 216; see also Tuchman, 1978).

Berkowitz says when high-prestige official sources appear in the news, the reporter-source relationship tends to legitimate or even reify the power structure of society (2008, p. 109). This occurs because the job of journalists is to produce news content that bears the aura of factuality: the statements of credible sources can be taken as fact, certifying the news without the need to research the veracity of that 'fact' (Ericson, 1999).

Earlier we highlighted global leaders as especially prominent journalistic sources, but it is not often that the local journalist can arrange a sit down with the president of the United States to discuss issues affecting their community. When powerful and famous figures do come to town, the local journalist might join the 'big media' throng that follows in their wake and experience a very different news culture where reporters and elites interact (Davis, 2007). In academic discussions of media and power elites, access is a key concept. In other words, those in supremely powerful positions have easy access to journalists, such as in parliamentary press galleries or the heart of the US financial system on Wall Street.

While local journalists do not usually enjoy this level of access to the centre, the power elite who control the state are served by various local agents who represent governments, the courts and/or police (Gutsche, 2015) and local journalists do have access to these sources which we will outline shortly. Increasingly, members of the power elite also employ specialists such as media advisers and public relations consultants to help them engage with the media at all levels of society.

Agents of the power elite

In a geo-social framework there are agents of the power elite, those who have delegated responsibility to manage political order in a local context. This is most identifiable with local governments, the courts and police. Local journalists play a valuable role as watchdog of those in power and their presence in communities helps to keep local government accountable. However, some argue that local media can be more like a guard dog of local authorities than watchdog (Donohue et al., 1995; see also Gilligan, 2012). For example, instead of watching for errors, fraud and other misdeeds among government officials and other leaders in a community, American community journalists of the 1990s were observed to produce much more content that appeared to protect these officials, leaders and the systems they worked in, especially in small geographic spaces. Journalists in larger, more diverse communities were found to be more conflict savvy, and tended to perform more of the traditional adversarial role of watchdog. Researchers concluded that where different local groups have conflicting interests, journalists are more likely to reflect the views of the more powerful groups (see also Gilligan, 2012 for full discussion). In a further example, Donohue and colleagues (1995) examined media coverage of national discount retailers moving into rural areas. While community leaders were concerned about losing locally owned businesses, consumers looked forward to the benefits of having big stores in their communities. The research found in these situations the media coverage was more likely to focus on community leaders' opinions while those of less powerful citizens received less coverage (Donohue et al., 1995, p. 122).

Prominent individuals and local identities

There are also key local sources who are not situated within the field of power but possess what Bourdieu refers to as symbolic capital, giving them the power to speak on behalf of a group or organization. We call them local identities. All routine news sources possess a type of symbolic capital. Bourdieu highlights that to possess symbolic capital is almost entirely specific and local. It can mean an individual who possesses any type of capital (economic, social, or cultural) that happens to be legitimated or prestigious to a particular field or space (Bourdieu, 1986, 1990). Symbolic capital is different to symbolic power – which we first discussed in Chapter 1 – as the latter refers to the ability to construct reality, rather than prestige or titles. Some sources possess a combination of capital that brings symbolic influence. Examples include the chief executive of the local hospital, an individual who owns much commercial or agricultural property in town, and the chairman of a water board. All bring specific knowledge, expertise and at times economic influence. Local football coaches or the president of a school council, political activist group or community fundraising committee, meanwhile, draw on the collective social capital of their respective organizations to stand in as the figurehead of their group. Such sources may not align neatly with traditional power structures of society – in fact some exist to challenge them – but they are regular and dominant news sources for local news outlets.

Public relations professionals as sources

Many elite sources of news, and increasingly not-for-profit and community organizations, draw upon the expertise of public relations professionals to help get their message across to news media. Public relations sources themselves do not possess symbolic capital, and they are not considered elite sources of news, but they do play an increasingly powerful role in brokering connections between elites and journalists. A well-written press release or quality audio or video grab can provide a ready source of information for local media outlets, already feeling the pressure of intense cost cutting (see Chapter 7 on business models). This is what Gandy (1982) terms 'information subsidies'. Scholarship across the Western world points to journalists relying increasingly on media releases to generate news stories, often running them verbatim in print and online (Davies, 2008). Sissons (2006) argues that in times of cost cutting and economic rationalism, journalists have become increasingly and excessively reliant on information supplied by public relations consultants via media releases as staff numbers have been reduced on local and regional papers (Sissons, 2006). Davis (2003) indicates that journalists feel increasingly compelled to react to what is made available free of charge rather than proactively finding and researching stories, which takes time and requires valuable editorial resources (Davis, 2003). Nick Davies coined the term 'churnalism', where reporters pay scant attention to context in the stories they are covering and instead rewrite information supplied to them in media releases. He declared all local and regional media outlets in Britain have been swamped by a tide of churnalism (Davies, 2008, p. 59), due largely to resourcing and economic restraints placed on newsrooms.

In our research, we have found regional journalists in Australia are using media releases verbatim and do not have time to even verify information before putting stories in the newspaper. This is because journalists face increasing time pressures and high staff turnover rates which make young country journalists new to a region dependent on information supplied to them from sources such as the local council until they 'find their feet' and make their own contacts (Hess & Waller, 2008). Consider this comment from a former journalist turned media adviser for local government in Australia:

I have 99 per cent success rate at getting my press releases in ... because I can write them up like news stories and I know that they often need fillers.

The activities of public relations professionals and news agencies in helping to shape news content in national and local news media is increasingly commonplace in the UK. Lewis et al. (2008) found journalists' reliance on these news sources is extensive and raises significant questions concerning claims to journalistic independence in UK news media and journalists' role as a Fourth Estate.

Events (planned)

News events come in two forms: planned and spontaneous. We will discuss the latter under the separate category of crisis/disaster. A planned event is something that elite sources of news might be involved in such as the opening of a new school, a media conference, fundraising event, festival, council meeting or election. Many local events occur on an annual basis, such as the agricultural show, and so journalists must be constantly creative and find ways to put a new spin on the story. This is where news values of human interest and narrative appeal are particularly popular, as well as the power of a quality image. Sometimes journalists write stories to provide context to a good photo taken at an event, or as a preview to it. This should not, however, come at the expense of providing basic information to audiences about where to go and what to do. Dates, times and schedules are often of paramount importance to audiences.

Many university-educated journalists in Australia felt it was 'beneath them' to focus on the banal and report trivial information such as times and event schedules (Hess, 2013b). They wanted to produce 'well-written' stories with narrative appeal – the types of articles that would be considered 'good journalism' by the wider profession. Yet a consistent theme among local news consumers interviewed in the same study was the lack of practical detail provided in stories by commercial news outlets. As a reader of one newspaper said:

> I would have thought including a contact number or starting time should be the most important thing a journalist thinks about, but a lot of the times you are left wondering where to go and what to do.

Another group of readers indicated that many locals were turning away from the region's newspaper and towards a volunteer-produced news-letter because it provided the 'little details' that the newspaper tended to leave out. As we will demonstrate later in this chapter, a return to basic information that helps bring people together is exactly the type of content appearing on new grassroots hyperlocal sites that emerge when traditional commercial news operations close their doors across communities. This information is a far cry from 'journalist as watchdog toppling governments', but providing basic information that brings people together, especially for planned events, is valuable all the same.

Crisis/disaster

Crisis and disasters come in many different forms, from organized protests to car accidents and devastating weather events. Local journalists help to create order amid chaos by providing information on what to do and where to go – from simple road closures to emergency contact numbers. Later in this section we will demonstrate how they contextualize these events for audiences and generate a sense of 'community'. This is in contrast to the role of big media that often descend on small towns and cities to cover a story when disaster strikes. While the term parachute journalism is often used to describe reporting of foreign affairs it is useful here as it is understood as the journalistic practice of flying into a region, reporting on a story and then leaving (Martin, 2011). Metropolitan reporters are often accused of being insensitive, with little regard for the people and situation they leave behind.

The international Federation of Red Cross and Red Crescent Societies distinguish between natural hazards (landslides, tsunamis, volcanic activity) and technological or man-made hazards (famine, displaced populations, industrial accidents, transport accidents, environmental degradation, pollution accidents). The geo-social framework of local news is important here because journalists report and must be prepared for different types of natural disasters and crises depending on their location in the world. For example, in northern Australia, cyclones are frequent, whereas in the south of the country they are extremely rare; roaring bushfires are known to ravage rural regions of the United States, whereas more densely populated areas within New York state are not affected. Journalists must prepare for crisis in the climates in which they work and this type of training is important for journalism students and reporters. This can influence everything from the type of equipment they carry to safety and training.

The power of local media to lead a community through crisis should not be underestimated. Increasingly, however, emergency services and elite sources of news are turning to social media to reach audiences. Journalists have come to play a much greater role in contextualizing information, rather than being the immediate go-to point for news and information. A study by Bruns and colleagues (2012) highlights the role of Twitter in bringing people together during extensive floods in the Australian state of Queensland in 2011. They argue that in times of crisis people seek basic information more than narrative. Their study found that news media tweets (including press releases and press conferences) were more likely to contain information that did not specifically provide emergency information, but rather more general news about the disaster. News media tweets were more common in the days after the flood crisis to highlight the human and economic impacts, or provide human interest stories. The study also highlighted that 'situational information' (tweets that provide information about the location of floods, areas to avoid, information about rescues, and so on) and 'advice' tweets (information about what to do and how to act for assistance and information) were among the most popular re-tweeted items by all organizations that posted content on Twitter in relation to the floods.

Man-made disasters such as accidents, pollution, displaced populations, industrial accidents and acts of mass violence can be especially difficult for local reporters when they know the people affected or involved in such crises. Car accidents might make a brief appearance in a metropolitan news broadcast but they are often leading news at the local level. The impact and intensity of such tragedies can be felt much more strongly across small communities, where people are more likely to be familiar with each other. The idea of journalist as 'neutral bystander' is often challenged in these situations.

Local reporters are sometimes among the first people on the scene at car accidents. In his account of community journalism, Lauterer (2006) gives the example of a photographer who views himself as a community member first and journalist second by helping emergency crews before taking photographs and gathering information because audiences expect he will serve the community before the journalistic field.

Journalists must always be mindful of their ethical duties when approaching people affected by tragedy or disaster. Big media that parachute into small communities to report on particularly shocking crimes often have less regard for the locals they seek to interview – to them they are sources they may never see again. For the local journalist, however, these 'sources' are people they have to deal with on a more regular basis, either professionally or personally.

The *Newtown Bee*'s coverage of the massacre at Sandy Hook Elementary School in Connecticut on 14 December 2012 is an especially powerful example of a small, local newspaper's community leadership and sound ethical practice during a tragedy that shocked the world. A feature article in the *New Yorker* (Aziz, 2014) explores the massacre through the experience of the *Bee*'s editorial staff. Aziz (2014) recounts an editorial written by the editor Curtiss Clark, published three days after the shootings:

> Clark counseled residents not to conform to the expectations of the 'legions of journalists who had arrived in caravans of satellite trucks as if drawn by some dark star of calamity'... Clark assured readers that Newtown (which Brian Williams, on NBC, called the 'saddest place on earth') had always been a place of civic action and responsibility. 'That story will not change' he wrote. He didn't intend to publish 'war stories', which would flatten the town's self-image. 'We need to extract ourselves from the sticky amber that freezes things in time.' (Aziz, 2014)

Aziz explains that in crafting a redemptive narrative, the *Bee* avoided much of the story:

> For weeks, the paper simply focused on documenting acts of benevolence: a group that had formed to promote random acts of kindness; another one that glued wooden stars, bearing messages of inspiration, to utility poles; a resident who set up a large tent near the highway

exit, so that out-of-town pilgrims, their hands full of dolls and baked goods, would have somewhere to place their offerings. (Aziz, 2014)

The residents of Newtown had to deal with the intrusion of a huge media pack that descended upon the town to cover the story. Their presence meant the locals also had access to state, national and international coverage of the massacre as a national tragedy. As the *New Yorker* feature article shows so poignantly, their local newspaper played an altogether different role, reminding Newtown of its strength, resilience and goodness and the newspaper's deep commitment to the community it serves. Curtis told Aziz: 'You don't have to worry – you're going to write this story and leave ... we're going to be covering this story forever'. There is much academic research across the globe that has emphasized the important role of local journalism in reporting crisis, from correcting facts appearing in big media news coverage to helping shift perceptions about a town in the wake of heinous crimes such as murders and mass shootings (see e.g.: Kitch and Hume, 2008; Hess and Waller, 2012). Kitch and Hume in their work around news coverage of Amish school shootings in the US highlighted the important role of the local press in reporting 'sensitively' as if they were seeing things through the eyes of fellow community members and allowing families affected by the tragedy to reach out to their communities (Kitch and Hume, 2008). Rather than just report the facts it became an avenue of hope and support. Local journalists in Australia who reported on particularly heinous crimes such as serial killings and murders were all found to play a community-building role and helping to re-establish their towns' reputations after being branded by big media as towns of horror or sites of evil (Hess & Waller, 2012). Local media also play an important part in collective memory, a less-examined aspect of crisis reporting. For example, Robinson's study of local news coverage of Hurricane Katrina in the US suggests that citizen journalists make an important contribution to collective memory by sharing their personal experiences in times of disaster (Robinson, 2009). It is worth mentioning that the preservation and archiving of news is changing as journalism moves further online and libraries and museums do the same. This may well become an area of scholarly interest in the future.

News media and social media

Social media sites such as Facebook and Twitter, content sharing platforms like YouTube and independent blogs and organizational websites are important secondary sources. So are other news outlets covering the same patch, or global and national events and issues. Local journalists have an increasingly important role in sorting through the plethora of online information for its news value and relevance, and sharing it with their audiences. However, Berkowitz (2008) warns there is potential for digital media to have a negative impact on reporter-source relationships, with less face-to-face or voice-to-voice communications between reporters and their sources and with email filling the gap. He says blogs have begun to blur the line between who is a journalist and who is a source. Furthermore, the practice of obtaining sources second-hand from the Internet has complicated questions about which sources count and what degree of sourcing is sufficient (Ruggiero, 2004). We, among others (see for example Livingston & Bennet, 2003), suggest the digital world has only reconfigured the tasks performed by journalists and editors, and standards of good journalism practice do not change. This is discussed further in Chapter 6. Using digital platforms to source information, and applying the same checks and balances that have always applied to finding and verifying information, local journalists can light the information runway for people. They must do more than report the facts. Good local journalism involves collating, contextualizing, sharing and making meaning of information for audiences. While user-generated content is celebrated for its participatory potential, a study by Williams and colleagues (2011) on BBC regional and network newsrooms suggests journalists and editors perceive such content as simply another source of news, a perception which is reinforced by the organizational framework established to elicit and process audience material.

Traditions and rituals

Rituals and traditions provide a powerful source of local news. It goes to the very heart of local news outlets' connection to 'community' – well beyond the traditional Fourth Estate function of the press. As we will show, local journalists not only report rituals and traditions – the very practice of engaging with a local media outlet itself can determine whether people see themselves as being 'in' or 'out' of community (Buchanan, 2009; Hess, 2015b).

A ritual may be understood as a pattern, form or shape that gives meaning to an action and is linked to a basic human need for order (Carey, 1989; Dayan & Katz, 1992; Durkheim, 1995; Soeffer, 1997; Rothenbuhler, 1998, 2006; Swidler, 2001; Couldry, 2012). Buchanan (2009) draws on the work of Appadurai, to suggest that small newspapers, in particular, play an important role in the production of local subjects as they feature sections and notices about rites of passage – for example, the publication of engagements and university graduation ceremonies. Reporting on marriages and writing obituaries and stories about wedding anniversaries are important ways to help people connect to their community. Obituaries have long been part of community journalism culture but they are increasingly becoming a lost art in some publications which are struggling with a decline in resources and arguably see this aspect of news as of lesser importance than the traditional Fourth Estate role. Obituaries provide an important way – for newspapers especially – to position themselves as central to the social in times of grief and to identify people who contributed to their communities, whether because they have lived in a local area all their lives, served as a dedicated community volunteer or been a well-known local identity. Kitch and Hume (2008) highlight the importance of obituaries in American community papers, arguing such commemorations are shared 'with an audience larger than the town, legitimizing these memories and values to a much broader audience than simply the families and friends of the deceased' (2008, p. 74). McNeill's distinction between the obituary and the newspaper death notice, however, highlights a form of 'media snobbery' 'which masks a more significant elitism about whose lives and deaths count in the public sphere' (2005, p. 190; see also Starck, 2006 on discussion on who makes obituary pages).

Many localities across the globe also have their own interesting or quirky rituals and traditions. Windsor in Nova Scotia, Canada, plays host to an annual pumpkin regatta, a water race where competitors attempt to float in brightly coloured giant pumpkins, to celebrate the significance of the seasonal produce. The *Brownsville Herald* in Texas reports on the annual Blessing of the Fleet ritual for the local shrimp association, where a priest prays for a safe and bountiful season, and blesses boats and crew in a ritual that 'raises the level of hope among shrimpers' (Brownsville Herald, 2015).

Local journalists also report on traditions and rituals that are important to particular organizations and cultural groups within the local area. They contextualize cultural and religious traditions practised across the globe. For example, journalists report on Thanksgiving, Easter church services, the start of Ramadan and Hannukah celebrations.

Birth, deaths and marriage column as media ritual

Sometimes a news outlet plays an integral role in people's ritualistic practices. The births, deaths and marriages column that features in local newspapers and their online sites serves as central to important rituals around life and death (Hess, 2015b). Announcing a birth, death or marriage in a newspaper has evolved into a powerful cultural practice among ordinary, everyday people across Western societies. Yet surprisingly, the role and place of these notices are rarely critically examined or studied in depth in scholarship about the news media. Such columns are identified within the classifieds section of a newspaper and include announcements of important birthdays, wedding anniversaries, engagements, funeral notices and an *in memoriam* section dedicated to the memory of those who have died (Hess, 2015b). People tend to publish these notices in newspapers that serve the places where they live or have social or genealogical ties. Aside from the official births, deaths and marriages register, these notices continue to serve as the informal public record for important cultural milestones and celebrations. Readers pay a fee to include this information and these announcements are often treated as a form of advertising revenue for publications. Amid the plethora of social media and new, free-to-access informational platforms, the idea that ordinary people across the globe continue to channel these important notices through traditional media – and often pay money for the privilege – deserves attention.

The births, deaths and marriages pages are a 'blind spot' within the news media and journalism academy that tends to be obstructed from scholarly view because of certain cultural values and norms that shape the field (Hess, 2015b). This blind spot is exemplified by a 'mythical divide' between political economy and culturalist approaches to the study of news (Fenton, 2006). Studying births, deaths and marriage notices highlights how local newspapers are positioned as the natural or legitimate social centre at a time when there is an abundance of social media options for ordinary people to share and publicize this type of information (such as social media sites like Facebook). People are under no legal obligation to place a birth, death or marriage notice in the news media. Yet newspapers possess an almost magical power in some contexts where people unquestioningly perform this practice.

Consider comments from readers of local newspapers gathered as part of a broader study in Australia. In being reflexive about their practices, participants revealed the almost invisible, subtle influences at play, such as:

You just don't think about it. It's just what you do. You put a notice in the local paper ... everyone does ... especially if it's a death. (35-year-old female) (Hess, 2016)

Everyday people as sources of news

Scholars admit it is quite surprising how little attention has been paid to ordinary citizens as actors and sources in news. Shoemaker and Reese (2014, p. 97) observe that 'only recently have we begun to take more seriously the non-institutional or citizen level' in the study of journalism and media.

Reich's (2015) study of ordinary people as news sources argues they cannot become substantial news players since they are granted a voice mainly during infrequent and ritualized circumstances such as unscheduled events; in online news, due to its participatory nature, and in TV vox pops; and in domestic rather than political and financial news. Journalists have lower esteem for them and the newsworthiness of the information they can provide. Citizens are considered less credible, informative and authoritative than 'regular' sources (Hopmann & Shehata, 2011) and more socially distant from journalists, who do not share their 'cognitive worlds' (Gitlin, 1980, p. 270).

There is little in the literature that discusses what 'ordinary' or 'everyday' people consider news and the role local media plays in their day-to-day lives. A reason for this may be because discussions about the everyday tend to be considered as separate from the domain of the public sphere – the latter shaping much scholarly interest about the news media. Craig (2004, p. 191) contends that the everyday is difficult to define: '[it] is highly individualised and amorphous and yet it also suggests activities that are shared and uniformly recognised and understood by a large number of people'. He highlights how scholars focus on everyday life in terms of consumerism and maintenance of the home as well as inordinate interests in personal relationships, romance and leisure activities, but ultimately a sphere 'drained of politics' (Craig, 2004, p. 192). Andersen and colleagues (1994, p. 9) suggest news editors continue to be:

> cloistered in newsrooms and reporters go where they can to get information as efficiently and economically as possible, and ironically many editors and reporters have little interaction with the people for whom they write and whose lives are altered by their news decisions.

Journalists are relying less on their readers for news, and stories of little consequence are being elevated to significant positions, or are filling news pages at the expense of more important stories, according to O'Neill and O'Connor (2008). Additionally, the reliance on a single source means that alternative views and perspectives relevant to audiences are being overlooked. Journalists are becoming more passive, mere processors of one-sided information or bland copy dictated by sources. Heider and colleagues' (2005) survey on reader views in the US found the public does not strongly endorse traditional journalism norms of watchdog and rapid reporting. Furthermore, when opinions of survey respondents and journalists were compared, survey respondents were significantly more likely to say providing a community forum was extremely important.

Calling for comments or story suggestions on Facebook and Twitter is considered a way of engaging more with the public, and social media now provides much insight into what matters to people. At times this may be considered tokenistic rather than a genuine attempt by journalists to listen to what is happening on the ground, especially among those communities where user-generated content and engagement with technology is not as strong (such as the elderly and disadvantaged).

The increasing number of hyperlocal ventures offers important clues about the types of news and information audiences seek beyond the professional norms and objectives of journalism. When commercial media shut their doors, leaving towns without information services, there are often amateur or other news services that pop up in their place. Nielsen (2015) argues members of the public and local community groups tend to get more of a say in hyperlocal outlets as news sources than in the mainstream local and regional news. Hyperlocals often challenge the 'parent' norms and conventions shaping mainstream news culture (Lewis et al., 2010). These include a return to basic information and a connection to ordinary people that rejects traditional news values and formulaic writing techniques (there is no mistaking the news value of proximity, however, in hyperlocal culture). Williams and colleagues (2014, p. 691) found that 'a key role that many (perhaps even most) hyperlocal sites play is the provision of often quite uncontroversial information about everyday life and activity in their communities'. Nevertheless, hyperlocal content, even the format and presentation, can be confronting to mainstream news culture.

On a recent research trip we visited a tiny town in Australia's southwest where the bakery distributes the area's photocopied hyperlocal news. A 'production error' resulted in the front page being stapled into the middle of the paper, but the baker said it did not matter. It was the content that 'locals' cared about. In other contexts it is the content that is troubling. Founders of the Mojo Movement said one of the challenges had been that the type of information relevant to neighbourhood reporting seemed 'insignificant' to some reporters. (Marymont, 2007, p. 19).

Summary

This chapter has considered where local news comes from, how journalists decide what makes news and the types of local information that matter to audiences, including births, deaths and marriages notices. Journalists working at the local level have a well-defined set of news values and sourcing practices for contextualizing information and events. They can also provide leadership in times of crisis. This underlines the importance of collectiveness and community to the local journalist's remit, an important theme throughout the book.

We began by acknowledging the disparaging view of local journalism as the 'parish pump' and set about showing why this is in fact an excessively narrow view of local journalism. It fails to account for the distinctive roles local journalism plays and its relationship to both the wider journalistic field and information flows and news that happens on a global scale. An important part of the professional news-gathering process is to contextualize events and we have taken a geo-social perspective to argue that local journalism's view extends beyond the parish boundaries to interpret the world through a local lens that makes meaning for audiences.

In the section on news sources at the local level we have shown some widely recognized 'key sources' are more integral to the local media scene than others. We outline six main sources of local news; elites and prominent individuals; events, crisis/disaster, news media and social media, traditions and rituals and everyday people. We have also taken steps to dispel the myth of objectivity when it comes to local journalistic practices. This is important, especially as a lead into the next chapter where we explore the value of practices such as public journalism and advocacy journalism. Here we shift from neutral observer to consider the types of journalism that help position local news as the beating heart and leader of any locality that aspires to notions of 'community'.

5 Connectors, Champions and Advocates

Introduction

This chapter begins with two unrelated news stories about bicycles, written by journalists working from different corners of the globe. They help to get the wheels turning in our discussion of the different ways local journalists connect people and advocate for their communities. The first concerns a man living in a small Australian town who is restoring some old bicycles that he plans to give to children living in remote Indigenous communities. At the end of the interview, the journalist asks if he is seeking more bicycles to repair. He shrugs and says 'why not?' and so the journalist includes a request for bike donations and puts his phone number at the bottom of the story. Several days later the man contacts the journalist in mock horror: 'What have you done?' he says. 'I've got 100 bikes sitting on my front lawn!'

About the same time in the United States, a local news outlet serving Fort Myers, Florida, begins a campaign to improve safety for local cyclists. A journalist there writes a story about road accidents involving bikes. She is then inspired to set up a 'share the road' community page on Facebook that invites visitors to join the newspaper's campaign. While the story is yet to prompt legislators to pass new laws increasing penalties for drivers who hit cyclists, the community has already raised money to distribute bike lights to those in need and local hospitals have joined the cause to preach road safety (Newsmith, 2015).

The above examples highlight two different but powerful ways local news providers maintain and/or reinforce their role as being central to the social. As we have outlined in other chapters, local news media possess a unique ability to connect people across different contexts; whether providing information that unites people at a social event, fundraiser or funeral, or that triggers a discussion about local politics between neighbours over the back fence. For example, a hyperlocal in the Netherlands takes pride in helping people find their lost cats and dogs, with the site's owners reporting people call in just to 'let us know how happy they are'

(Kerkhoven & Bakker, 2015, p. 198). There are also cases of journalists serving as community champions or advocates where they take a conscious, active role in bringing people together to discuss community and political issues or to campaign for change, as in the example about bike safety in Florida.

The concept of 'mediated social capital' (Hess, 2013b; 2015a) offers a way to understand how local journalists bring people together, connect and advocate on behalf of audiences. Mediated social capital is the power of news outlets to connect everyday people with each other (bridging/brokering) or with those in positions of power (linking) (Hess, 2013b, 2015a). Specifically, we will explore practices of public journalism and advocacy/campaign journalism (Waisbord, 2009; Maslog, 2012) that are widely associated with local media. The differences between these roles, however, are not often made clear or properly understood.

Public journalism is seen as an opportunity for media to listen to the conversation the public is having with itself, to facilitate discussion and debate rather than merely report on matters generated by the political elite. Advocacy journalism, meanwhile, is a news outlet's ability to campaign or advocate on behalf of a perceived collective on matters of public interest. It has also been referred to in the literature as campaign journalism (Aldridge, 2003; Birks, 2010) development journalism (Bowd, 2007) and boosterism (Gutsche, 2015).

These journalistic practices are important for local news outlets if they are to maintain credibility, and for hyperlocal ventures to build legitimacy in the digital environment. We suggest the future of local media may, in part at least, rest on their ability to be seen as connectors, advocates and champions for the localities they serve. In highlighting news media's power for good, however, the chapter concludes by reminding us of media's privileged position to serve as a form of social control, and its potential for misuse and the importance for journalists of being reflexive about what they do and the power they possess.

Understanding mediated social capital; bonding, bridging and linking

This chapter situates the media's ability to connect people and campaign on their behalf as forms of 'mediated social capital', so it is important to provide an overview of the concept before examining the specific practices that sit within this framework. Chapter 1 outlined some key concepts from Pierre Bourdieu's theoretical toolkit that have helped shape our understanding of local media. One of those tools is social capital – what Bourdieu defined as:

> the aggregate of the actual or potential resources which are linked to possession of a durable network of more or less institutionalised relationships of mutual acquaintance and recognition. (Bourdieu, 1986, p. 248)

Hess has drawn inspiration from Bourdieu, among others (Jacobs, 1961; Burt, 2001), to conceptualize 'mediated social capital' – the power of local media outlets to connect people, both consciously and unconsciously, across various social, economic and cultural spaces and to link people with those in positions of power. Mediated social capital also recognizes the ability of the news media to control the information that brings people together in physical and digital spaces (see Hess, 2013a; Hess 2015a). It represents a breakaway from other scholarship that examines the relationship between local media and social capital because it argues this social power is a resource that commercial news media can utilize to maintain or build a position of advantage (Bourdieu, 1986).

Traditionally, social capital is considered a societal level resource – it is associated with terms such as 'civic participation', 'community' and 'volunteerism'. Social capital is the glue that holds communities together, makes them work as a collective and supports the idea that we rely on relationships with others to fulfil social, cultural and economic needs (see especially Putnam, 2000). The news media, and local journalism in particular, is seen as essential to this, largely in providing information important for the accumulation of social capital. For example, a study of more than 300 residents in a mid-west metropolitan area in the United States (Jeffres et al., 2007) found newspaper readers were most involved in 'community', most attached to their neighbourhoods and most active in discussing public affairs. In his study of 'local' media in Australia and Canada, Richards (2013) draws on the work of Robert Putnam to suggest such outlets are influential in facilitating community communication and hence contribute to regional social capital (see also Bowd, 2012). Other scholars have attempted to use community newspaper content as a measure of collective social capital (Kreuters 1998; McManamey 2005), or link circulation size of community newspapers in certain geographical areas to community social capital (Galper, 2002).

We do not discount the importance of the media in providing information that lubricates the wheels of democracy, but we do resist a functionalist account (see Chapter 1) that positions the news media as a neutral conduit that helps to develop social capital as a societal level resource, or views media as always being able to put the common good ahead of its own (Hess, 2016).

Mediated social capital takes three main forms: bonding, bridging and linking. *Bonding* is understood as the news media's ability to foster, both consciously and unconsciously, the idea of 'community', 'close ties' or 'psychological bonds' that audiences have with the 'places' and networks that news outlets serve in a geo-social context. We have discussed this idea extensively in Chapter 2 and will return at the end of this chapter to discuss its relationship to issues of social control that can be enacted by recognized or established 'leaders' and power structures within a community. The emphasis for now will be on *bridging* and *linking*.

Bridging

'Bridging' outlines the unique position of the news media to control the types of information shared between individuals and to connect or broker (Burt, 2005) connections between people (mostly horizontal networks)[2] across cultural, social and economic spaces. The role of public journalism is an important exemplar of bridging social capital which we will discuss shortly. At the heart of the public journalism, or civic journalism movement, is the belief that journalists do not merely transmit information and that the news media should do more than simply cover the news (Haas, 2007). There is a key difference, however, in the way public journalism scholars view social capital and how the theory is utilized here. Most public journalism supporters view social capital as a societal level resource and see the primary role of journalism as enhancing civic participation or 'revitalizing public life' (Merritt, 2009). In contrast, proponents of 'mediated social capital' argue certain local news media possess the legitimacy and symbolic power to connect people and that this role should be examined through a critical lens.

Linking

Linking social capital is the ability of the news media to connect everyday people with those in positions of power. Linking provides a prism to consider how the news media, in performing a bridging/brokerage function, has the ability to consciously and deliberately connect individuals and groups in wider social space with those in positions of power (vertical ties). The practice of advocacy journalism and associated ideas of campaign journalism, boosterism and developmental journalism are all examples of linking social capital that must be examined for issues of inequality as well as any advantages they might present.

Bridging social capital and the practice of public journalism

The idea of public journalism, which has also been called civic journalism, emerged in the early 1990s. Its roots can be traced to the newspaper industry in the United States and the academy, as those concerned with both journalism practice and theory tried to address declining interest in newspapers and civic life. Poindexter and colleagues (2006) trace the beginnings of both arms of the public journalism movement. Firstly, how Davis 'Buzz' Merritt, the editor of the *Wichita Eagle*, a Knight Ridder newspaper in Wichita, Kansas, spearheaded a voter project that is considered one of the first examples of public journalism practice. Secondly, how Jay Rosen, a New York University journalism professor, directed the Project on Public Life and the Press. The editor and the scholar inspired this movement and new area of research that became known as public or civic journalism.

It gained immediate support from cultural studies scholars including James Carey, who sought to turn conventional understandings of journalism on its head (1989). Rather than simply report the news, public journalism encourages reporters to listen more closely to the conversations audiences are having with themselves, facilitate discussions and enhance civic participation. It differs from advocacy journalism, which is outlined later in this chapter, in that key proponents of public journalism: a) emphasize the importance of civic participation/discussion over orchestrated outcomes; b) focus much more on facilitating horizontal ties than vertical ties; and c) reinforce the importance of balanced reporting where possible in discussing civic affairs – points we extend on soon.

One of the most widely cited scholars in this space, Rosen propounds public journalism as a multifaceted phenomenon (see also Haas, 2012) that has been represented in three main ways: as a philosophical argument about where the Press should be going; a set of practices that have been tried in real-life settings; and a movement of people and institutions concerned about the possibilities for reform (Rosen, 1995 as cited in Haas, 2012). Public journalism should not be mistaken for practices such as citizen journalism or participatory journalism, as the former is largely the role of professional journalists working for news providers who possess the symbolic capital, or at the very least cultural capital (see Chapters 1 and 2) to represent the interests of the locality.

It is also worth considering that while there has been much academic and news industry interest in public journalism, it tends to be approached from a Fourth Estate perspective with a focus on politics, democracy and the news media's view of itself as society's watchdog. Poindexter and colleagues (2006) take a different approach through their research on how audiences understand public journalism at the local level, and its benefits. They argue the techniques that epitomize public journalism also resonate with the beliefs of what it means to be a good 'neighbour' such as caring about the community, reporting on interesting people and groups, understanding the local community and developing solutions.

We suggest public journalism is best viewed as a journalistic practice, rather than advocate its place as a philosophical movement. While we encourage reporters to actively seek ways of bringing people together to discuss matters of civic importance, we do not contend, for example, that they should base their entire journalistic *modus operandi* around Fourth Estate conceptualizations of public journalism. Rather, that is one way for journalists to enhance their contribution to society and can also serve as a valuable point of distinction for local media.

Facilitating civic conversations

Public journalism proponent Jay Rosen cites James Carey to suggest the true subject matter of journalism is the conversation the public has with itself (Rosen, 1997, p. 191). As Glasser and Craft (1998, p. 204) formulate it, the purpose of public journalism is 'to promote and indeed to improve, and not merely to report on or complain about, public or civic life'. Andersen and colleagues (1994) argue that conversations among the public cannot be one-sided; journalists must listen more and speak less as they become full-fledged participants in the public dialogue. As a result news will become a legitimated and sanctioned topic of conversation among all cultural groups. In this way journalists are recognized as facilitators – not providers – of public discussion.

Rosen gives the example of newsrooms initiating conversations about civic affairs among key publics. The aim is to create a 'bottom-up' orientation to public affairs reporting by letting citizens shape the news agenda, instead of elite sources such as 'City Hall' (Rosen, 1999). Other early examples of public journalism include media outlets offering free pizza to any group that would talk about teen violence and send its comments back to the newspaper (Charity, 1996) and the *Savannah Morning News* in the US state of Georgia convening the public for problem solving (Nip, 2008). Friedland (2004) highlights some of the pioneer experimenters such as the *Charlotte Observer* 'Taking Back Our Neighborhoods' series, which led to the creation of more public housing and 'neighborhood leaders talking to each other ... sometimes for the first time'. Meanwhile, Voakes (2004) highlights the work of scholars who engage in civic mapping (see especially Harwood, 2000), which involves working more like an anthropologist than a daily news reporter. It enables exploration of a community's various 'civic layers' by listening and talking in places that traditional journalists have often ignored. America continues to boast hundreds of examples of civic and public journalism. Undertake a Google search of public journalism initiatives by community newspapers and it is likely to reveal hundreds of examples of journalists attempting to instigate public conversations on key issues, especially in the US. For example, The *Steamboat Today* paper, established in 1989 to serve Steamboat Springs in Colorado, ran a forum in 2015 to discuss the 'positives and negatives of allowing marijuana-growing operations in the region' (see www.steamboattoday.com) while in 2016 the *St Louis Post-Dispatch* facilitated public debate around the stresses of parenting and grandparenting as part of a special report into the toxic effects of stress on children. The newspaper gathered key community representatives and healthcare experts to participate in discussion around the issue and reach some potential solutions. It should be noted, however, that public journalism is not the exclusive domain of the US. Japanese newspapers, for example, have outlined early practices of civic journalism from the 1980s. Kitamura (2009) describes the work of the *Kahoko Shimpo* newspaper that ran a series on the question around why its region had so much dust in the air. The series led to much public deliberation; the problem was eventually linked to the use of spiked tyres on roads and led to a public campaign to outlaw such tyres on vehicles (see also Rausch, 2012).

In Australia, some local journalists involved in a unique education and training programme, the Country Press Australia/Deakin University cadet journalism course, are encouraged to listen to and convene conversations in cafés, pubs and Facebook to source story ideas for news or hold informal focus groups with people representing various civic layers outside political establishments to determine what the key issues are 'on the ground'. One Queensland newspaper held a forum of key stakeholders to discuss a shortage of volunteers in the region, which was met with overwhelming support and applause from the community (see Beaudesert Times, 2014).

In the United Kingdom, newspaper and hyperlocal publications engage in and exemplify the practice of public journalism. One example is the hyperlocal site *The Lincolnite*, an independent news provider founded in 2010 to serve the county of Lincolnshire in the east of England. It facilitated a political forum in 2015 that involved candidates for the seat of Lincoln in the British Parliament. The site drew on the symbolic capital and resources from established news providers such as BBC Radio, the local newspaper and FM radio to share resources and production costs to run the event. *Lincolnite* founder Daniel Ionescu said that at its heart, the public aim of the collaboration was to engage more people in politics and to help them place an informed vote. More than 200 people attended the live debate, which included multiplatform content such as video, audio, live blogging and questions from the audience.[3]

Objectivity and 'taking sides'

Public journalism challenges the role of objectivity as it applies to news because it does not view journalists as neutral observers, rather as active participants in news selection and discussion. However, it stops short of encouraging journalists to take sides over an issue of civic importance. A distinguishing factor of much scholarship on public journalism, as highlighted by Haas (2012), is that scholars have spent more time delineating what journalists should not – as opposed to should – do in the interests of remaining politically neutral. Specifically, advocates have argued that 'journalists should be concerned with the process, but not with the outcomes of citizen deliberation, refrain from endorsing particular politicians and political proposals and avoid partnering with special interest groups that seek to further particular interests' (Haas, 2012, p. 6). This is what distinguishes it – in part – from the practice of campaign or advocacy journalism that we will examine shortly.

Many US newspaper journalists approve of three tenets of public journalism practice: using ordinary citizens as sources for stories on public issues; holding public meetings to begin community discussion of issues; and reporting enterprise stories that begin to look towards solutions to problems. Voakes (2004) argues that journalists working in smaller communities are the most receptive to these ideas. Public journalism scholars have at times come under attack from journalists working for large media organizations who hold the Fourth Estate function of the press and role of neutral observer as central to their professional practice. Davis 'Buzz' Merritt (2009, p. ii) argues 'public journalism has had journalism done to it'. In other words, journalistic norms and conventions cannot deal with such a challenge to traditional practice. But he contends the opposition is based on ignorance or a different appreciation of journalism. He offers this insight and advice for those practising public journalism:

> A public journalism project must be seen as such from the very conception of the idea. Trying to apply public journalism principles only in the writing will not work; it must begin with the concept and the basic reporting because applying public journalism principles presents an additional set of questions. For instance, staff doing a project on a community problem would traditionally ask itself questions such as 'is the reporting fair, accurate, complete, thorough?' It would explore such questions as 'Why does the problem exist/persist; what mechanisms exist to deal with it; why are they not working?' Yet it might also ask itself an additional set of questions: 'what would be; in the broadest sense, good outcomes. What is the goal? What mechanisms, government, private, public might come into being to help attack the problem? In other words, what capacity to deal with the problem is missing and how can that be built and maintained. Who needs to talk to whom to resolve the problem' ... The level of questioning and reporting will not occur unless the journalists thinking about the issue have adopted a purpose beyond telling the news. (Merritt, 2009, p. 129)

Public journalism: the public, press and issues of power

The Internet makes it possible to build a publicly held and publicly controlled space of local civic communication (Sirianni & Friedland, 2001). Such ideas are reinforced in scholarship celebrating the democratization of the Internet and the belief that new communication channels provide scope for people to connect on much deeper, more constructive levels. But Friedland (2004) rightly points out that both the resources and imagination must first be available if this type of media space is ever to become a public resource. In order to connect people effectively and meaningfully, there is often an 'information broker' who has the available time, resources and credentials to perform such a role (Hess, 2013b).

As highlighted in Chapter 1, it is important to recognize issues of power in discussions about media in digital space. There must also be scope to consider the context and influences that shape drivers and practices of public journalism. For example, it would be unreasonable to suggest anyone with access to the Internet has the ability to bring people together to discuss issues of civic importance in a given community and expect to be 'heard'. We need to consider the legitimacy/reputation of the 'broker' facilitating these connections, their practical know-how and degree of local knowledge that assists them to perform such a role. However, public journalism scholars have paid relatively little attention to how deliberation may be affected by social inequality, according to Haas and Steiner (2001). They argue 'community' has been viewed as a unified, tangible site where people share an overarching vision of the common good that enables them to reach consensual solutions to problems (Haas & Steiner, 2001, p. 126).

Positioning public journalism as a form of bridging social capital helps us to appreciate these issues along with understanding the advantages of public journalism to those who practise it, and why they possess the ability to perform this role. In 2014, Hess interviewed journalists working in regional media in Australia as part of a study on the role and place of local newspapers. One reporter/editor who was involved in setting up a debate between candidates for a local election said the benefits of public journalism were immense from both an economic and a symbolic perspective:

> It brought democracy to the people and connected people with each other, because people got to discuss what was important to them. But if you want me to be totally honest, we did it because it generated lots of copy, it filled news pages, but you would never repeat that out loud. We were so surprised because the hall was filled to capacity, people were standing up at the back, which shocked me because I didn't think there would be much interest.

The journalist also made this observation:

> I think it absolutely enhanced the newspaper's reputation because it showed we were willing to put our hands up and try it. Every other media outlet in the area, radio, television, ABC all piggy-backed off our forum and cited us in their coverage. (see Hess, 2013b)

These comments illustrate that the motivations to perform this type of journalism are shaped by cultural and social forces within the journalistic field, such as a need to fill news pages and be perceived as the legitimate news provider over others. Further, the journalist's 'confession' to the motives of running the public forum resonate with Bourdieu's observations that while the formal presentation of the principle of social capital is that of altruism, the economic realities behind its accumulation must be masked in order to produce any effect (Hess, 2013b).

Advocacy, campaigner, champion: Journalism and linking social capital

An examination of power dynamics is particularly helpful in distinguishing public journalism from advocacy journalism, which is a well-documented but not often critiqued practice of local journalists. We situate advocacy journalism under the umbrella of linking social capital. Journalists perform the role of translating information from elites in a way that is understandable to the masses (Carey, 1969), but linking social capital suggests there is value in journalists facilitating direct engagement between these elites and wider audiences, drawing on local journalism's role as leader of 'community' to enact change.

Bourdieu suggests that within any given network, a figurehead represents a group with the aid of collectively owned social capital (Bourdieu, 1986). In regards to 'mediated social capital', this not only enables the news media to speak on behalf of audiences but also provides an opportunity to address power imbalances by 'brokering' connections between those in power and those who are not. In other words, journalists use their agenda-setting role to identify issues that affect everyday people or 'communities' and link to and lobby those in positions of power to instigate a desired action. A key difference from public journalism is that advocacy journalism requires local media to set the agenda and advocate for a desired outcome. Before we outline this practice in more detail, however, it is important to provide an overview of how advocacy journalism is understood in wider academic scholarship and situate this in the context of local media. We will also outline literature that prefers the use of other terms to describe practices such as development journalism, campaign journalism and boosterism.

Advocacy journalism – an overview

Advocacy journalism takes a key tenet of public journalism – to listen to audiences and involve them in problem solving – a step further by embracing the role of champion. In this model, journalists lobby for a particular cause or advocate a solution to an issue. They don't stand back 'objectively' – they take sides. At times it resonates with the radical democratic model of the press we outlined in Chapter 1, where journalists oppose or challenge power structures in society and become advocates for change in their communities. Advocacy journalism has been practised for several hundred years, with newspapers seen to take a stance on issues from civil rights to the world wars, according to Applegate (2009, p. xiii). He quotes Ernest C. Hynds, who defines advocacy journalism as:

> based on the premise that the journalist has both a right and an obligation to become involved in the events that he reports. The advocate ... says that since objectivity in reporting cannot be obtained, it should not be attempted. The reporter should instead tell the truth of the event or the situation as he sees it. (cited in Applegate, 2009, p. xv)

Studies show that small newspapers are important to towns and their development (Poindexter et al., 2006; Bowd, 2007; Meadows et al., 2009). Historian Rod Kirkpatrick (1998) argues that local newspapers in Australia have shown leadership and advocated on behalf of their communities since the 19th century. He suggests that in many instances the establishment of a town's first newspaper predated the advent of local government and placed a heavy onus on the newspaper to represent or advocate the interests of a town (Kirkpatrick, 1998). Maslog (2012) observes that in discussions about 'community' newspapers, 'advocacy' has become the new buzz word, which 'runs counter to the age-old concept of objective journalism' (Maslog, 2012, p. 127). Small newspapers especially are seen to have a strong association with the towns and cities they serve, not just in terms of being information sources but also as 'voices' for their communities (Bowd, 2007; www.iswne.org). It is important to note, however, that while the term 'advocacy journalism' is used to understand local media practices, internationally it is a practice much more at home with alternative media and scholars who study this form of journalism.

Alternative media and advocacy/campaign journalism

Alternative media journalists have long been distinguished by belonging to a campaign or movement for which they write or broadcast (Forde, 2011). Unlike local media that intermittently campaign on behalf of audiences, alternative media are almost entirely defined by their advocacy work. They have an overriding commitment to their public sphere, and always their public sphere is quite simply that which is not being served, or served properly, by the mainstream news media. A primary aim of alternative media groups and journalists is to have an impact on politics and policies across a range of issues (from the environment to social justice, trade agreements and international relations) by influencing public debate and agitating for change. For example, Howley (2010) defines alternative media (which is also referred to as 'community' in some contexts) as an alternative to profit-oriented media that caters for the wide range of tastes and interests of ethnic, racial and cultural minorities, who are often ignored, silenced or otherwise misrepresented by mainstream media:

> For those with little or no access to mainstream media, community media provide resources and opportunities for marginalized groups to tell their own stories in their own voices. They are instrumental in protecting and defending cultural identity while simultaneously challenging inaccurate, prejudicial media representations. (Howley 2010, p. 5)

Forde (2011) suggests alternative media is more closely aligned than any other form of journalism with the unrepresented, the 'poor and downtrodden' (Downing, 2003, quoted in Forde, 2011). In some contexts local media can also be understood to dwell on the periphery, especially when considering hyperlocal sites, small newspapers and radio stations serving remote and rural communities. These media outlets are located far from the powerful centres where decision makers in politics and business are based. However, we cannot ignore the fact that local news outlets are increasingly owned by powerful media conglomerates and elites and are part of global information flows and movements (see Chapter 2, see also Hess & Waller, 2015 for full discussion on differences between alternative, community and local media). Another difference is that local journalists arguably have more power than many alternative media sites to influence public debate in the social spaces they serve. This power derives from their relationships with routine sources, such as police and local government officials, which help them to set the news agenda. They often have a regular working relationship with the political elite which places them in a position to instigate change.

Unpacking the pecking order: Local media's influence in advocating for change

Earlier in this chapter we highlighted the importance of examining issues of power to consider why certain media are more influential than others when it comes to practices like public journalism and advocacy journalism. Even though we live in an increasingly media saturated world, full of 'citizen journalists', bloggers and social media users, there is evidence that a pecking order of power still exists. It is necessary to consider the relationship of certain local media organizations to other elites to examine the degrees of legitimacy they wield. In discussing the media's relationship to the law, we have drawn on the work of Bourdieu to suggest a reason that traditional mainstream journalists maintain symbolic capital in the communities they serve is partly because of their unique position to other fields of power.

It is no exaggeration to say that the activities of the state are bureaucratically organized for journalists. For example, in Australia reporters are provided with office spaces and specially designated seating in courtrooms and parliamentary chambers. Few hyperlocal publications or citizen bloggers are given such 'seats at the table'. To be taken seriously as a spokesperson for a community takes time to generate. As we will demonstrate in Chapters 6 and 7, many start-ups and hyperlocals that seek to generate a profit struggle to stay afloat, especially to begin with. Time is money, however, and is not always on their side.

Consider this example from our Australian research on local media (Hess, 2015a), which demonstrates the power of local newspapers to lead change in the community. Several participants identified as being particularly prolific on social media all noted the continued power of traditional news media, particularly in instigating change or engaging with elite sources. As a contributor/activist engaging with the daily newspaper said:

> With Facebook there's a chance for people to become real activists and I think it's a fantastic thing ... but the newspaper has that continued legitimacy, and that's where you want to get your views heard because it reaches so many people. (Interview with author, 3 April 2012)

She gave the example of a Facebook site where teenage boys in the region were rating the 'quality' of their sexual encounters with girls. She said she contacted police to highlight that individuals were making comments about girls under the age of 16 when sex with minors was illegal under Australian law:

> I went to the police and they told me they [couldn't] do anything about it and just told me to tell people to get off Facebook. That didn't help. So in order to get anything done ... to reach the general public, particularly parents and kids, I went to the paper. I can put this stuff up on Facebook by myself, but it's not going to reach the people I'm

trying to target. We wrote a press release on what to do about this site, it was [published on] page one. The newspaper then went to the police asking what they planned to do about it and it was only then that the police said 'they were looking into it', when they were dismissive of me initially. (Interview with author, 3 April 2012)

Those who perform linking practices work best when they are in a position to broker connections between elites and everyday people, or to enact change with elites on behalf of audiences.

Examples of advocacy journalism at the local level

As we outlined earlier, by far it is the local newspaper that serves as the greatest exemplar of advocacy and campaign journalism at the local level. In America and internationally, for example, hundreds of newspapers aligned with the International Society of Weekly Newspapers celebrate successful campaigns where they have lobbied on behalf of audiences for a better deal for their communities. Topics include the need to upgrade roads and public transport as well as campaigns for new hospital funding equipment and improved education and community health services. *The Guardian* has provided an extensive overview of 30 powerful local newspaper campaigns in the UK. They included the *Eastern Daily Press*'s push to help flood victims and the *Manchester Evening News*'s campaign to save its local science museum (Greenslade, 2014). In Australia, an increasing trend is emerging at the local level where major media conglomerates with interests in local newspapers pool together resources from newspapers in the same fold to run joint advocacy/community campaigns. In this way, they are combining resources and their symbolic capital to identify issues that are of common concern and lobbying politicians at a federal level for change.

News stories that aim to promote and raise funds for a particular cause can be described as both bridging and linking social capital. An example of bridging is a campaign to raise money for a family whose child is dying of cancer, which draws on everyday people, or horizontal ties, and does not involve lobbying elites. A further example involves a hyperlocal site in Australia that launched a fundraising campaign to restore a dilapidated mural painted years earlier by an important local artist who had since died (see www.bluestone.com.au). In contrast, raising high-level funds for big projects (such as a fire-fighting/rescue helicopter) to serve a local community requires lobbying elite news organizations for support and fits under the framework of linking.

Campaign and development journalism

Other terms used to describe the role of local media lobbying on behalf of audiences include 'developmental journalism', 'campaign journalism' and 'boosterism'. Bowd (2007) argues small newspapers have benefited from the perception that they are a valuable promoter of the community – a concept often associated with developing nations where stories are written to advance special local interests (Bowd, 2007; see also Hatcher, 2012a). Maganaka (2004) argues development journalism tends to address pervasive problems in countries with post-colonial backgrounds. It gives 'painstaking' attention to topics such as government plans and budgets, land reform, taxation, banking and finance, industry, agriculture, population, manpower, education, community development, public health, social welfare, the environment and science and technology. It is characterized by its purposiveness, pragmatism and relevance where journalists should be active community participants in social change. Hatcher says development journalism is often critiqued as being a propaganda tool for government-driven work, or embodies the ideals of journalists operating in economic systems that do not support commercially driven media (Hatcher 2012a, p. 244).

Scholars such as Birks (2010) and Aldridge (2003) use 'campaign journalism' to describe the role of local media that make claims to represent the interests of publics such as their audiences, or groups affected by an issue. Aldridge is interested in issues of inequality that arise from such practices, which we will demonstrate in a moment. Birks highlights that journalists' first criteria for 'campaign journalism' is reporting that is labelled as such, with a title and logo attached to every article on the topic. This is arguably to distinguish it from traditional news stories influenced by norms such as objectivity and neutrality. Secondly, campaigns have an objective by which success can be defined.

Birks (2010) gives examples of campaign journalism in Scotland. She found newspapers such as the *Daily Record* to be most active in performing the practice. It ran regular, short campaigns calling for tougher action against drug dealers, loan sharks and anti-social youths. Meanwhile, the *Evening Times* ran a year-long campaign – 'Hands off Yorkhill' – rallying against the closure of one of Glasgow's three maternity hospitals.

Boosterism

In rural areas of the US, 'boosterism' has been a long-standing and well-documented editorial practice. It dates back to the 19th-century frontier and the efforts of struggling newspapers to attract settlers to the West.

According to historian Daniel J. Boorstin in 1965, the 'pioneer newspaper of the upstart city ... had to call into being the very population it aimed to serve' (in Baker, 2010, p. 170). However, 'zealous editors carried boosterism into the twentieth century, extolling and exaggerating the virtues of their towns' (Baker, 2010, p. 170). This journalism often reflected the aspirations of a community, not necessarily realities, and 'the optimistic language of boosterism was often slathered with adjectives and superlatives to entice settlers to the vision of what the town could become'. We will highlight how this relates to the evolution of editorial writing a little later in this chapter.

In his discussion of the challenges facing US small town newspapers, Guth (2015) quotes from the 1937 textbook *Country Journalism*, in which the author Charles Laurel Allen wrote that being a 'community booster' was the most important element in becoming a successful country journalist: 'Boost, even when something needs correcting; a positive suggestion showing the way to better the town will accomplish far more than showing how poor the town is' (Allen, 1937 in Guth 2015, p. 266).

A survey of mid-western rural weekly newspaper publishers (Tezon, 2003) found widespread agreement with the proposition that they have to be 'married' to their communities by devoting many extra hours to civic duties. Most of the respondents indicated that they felt that they could handle any conflicts of interest that could arise from this kind of relationship (see Chapter 6 for discussion of relationship issues). Tezon (2003) observed that the majority of recorded mission statements for these community weekly publishers included some reference to promotion or the role of cheerleader for their towns (Tezon, 2003). Guth (2015) says these findings echo those of a 1960s study that found a majority of small town community leaders believe the proper role of their hometown newspapers was to work jointly with community leaders to initiate projects (Edelstein & Schultz, 1966 in Guth, 2015).

Guth (2015) interviewed journalists and their managers about the expectation of small town US journalists to promote the local area:

Doug Anstaett, executive director of the Kansas Press Association, said he felt this pressure early in career. While serving as the editor of a small-town newspaper, he said he had to remove one of his journalists from writing a weekly column after the writer – to the horror and disgust of local merchants – suggested it was easier find [sic] Christmas gifts for his family at a mall in a nearby town. (Guth, 2015, p. 267)

The value of editorials

The practice of boosterism serves as a useful reminder that before the rise of the 'professional' journalist and the importance of objectivity, newspaper content was brimming with editorial comment. Opinion was not only reserved for clearly identified column pieces, but littered throughout news stories. News outlets were fierce advocates for their communities, especially in newly established settlements in North America, Australia and New Zealand during the 1800s. Town leaders relied on the press as an instrument to promote population growth and attract industry and infrastructure, and had strong political agendas. Consider *The Oregonian* (the oldest continuously published newspaper on the US west coast) whose staff won a Pulitzer Prize for editorial writing[4] in 2014, continuing a proud journalistic tradition. The newspaper was established in 1850, one year before the incorporation of the tiny community of Portland, Oregon. At the time, prospective leaders of the new settlement elected to establish a local newspaper. This was seen as a prerequisite to urban growth, and they went hunting for an editor from the big smoke.

Opinions and editorials in the news pages have long been considered essential for community prosperity, but they have received relatively little attention in scholarship that understands journalism practice at the local level (see Lauterer as an exemption here, 2006). This is surprising when they are an instrumental part of both public journalism and advocacy journalism initiatives.

The editorial

A good editorial researches, summarizes, celebrates or suggests ways to enact change. Lynch (2013) highlights that editorials are the voice of the newspaper and are usually a reaction to the news, or a community event or issue. The purpose of the editorial is to influence the reader and the editorial writer uses facts to make an argument to support a point of view or an opinion. Yet, too often, the editorial is written in a hurry and against a deadline. In some countries, the editorial has not been included in digital editions and remains the domain of printed news. As newsrooms shrink and there is less and less time to produce the news, the editorial is losing priority. Even in the university setting, journalism graduates are often taught the importance of objectivity over the value of opinion writing.

A study on the status of editorial writing in Australian, Canadian and US weekly newspapers (Selvin, 2015) found the practice of writing editorials was under increasing pressure as staffing cuts shrunk news-rooms. An award-winning editorial writer for a small Canadian news outlet argued:

> 'At a community newspaper, an editorial is something you do on the corner of your desk when you're not being interrupted.' Though modest about the general popularity of editorials, he added, 'I like to think people find mine interesting now and then' (cited in Selvin, 2015).

Academics and industry experts have noted an exodus of senior writers from local newsrooms, with many retrenched and replaced by more inexperienced but cost-effective early career journalists. This means deep community knowledge and understanding of key issues that give journalists the confidence to craft editorials are at risk of being lost. When it comes to more general column pieces, newspapers are producing more generic articles that can be published across a network of news providers owned by the same media company, devoid of any local content.

In serving the interests of the locality, journalists should be mindful of providing a voice for all sections of the community, appealing not just to popular opinion but representing the under-represented. They must select their topics carefully and write thoughtfully. In other words, good editorials display community bias not personal bias. Faith Wylie, co-publisher of the *Oologah Lake Leader* in the United States, wrote an editorial outlining the importance of community bias. She wrote:

> Is the *Oolagah Lake Leader* biased? Of course that's what you expect of us. We're biased in favor of our community. Our methods of communication have expanded but we're still biased in favour of you. (Wylie, 2015)

Consequences can be damaging if personal self-interest or views that exclude certain members of the community on the basis of gender, race or sexuality get in the way. One Australian country newspaper editor boasted at a journalism conference about a recent editorial he published that called on townsfolk to 'take pride' in themselves if they were homophobic or opposed marriage equality.[5] This is risky and potentially polarizing. Editors must abide by professional ethical codes that are in place in countries around the world – principles that attempt to ensure journalists do their best not to incite violence, hatred or racism.

Opinion and editorial writing has many styles including the erudite, the plain-spoken and the provocative (Standring, 2008, p. 115).

Attention to detail, comprehension, synthesis, introducing a call for action and reciprocity are keys to a good editorial (Lauterer, 2006). Local knowledge and an understanding of what makes a place tick are essential for editorial writers. Lauterer (2006) quotes working journalists who strongly believe editorials do no harm and the point of such columns is always to effect positive change. Column and opinion writers are strongly advised to do their homework. Tate and Taylor (2014) argue opinion stories, from editorials to blogs, can educate people, help a community grasp a complicated problem, rally citizens to an issue or publicize the perspectives of the voiceless or underrepresented:

> An opinion piece is only as strong as the writer's knowledge of the subject. Opinion writers who talk to multiple sources and explore multiple sides of an issue develop persuasive arguments that give readers insight. (Tate & Taylor, 2014, p. 114)

Audience opinion: From letters to the editor to 'texts' and Facebook posts

The role of the news media as a credible, legitimate space or platform for people to share their opinions and views with others in a 'community' is an important issue in the digital world. Throughout history, local newspapers provided opportunities for townsfolk to pen their concerns on key matters and share them with wider audiences. Sometimes this would generate fiery responses from those with different views, and so letters to the editor pages became an important, early feature of media and helped establish news providers as the alternative 'town square' for political debate as communities grew in size and stature. Today, traditional letters to the editor continue to feature in the local press, but in a technological landscape these sections are increasingly morphing into practices such as 'texts to the editor' or 'Facebook posts' on stories and issues. It could be argued that these pages provide a good barometer of how active and engaged a community is about political and civic life. This must be considered with some trepidation, however. Letters to the editor, for example, are often the domain of just a small section of a community (such as political candidates, leaders and community activists) and journalists also play a 'gate-keeping' role in deciding which letters should be published in print given space restrictions on pages. Online – where everyone with computer access and an Internet connection has the option to comment and participate in key debates – has its own challenges.

Often social media is celebrated as an important tool for participatory democracy, but local journalists must work to ensure content featuring audience opinion is civil and reasonable (see Prochazka et al., 2016 for full discussion). Journalists increasingly perform the role of umpire in determining what is acceptable and unacceptable discussion online. This can be a time-consuming task in a resource-poor media environment. Freelon (2015) found insults in almost 40 per cent of newspaper comments, making them 'far ruder' than posts in Twitter. Some studies also argue news articles that include user comments are judged to be lower in journalistic content than those without comments, regardless of the quality of the discussion (Ash et al., 2010) A study by Prochazka et al. (2016) found that neither uncivil nor civil commentary enhanced perceived journalistic quality of articles among audiences. They argue the crucial challenge is for news companies to enable participation and feedback on stories without risking damage to quality perceptions of journalistic content through poor comments.

While social media dominates academic and industry discussions about engaging public opinion, the role of local talkback radio should not be overlooked in discussions about media. Talkback can be distinguished from other forms of radio because it invites people to listen and to call with their views and opinions (see Ewart, 2010). A report into the role and place of talkback radio in Australia found the medium to 'provide a homeland and heartland for audiences' – a relatively free space where people can air their opinions. It also found that talkback radio uses a variety of mechanisms to screen and facilitate callers and often sets the agenda as to what opinions and views it is seeking from the community on a given day (Ewart, 2010).

Bonding, bridging and linking: The flip side of media power

The dark side of 'community' and the media's relationship to constructing reality was discussed in Chapter 2. In outlining practices such as advocacy or campaign journalism it is important to acknowledge that any talk of media as 'champion' implies there are always winners and losers. Not everyone, for example, makes the team or has the ability to speak on the team's behalf.

Gutsche (2015) works to address issues of inequality through his critical engagement with 'boosterism'. He contends that in advocating on behalf of 'communities' journalists can also engage in a form of social control. He argues that boosterism promotes mediatized notions of a community's dominant traditions, identities and potential for future prosperities. It includes practices that maintain and empower dominant cultural positions of collective identities that then deploy messages of approved behaviours, including consumption and patriotism. This also serves as a form of 'social banishment and removal of undesirables from society' (p. 507). Gutsche demonstrates how local news representations in mid-western US states normalize protectionism of white space. He highlights how place making in news divides geographies and people.

Aldridge (2003) takes issue with campaign journalism at the local level as it seeks to appeal to as many inhabitants with a stake in an issue as possible. She argues there has been a growing reliance on campaigning as newsroom resources shrink because it is reliable and delivers a predictable flow of news when reporters are scarce. Campaigns are also believed to be a powerful tool to draw in audiences. This means newspapers run the risk of placing important social issues in populist interpretive frames. Aldridge (2003) argues such journalism promotes public debate that appeals to universal values and generates a blandly consensual discourse of sentimentalized 'insiders' with the demand that we identify with them. In other words, news outlets choose campaigns that critics of this type of journalism find hard to contest – whether it be supporting the retention of nursing homes for frail and dependent elderly people, or the safety of young women.

Journalists should engage in critical scrutiny and self-questioning about the types of issues that require attention, according to Aldridge (2003). This includes considering even more controversial topics that might not appeal to the majority but deserve society's attention all the same.

Naming and shaming

In the previous section we touched on issues of social control generated when local media play a role in defining and conceptualizing understandings of 'community'. In acknowledging issues of power, it is important to examine the media's disciplinary role that comes alongside its position as advocate and community leader. To highlight this we will outline the role of 'media shaming', especially of those who do not comply with expected moral or community values. We position 'media shaming' as a powerful cultural practice that was assumed by news media when brutal shaming punishments were all but phased out across Western societies by the 19th century.

The practice of shaming others has intensified in the digital age. There is much literature that highlights the role of social media in exposing the wrong doings of others, via the practice of i-surveillance (Hess & Waller, 2014). Armed with mobile phones or other devices, everyday people are quick to expose the wrongdoings of others, from racial abuse on trains or people who flee car accident scenes to those who urinate in public places. Our research has found that quite often it is traditional media that amplify shameful behaviour – determining which cases should be elevated from archives like YouTube and Facebook, contextualized and shared with audiences. At times they identify faceless perpetrators exposed on social media for the sake of a story, acting as a law unto themselves. Local media outlets have also been known to shame vigilantes who use social media to expose the wrongdoings of others if they deem the practice inappropriate, reinforcing their mantle as community leader with the power to determine 'right' from 'wrong' – at least symbolically (see also Noelle-Newmann, 1993; Nussbaum 2004; Petley 2013; Lupton, 2015 for other important work on the topic of media and public shaming).

Consider the example of a woman caught urinating one night outside a McDonald's restaurant. A passerby captured the incident on camera, and the footage was uploaded to YouTube and Facebook. After attracting thousands of hits, the local newspaper was alerted to the story. Rather than report the details, it ran an article saying the woman did not deserve such humiliation and they would not be showcasing the footage or naming her publicly (Hess & Waller, 2016b).

Summary

We return to the news stories about bicycles that framed the introduction to this chapter. American journalist Janine Zeitlen, who was responsible for the campaign to improve bike safety in Florida, told the *Columbian Journalism Review* that this type of journalism felt natural to her. She argued: 'You don't have to be a reporter divorced from humanity. I care about bicyclists getting killed. If can do something more proactive to stop that, I want to do it'. (Newsmith, 2015). Zeitlen resists the widely held journalistic norm that journalists exist 'outside' of society and their job is to report and provide information objectively. This chapter has demonstrated that serving as advocates and leaders on behalf of a community generates and reinforces power in different ways. Problems arise when we seek to determine what we mean by 'community', who fits in and who deserves representation. It is necessary that journalists sometimes embark on advocacy and campaign journalism on topics that appeal to a majority, such as the desire for safe neighbourhoods, clean air and water. However, they must at all times consider the under-represented and serve as champions for those without a voice in the very interests of preserving the importance of 'community'.

6 Changing Journalistic Practices

Introduction

Media that informs, educates and entertains us is retrievable from just about anywhere. It's available in 'the cloud', on our phones and computers, in cars and even accessible from the watches we wear. There are old media habits, too, that die hard, with local television, radio and printed news still in demand everywhere from the breakfast table to cafés, trains and hospital waiting rooms. In this digital world it is important that local news outlets are in tune with audiences' range of mediated habits. They also have to be sure that when people do come looking for their content it can be found easily and in a suitable format, whether the written word, video, images, audio or a quick link. Consumers, it seems, are demanding more and more 'choice' on the information menu. Providing an all-you-can-eat information buffet, however, is costly and time consuming. There's also the argument that the information being produced is not as 'nutritious' because news outlets are more interested in how it looks than the quality of its core ingredients.

What we do know is that these ongoing changes in newsgathering and news consumption have created constant demand for media workers with cutting-edge digital and technical skills. Different ways of 'doing journalism' have emerged and are being interwoven with old ideas. There is also the once taboo topic of business skills that still receives less emphasis in journalism practice, scholarship and education. Yet this is an increasingly important skill set for local journalists as profits slump and new start-up enterprises emerge. Local journalists must not only produce the news; often they are media entrepreneurs or part of small operations looking to produce profits. Necessity demands a greater understanding of business culture alongside technological change, yet they remain uneasy bedfellows. For much of the 20th century, journalism scholars and industry worked hard to establish distance from those who produce revenue to preserve the 'purity' of the journalism profession.

This chapter emphasizes that technological change has been a key contributor to the economic and social conditions that are transforming journalism practice at the local level more broadly – and profoundly. We set out to show that changes to the professional role and identity of journalists involve not only employing a different set of tools; journalists working at the local level are doing different things, including curating user-generated content and setting up, managing and generating revenue sources for their own hyperlocal news outlets. All the while, an emphasis on traditional skills and practices such as investigative journalism remains (Deuze, 2007b). Debates about the neutral 'observer role' also persist, especially in smaller communities, where some journalists can find it difficult (and undesirable) to maintain a distanced, objective stance, while others insist it is imperative.

In the sections that follow, we explore how digital news skills and local journalists' new roles overlap and intermingle with traditional practices, highlighting how they assist newsmakers to perform their important roles. This includes the ability to listen into and facilitate conversations among audiences, as well as moderate and curate content on social media platforms.

The chapter is divided into four sections. We begin with the technical and multimedia skills necessary for work in 21st-century newsrooms. We then explore some of the community and social tasks local journalists are now performing, before considering the range of skills related to content curation. To be a curator in the world of social media involves sourcing online content produced by others, and repackaging it for a specific audience. Much like an art curator, journalists work within the space of a given theme (in this instance localness) to find the right pieces that complement the aim and scope of the gallery (news outlet). Sometimes they even provide the media platforms for people to create their own content (discussion boards, citizen journalism, photography) and then exhibit the best of it for audiences.

Finally, we look into commercial skills and entrepreneurial journalism at the local level to show that the news business is no longer the domain of a select few. Technology has changed the rules of the game. We draw on the wisdom of some entrepreneurs to show it takes a lot of determination (and a small dose of naiveté!) to start up your own local media business, but the rewards can be great.

By the end of the chapter it will be clear that a new generation of local journalists is developing a different mindset and skill set, thereby enriching traditional community journalism roles. As McQuail (2013, p. 182) argues, 'the journalist workforce is likely to have a range of new and different skills that reduces an older sense of identity and vocation'. On the other hand, 'despite enormous changes over the last century or so, the central core of what journalism does or is expected to do for society has not changed all that much' (McQuail, 2013, p. 196). A way to cope with this dilemma is to acknowledge that what society expects of its news providers might not have changed, but what many journalists actually do has undergone fundamental transformation. Furthermore, as Bakker (2014) argues, the changing roles local journalists play are not necessarily a sign of an overall downgrading of journalism. Some research we draw on in this chapter does suggest tasks such as harvesting information from online sources are of concern for a number of reasons; but others, such as moderating discussions, data journalism and social media curation can arguably be considered as 'upgrading' journalism.

Technical, multimedia and 24/7 skills for local reporting

Digitization and convergence are reconfiguring newsrooms and news practices, which means that increasingly journalists need to be able to produce and process text, video and sound in their reporting, especially for the web. As job opportunities continue to shift online, those who have the ability to work in different digital formats and handle many types of technology across multiple platforms will get these jobs. For example, a survey of US network affiliate television news directors found 91 per cent said new media skills were important when making local TV hiring decisions (Cremedas & Lysak, 2011).

As most local news outlets now have online platforms, journalists who may have once focused on meeting a daily deadline, or producing one or two broadcasts or newspaper editions, must now be able to report and update online news quickly and continuously in response to the around-the-clock demands of the digital newsroom. They also work with an array of digital technologies to find stories and sources and provide additional content, such as video, blogs, slideshows and podcasts. Willnat and colleagues (2013) conclude from the findings of their research in 31 countries that there is no clear pattern when it comes to journalistic competencies, although they also state that multimedia skills are crucial. These include online research, producing news for different platforms and IT skills, including the ability to design and run websites. These competencies are commonplace in newsrooms now. For example, research on regional media in the UK and Sweden (Witschge & Nygren, 2009) found high levels of multi-skilling among journalists working on all news platforms, who are described as 'multi-reporters'. Witschge and Nygren (2009) also observe that journalists on regional media use on average 4.4 different software packages per day. These often include content management systems (CMS), web browsers, e-mail, software for pictures, layout, editing sound and video and spreadsheet software.

A nationwide survey to assess the impact of multimedia demands on American television reporters and producers from a range of market sizes shows that TV news staffers 'are doing much more than just TV' (Smith et al., 2007, p. 555). According to the study, nearly 70 per cent of news workers who responded to the questionnaire perform tasks associated with digital spaces; most notably, producing content for their station's website. Their duties (in order from most common to least) include writing stories for the web, posting content, hosting Q&A sessions with viewers, showing unaired video, providing links to sites related to stories, providing still pictures, creating blogs, and creating Internet-only stories (Smith et al., 2007). A majority agreed that their workload was increasing because of multimedia activities. One respondent stated: 'Convergence places a lot more responsibility on my shoulders. I have far more work to do here than if my station did not practice convergence' (Smith et al., 2007, p. 567).

Considering this, it is not surprising that much scholarly research on multimedia journalism indicates that it 'seems to bring with it a limitless number of potential tasks for journalists to fit in their workday' (Singer 2004, p. 3). In Singer's research on the work practices of print, television and online journalists, the integration of digital media demanded more from reporters as they produced content for multiple platforms. Duhé and colleagues (2004) describe how some television reporters have morphed into video journalists, commonly referred to as multimedia, digital or backpack journalists. 'This [video journalist] describes an individual reporter who writes, shoots, and edits a story' (Duhé et al., 2004, p. 87). Positions such as 'photo journalist' have been eliminated at some television stations as new technology makes it possible for one person, such as a reporter, to assume those duties. Huang and colleagues (2004) referred to this as 'role convergence', which is leading some managers to eliminate positions. As a result, journalists accustomed to performing certain day-to-day tasks now assume a number of duties that would have been handled by several news workers previously (Deuze, 2004).

In their study of demands of daily news work in Sweden and the UK, Witschge and Nygren (2009) found journalists working in regional media produced two to three articles per day, and those involved in wholly online news produced between five and 10. Their research highlights not only the intensification of work, but also the impact of organizational changes on newsroom practice. The journalists surveyed reported that their work was now more team-based and planned than in the past. They also said the way they gathered news had changed. They spent far more time in the newsroom, rather than out in the field. This was attributed to the fact they were dealing with so much information that came through email and was found on the Internet. It was once the norm for local reporters to spend most of their time out covering events and meeting with sources. Witschge and Nygren (2009, p. 43) observed a distinct drop in time spent out in the community, but said: 'At least every second regional and local journalist leaves the newsroom every day for work, according to the Swedish survey'.

There is evidence of frustration among some journalists who are dealing with technological and organizational change. A number of studies have found one of the main reasons for this is that reporters believe the changing job responsibilities brought about by digital media take away from their traditional journalistic routines – routines they consider important to carrying out their journalistic responsibility (Ursell, 2001; Sylvie et al., 2004). For example, a number of reporters said they were spending less time contacting sources, fact checking, investigating leads and developing their material – all part of their previous day-to-day routines – because of the time constraints associated with generating stories for multiple platforms and the added responsibilities they have had to take on due to job cuts in their newsrooms (Sylvie et al., 2004). Witschge and Nygren (2009, p. 44) found many journalists did not think multi-skilling would make journalism better. They suggest these negative attitudes might lie in the fact that journalists believe multi-skilling is mainly used by management to lower costs and increase productivity, rather than to provide them with new creative opportunities.

On the other hand, studies such as those by Pavlik (2000), Lysak and colleagues (2012) and Adornato (2014) offer more positive journalist perspectives. They all argue that digital technology enhances local reporters' potential, despite the additional pressures brought on by digital innovation. Pavlik says 'reporters can now effectively use online tools to gather news and information, check facts and even find resources' (2000, p. 230). Lysak and colleagues (2012) found 80 per cent of local television news directors agree or strongly agree that social media – especially sites such as Facebook and Twitter – enhance reporting of stories. Journalists also said new media had become an important way of interacting with

the audience. The editorial team at the *Plymouth Wicked Local* news outlet in Massachusetts outline their use of Twitter on a day-to-day level:

> We often use Twitter to get our followers to click on links that redirect
> them back to stories and photos on our *Wicked Local Plymouth* website,
> but there's much more to Twitter than that. We also use it to seek and
> gather information, and we follow people, organizations and town
> departments to help us stay in touch with what's going on in Plymouth.
> Twitter has taught us to get right to the point. It's amazing what can
> be said in 140 characters or less. The power of Twitter as a news source
> continues to grow. We follow presidential elections, severe weather
> events, high-profile trials such as [the] Boston Marathon bomber ...
> and much more through social media. Locally, having a Twitter handle
> has been a requirement for our reporters for several years, but beyond
> being mandated, we realize it's another valuable tool in the toolbox.
> Mobile devices put the news of the day in our hands. While we post
> timely material to our *Wicked Local Plymouth* website and share inter-
> esting items on our Old Colony Memorial Facebook page, Twitter let's
> [sic] us reach an audience with a greater sense of immediacy, often as
> a story is developing. (Wicked Local Plymouth, 2015)

Adornato (2014) interviewed reporters working at a local television station in the north-east of the United States. They said they had underestimated the power of digital media as a tool to track down both stories
and sources. This was an unanticipated, yet desirable, consequence of
the adoption of new media. Adornato (2014) also found reporters' interactions with their routine, institutional contacts, such as communications officers in government departments and local companies, were
changing. Traditional sources were increasingly posting information
online before, or instead of, contacting media outlets directly. Reporters
must therefore routinely monitor the online platforms of their major
sources of news.

The place for printed news?

We should acknowledge that while digital sensibilities are important,
some local news providers continue to find that print remains the most
legitimate platform to share news and information, regardless of the
strength of a town's ability to connect online or the availability of its
wifi. While there has been a plethora of reports pointing to the decline
in revenue and circulation for print, there are signs it is not all doom and
gloom. There are thousands of small community newspapers operating

successfully in the US (see www.iswne.com) and in Australia many local journalists report that their readers still prefer the print product over online.[6] They are quick to point out that the transition to digital does not spell the end of newspapers, only the format in which they are read. A cultural studies approach to news encourages us to consider the needs and wants of communities in their specific contexts, from demographics to digital connectivity and capabilities.

Consider two new hyperlocal publications in the United Kingdom. The *Caerphilly Observer* in Wales began in 2009 as a printed product. This was because its founder, Richard Gurner, discovered that in the local area advertisers continued to want to work with print rather than digital platforms. The hyperlocal began by providing a low-cost platform for legal notices and also received funding from local government to get the first four editions off the ground. Then there is the success of the *City Talking* in Leeds, which began as a Facebook page focusing on fashion, food, music, culture lifestyle and sport. As the page grew in popularity the proprietors expanded from Facebook on to a website and then into print. The hyperlocal now collaborates with the *Yorkshire Evening Post* to distribute its print edition and has also hosted special projects such as the Leeds Digital Fashion Week. These examples highlight that while being digitally savvy is important – especially for start-up enterprises – print remains powerful. An article published by the Nieman Foundation highlighted that in 2013, newspapers were still distributed to as many as 40 million people in America and 1.4 billion worldwide. The report's author Ken Doctor highlights that many newspaper subscribers are affluent and strongly represented among baby boomers. While many of them own i-devices to read news and information digitally, they seem to prefer the print paper. This creates a conundrum for publishers opting to cut news print usage (Doctor, 2013). The World Association of Newspapers has also reported that circulation revenue from newspapers (in print and digital formats) now outweighs advertising revenue. This is largely because advertising revenue had plummeted dramatically in recent years. But Secretary General of the World Association of Newspapers, Larry Kilman, said the figures meant publishers were relying on audiences more than advertisers to help fund journalism and circulation across a newspaper's multiple platforms was stable.

> ...it is clear that the story of the newspaper industry is not one of doom and gloom and decline. Newspapers around the world are successfully proving their value to advertisers, discovering new markets and new business models. (Kilman, 2015)

Radio journalism and digital innovation

Local radio is a worldwide phenomenon that has been in existence for about 100 years and is grappling with many of the same techno-logical, economic and cultural issues as local newspapers. The diminu-tion of localness in the local radio sector is occurring in a number of ways, according to Starkey (2011). Locally owned, locally originated and locally accountable community radio stations are falling under the control of national and even international media groups. Local radio journalists are now expected to produce content for their news organi-zation's websites, which involves writing, image making and IT skills that were probably not part of the job a decade ago. Live streaming and podcasting are now regular features of news radio.

Journalists working for local radio have had to adapt their practices, but they also have the advantages of audio skills and instant reporting that are well suited to digital news production and therefore of advan-tage to newspapers seeking to enhance their online offerings, as we will see from the case study below.

Local radio has always enjoyed the benefits of immediacy, getting the news to people as it happens or certainly much faster than the local newspaper of bygone days could manage. As a medium, it creates an intimacy between broadcaster and listener, literally amplifying local voices, concerns and culture. Local talkback radio is an exemplary site of participatory media practice. Radio remains popular with audiences who have it in their homes, their cars and workplaces, and on their digital devices. In the UK, 45 million people are regular radio listeners (Chantier & Stewart, 2009). In the US, NPR produces and distributes to its 764-member stations more than 120 hours of original programming and reaches more than 34 million listeners weekly (Halbert & McDowell, 2013, p. 19).

Local radio differs from country to country, according to culture, his-tory and perhaps most importantly the regulatory environment estab-lished by different governments. We acknowledge that broadcasting policy is a key factor in this, but it is a complex topic (Starkey, 2011) that we cannot do justice to here, so we will not delve into it. There are also some significant differences between commercial and not-for-profit radio.

In the commercial sector, the fierce battle for audiences and advertis-ing revenue has resulted in programming and promotional techniques designed to be profitable. Music tends to dominate the airwaves and some commentators warn that these outfits neglect local news at their peril because it is what makes local radio distinctively local (Chantier & Stewart, 2009). Local public broadcasting, most notably BBC Local Radio, takes a more serious approach featuring talk and speech. This has led to the public broadcaster establishing a niche among a generally older audience.

Producing high-quality journalism in cost-effective ways is a challenge for all local news providers. One recommended survival strategy is to form a strategic alliance with another respected community news organ-ization (Kaye & Quinn, 2010). One such US case study of a partnership operating in Miami, Florida, is worth considering because it points to the kinds of innovations that are transforming local journalism practice.

Several years ago WLRNFM, a non-profit National Public Radio (NPR) member station, developed a news partnership with *The Miami Herald* newspaper that has become a respected source for locally produced radio news. Halbert and McDowell (2013) argue this business model embraces the advantages of not only sharing people and resources, but also shar-ing the intangible asset of brand equity exhibited by both parties.

The alliance began with one radio news director and two part-time reporters, who were based in the *Herald*'s newsroom and were made employees of the *Herald*. This was done purposefully so the two news cultures – writers and broadcasters – would be side-by-side, in hopes of eliminating any 'us versus them' tensions between departments, accord-ing to Halbert and McDowell (2013, p. 27). Following a pilot phase, the news staff was expanded to five full-time reporters and two part-time reporters, who participate in anchoring newscasts, editing audio, pre-paring copy for broadcast and other necessary functions of the news operation. In addition, newscasts expanded from mornings into the middle of the day, providing more news and more advertising oppor-tunities. WLRN/Miami Herald News produces newscasts 16 times per weekday. News bulletins are also available for online listeners through links on *The Miami Herald* website and through iTunes.

Halbert and McDowell (2013) argue that the WLRN/*Miami Herald* strategic alliance has a defined purpose that goes beyond a superfi-cial promotion or sharing content basis. Under this arrangement, the news employees and news studios of WLRN are fully immersed into the newsroom of *The Miami Herald*, both physically and as organized by management. WLRN/Miami Herald News employees are considered internally as another department of the *Herald* (although they truly are employees of a WLRN subsidiary organization named 'South Florida Public Media'), and given access to the additional resources of the *Herald*. The radio reporters have published news stories in the *Herald*, while print journalists have been put on air during breaking news events (Giovannelli, 2012).

Interpretation and curatorial skills

International surveys show that local journalists from diverse nations including Canada, Brazil and the Netherlands now consider 'interpretation' to be one of their most important roles – even more important than the dissemination of information (Willnat et al., 2013). This reflects the fact that the changing political economy of news and the proliferation of user-generated content on social media have disrupted the monopolies traditional news media held over the circulation of knowledge and the power this gave them to shape public debate. The disruptions are profound, prompting a rethinking of journalism itself (Peters & Broersma, 2013; Schudson, 2013).

Local reporters no longer have the privileged position of exclusive access to sources and the public sphere, except perhaps in specific cases such as breaking news. Now, both the sources of local news and the audience can establish their own public channels. As a result, a new need has emerged for journalists who can synthesize and make sense of the many voices in the town square. For this reason, 'interpretation skills' and 'digital curation' are fast gaining importance alongside technical and multimedia competencies. Straight and factual reporting has long been the ideal in journalism. However, due to the rise of online media, 24-hour news and the subsequent flood of raw and unfiltered information, the dominant role of journalists in many countries is shifting toward offering interpretation and organization of the information reported on.

Two aspects of the changing communication environment are promoting the importance of interpretative journalism, according to Tumber and Prentoulis (2005). They highlight the increased number of news providers and the ability of organizations to communicate directly with the public, bypassing journalists and traditional media. Therefore, given the abundance of raw information available, journalists need to show their abilities in sorting out meaningful facts and interpreting them for local audiences. This is where concepts of proximity and scope (which we outlined in Chapters 2 and 4) are important. Journalists must be seen to be capable of interpreting information for local audiences. They must have a detailed understanding of the region they serve so they can identify questions to ask sources and 'localize' information circulating in global information flows.

Interpretation

A comprehensive review of the literature shows that there are different conceptualizations of interpretive journalism (see Salgado & Strömbäck, 2012). It also shows that most studies of interpretive journalism focus on political and national journalism, rather than the local level. No matter where this type of journalism is practised, it is almost always defined as in opposition to, or going beyond, descriptive, fact-based journalism, and some definitions point to a shift of emphasis related to the five Ws of journalism: What, Where, When, Who and Why. Salgado and Strömbäck (2012, p. 146) conceptualize interpretive journalism as entailing a greater emphasis on the 'meaning' of news beyond the facts and statements of sources, and a greater emphasis on the Why of the five Ws. It is characterized by a disbelief in the notion that it is possible to separate facts from values.

According to one critic of interpretive journalism, this style is driven by themes, where facts are used mainly to illustrate the theme chosen by the journalist (Patterson, 2000). This perspective should be understood within the larger context of the relationship between journalists and their sources. A journalism focused on the What, When, Where and Who enables sources to set the news agenda and news frames, reducing journalists to collectors and amplifiers of sources' messages. In contrast:

> The interpretive style empowers journalists by giving them more control over the news message. [...] The descriptive style places the journalist in the role of an observer. The interpretive style requires the journalist to act also as an analyst. The journalist is thus positioned to give shape to the news in a way the descriptive style does not allow. (Patterson, 2000, p. 250)

There is a broad consensus that providing people with the kinds of information they need to be free and self-governing is one of journalism's most important democratic functions (Kovach & Rosenstiel, 2007). But as Salgado and Strömbäck (2012) observe, agreement breaks down when the discussion turns to the kinds of information that people need. They say that for those who defend interpretive journalism, the answer may be that people need analytical and contextualized information – information that makes it easier for them to make sense of facts and what is happening. For critics of interpretive journalism, the answer is instead that people need information unfiltered by journalists – information that comes as directly as possible from the original sources.

The following section considers the important role for journalists in an age of information abundance, where people are also time poor, and how this has created the need for journalists with curatorial knowledge and skills.

Curation

The concept of curating news is not new. According to Bakker (2014, p. 599), it involves consciously seeking out content, editing content, enriching content or combining content from different sources. At the most general level, it has always been a core competency; that is, organizing the information filed by reporters into a deliverable package for audiences. However, 'digital curation' has entered journalism's lexicon as an extension of a specific newsroom role that old school journalists in the UK, New Zealand, Australia and many other places call 'copy tasting'. In fact, the copy taster remains a key figure on traditional news desks. Usually senior journalists with well-developed news sense, copy tasters sift through the incoming reports from national and international news agencies – including Reuters, AP, PA, Agence France Presse and the rest – rejecting some, selecting others and pushing the most promising ones towards staff reporters, or the relevant specialists, for their assessment and follow-up. Through this process some of those stories are developed, expanded and taken to a new level. Others are simply edited and published. On local newspapers, especially in regional areas, a national story is often developed with a local angle, while international stories are run straight from 'the wire'.

In today's world of journalism, the sources for stories have multiplied well beyond the news agencies and become available to all. There is far more information being disseminated, on a wide range of open publishing platforms. So the old-school skill of copy tasting has had to be reinvented in the modern world as one in which many news sources – both official and unofficial, eyewitness, citizen journalist and/or expert – can be scanned, appraised and either incorporated into news reports or rejected. It still comes down to a fundamental journalistic skill – the ability to present information in the most dramatic and engaging way.

Howarth (2015) argues that the relationship to original content is the key factor for distinguishing news curation from traditional newsgathering. She contends that while the reporter generates the journalistic equivalent of original content in the form of news, the imaginative curator re-mixes and re-presents existing content in potentially novel ways. However, debates have polarized between those who view news curation as part of the death of journalism and others who regard it as part of a wider revival of the profession, freed from monopolistic institutions to circulate a greater variety of knowledge and viewpoints (see Picard, 2014). We draw on Robert Picard's nuanced argument that journalism is undergoing a transformation that involves adapting to the age of curation but that those traditional news providers that fail to adapt will most likely decline. Changes to the way journalists gather and disseminate news do not mean that professional standards should slip. For example, building and maintaining trust is important to validating curation as a new form of journalism. News curators should therefore operate within the same professional framework as traditional journalists. For example, ethical standards (including verification and disclosure) and transparency (including citing and crediting sources) are essential in building trust in a curator.

In the fast pace of change, digital curation is experiencing developments of its own. Bakker (2014) points to live-blogging as extending the concept. He says it involves finding as much relevant and recent information as possible from all kinds of sources, including social media, and combining these in one continuing storyline. It utilizes software like Storify, Scribble and Coveritlive, and consists of publishing as fast as possible. Live-blogging is often seen during disasters, crime coverage, sports, elections and other news events that need continuous updating.

Curation and hyperlinking

Hyperlinking is now part of the modern-day lexicon and involves using a word, phrase, picture, icon and so on in a computer document or website on which a user clicks to move to another section of the document, or jump to another webpage or site. Journalists assume a role in sourcing a range of available websites and information about an issue and include them as hyperlinks in their stories. For example, a journalist might be writing a story about council plans to redevelop the central business district. As part of their story, they might include links to the council website, architectural plans, a Facebook page set up to discuss the development or a flier expressing community opposition. In this way, curating involves creating a 'one-stop shop' of available information about an issue that audiences might benefit from. It may be argued that the practice of hyperlinking makes a news site more useful and also builds on its authority as a leading source of information. McAdams and Berger (2001) observe that hypertextuality allows a reader to surf within a story and provides the feeling of being in charge, which might be reflected in the website's sense of reliability and legitimacy. But they maintain that the author does not give up control and by choosing which hyperlinks to include they maintain power over content accessible from their homepage.

Curation and social media – a theoretical perspective

As we highlighted in the introduction to this chapter, local journalists who engage with social media content uploaded by everyday people on sites such as YouTube and Facebook work much like any curator in an art gallery space. First they must locate, or be alerted to, interesting pieces related to a particular theme ('local appeal') that will generate talking points among audiences. Journalists must then extend the narrative of the content to give it new life and context before they launch it in the news media space. There are many influences at work in this process, such as the range of news values discussed in Chapter 4 that help journalists determine what is news. Most importantly, however, it is political economy influences that make social media especially significant to the practice of digital curation. The role of drawing attention to and exhibiting certain social media content is an especially attractive proposition to news media because it is perceived as 'free'. Social media content is often viewed as a cultural, participatory resource available to us all, rather than as a competitor in the news media environment.

Imagine walking into a supermarket with its shelves brimming with goods. Journalists can browse the aisles, pop anything of interest into their trolley and walk away with their goods without paying for them at the checkout. They don't mind attributing the information to media sites such as YouTube, Facebook or Twitter because of its 'participatory' nature. And to make it more irresistible, social media content often comes with its own free market research in terms of 'Facebook likes' or YouTube 'views'.

Robert Gehl (2009) provides a useful theoretical framework, which we extend to understand the news media's role and power as curator in digital space. He conceptualizes sites such as YouTube as an archive where information is filed and stored. Gehl (2009) argues that the YouTube archive has two curatorial functions – the storage and classification of material and its exhibition and display. He says that YouTube users are the curators of storage. This is where content is kept, titled, described and tagged, while curators of display create meaning and facts from the archive by contextualizing, interpreting and exhibiting material. We have argued that the 'curators of display' role is one performed by traditional news media (Hess & Waller, 2009). Gehl (2009) argues that the curators of display benefit from the unpaid labour of the curators of storage who have invested significant capital costs in equipment (such as smartphones, video recorders, computers) and Internet access to produce, gather, edit, upload and tag videos. In previous studies we have highlighted examples where the news media has been a curator of display, including its elevation of YouTube footage of a little koala named 'Sam' who survived an Australian bushfire to become an international media sensation (Hess & Waller, 2009) and turning British spinster songstress and YouTube hit Susan Boyle into a global superstar (Hess & Waller, 2011). Local journalists also draw on popular social media footage around local topics for news. The *Northfield News* in Minnesota, for example, writes about a local musician who has attracted millions of hits on YouTube (Krein, 2015).

Curating local news

Local journalists can enrich their reporting through digital curation that provides context and background detail, verification and scope for follow-up. Journalists operating online can be both reporter and publisher, able to curate content at the article level and that of publication – whether it's a Twitter stream, a Tumblr blog or a Flipboard magazine. A good curator of local news will remain close and listen carefully to their community, as in many ways they are the sources of news.

Image curation is perhaps the most established form of this news work, and has also spawned a host of apps from Instagram to Pinterest and Flickr. Journalists working across all platforms can make great use of these apps in their work, but compiling slideshows for news websites is perhaps the most popular and effective form of news image curation at the local level. Slideshows can be curated according to themes, for specific events or general information. We know from our research that great images of the local environment, people and events resonate strongly with local audiences (Hess & Waller, 2016b), so curating galleries of images and sourcing outstanding photos and graphics online is highly worthwhile at the local level.

When it comes to eyewitness accounts, Twitter probably comes first to mind. There's also a lot of material filed to Facebook, and video to YouTube and other platforms. RSS, Twitter, Storify, Storyful and any number of other tools can be used to stay on top of what's happening and be human filters for local news.

Twitter lists are curated channels from particular users who pass on information in a specific field – in the case of local news and information journalists can seek out lists relating to a specific geo-social space. Large numbers are not essential; 10 or even five is a good start and users can always be asked to suggest more, which can spark an interesting discussion. Benefits include that the list is based at your Twitter account, bringing you more followers.

There are also examples of new news ventures that aim to generate revenue by performing a curatorial role on behalf of audiences and news sites. They are attempting to harness new software and computer programming to assist this function. For example, *Near You Now* in the UK identifies the most relevant stories for each unique customer based on where they are and the places that matter most to them. There is also scope to curate social media content from people targeted in a given locality to help journalists in their curating role. Professor David Weir at the University of Sussex is helping to develop the *Near You Now* platform to enable such curation to take place. He said:

> In the future we expect that people will be able to check their smartphones not just for news on a national or regional level, but to find out what is happening at the end of their street. (University of Sussex, 2014)

Community and social responsibilities

Technological and economic developments have not only changed daily journalistic practices, they have also transformed the journalist's relationship to the audience. In journalism scholarship, the audience is also understood as a driving force behind changes in newsrooms. A constant theme in the literature is how media managers and journalists are increasingly recognizing the importance of changing with the times: keeping up with the shifting demands of audience members, most notably the way in which they consume information via multimedia platforms. For example, nearly 80 per cent of Internet users regularly visit social media sites, and 50 per cent of Americans get news from one or more media platforms (Nielsen, 2011; Pew Research Centre, 2012). These changes mean journalists working at the local level have more community and social responsibilities than ever before. At the same time, however, they must negotiate their relationships and responsibilities to members of the community. Many of these revolve around the power of the media in people's everyday lives – for better and for worse.

Staying close while maintaining distance: The local journalist's dilemma

There has traditionally been a 'philosophical difference' in the way journalists working at the local level approach audiences, advertisers and news in general, because often local journalists know intimately or through their personal social networks, the people and places on which they are reporting (Lauterer 1995, p. xiv).

As discussed in Chapter 2, local journalists need to understand the essence of community, the importance of place, of the relationships people maintain, and of the values and goals they share. Wotanis (2012) argues, 'They also realize they cannot hide behind a masthead. Their readers are their neighbours, their fellow church members and the people they see in line at the local grocery store or at a table in the coffee shop' (Wotanis, 2012, p. 14). In her study of 'wonderful weeklies' in the US state of Mississippi, Cass (2005) discusses how the owner-editors of four small, rural newspapers carry out their journalistic roles. She argues that the editor of the *Carthaginian* in Carthage, Mississippi, Waid Prather, gets involved in local news in a way an urban editor never would. For example, when a storm downs trees and power lines, he does not leave the scene after taking a photograph and gathering information for the news. Instead he pulls out his chainsaw and helps emergency workers to clear the road (Cass, 2005, p. 21). Despite these kinds of examples, US research has shown that mainstream local journalists tend to disregard the need to be involved with, or live in, the community on which they report. For example, Gaziano and McGrath's (1987) survey of 100 journalists demonstrated the discomfort many feel when living or getting involved within the communities they cover:

> While nearly 9 in 10 agreed that 'it's important to know a lot of people in the community' ... fewer than three in 10 agreed that 'it's important for people who work for newspapers to be involved in community organizations'. (Gaziano & McGrath, 1987, p. 320)

Overall, the survey concluded local journalists seek to keep distance between themselves and their audiences to maintain a level of credibility for their news outlet (Gaziano & McGrath, 1987, p. 325). This belief probably stems from the journalistic codes of ethics, like that of the US Society of Professional Journalists, which is 'voluntarily embraced by thousands of journalists' and states that journalists should act independently and 'remain free of associations and activities that may compromise integrity or damage credibility' (Society of Professional Journalists, 2000). This trend identified by Gaziano and McGrath in 1987 has apparently not waned. Mayer (2011) found:

> Journalists still foster and celebrate otherness more than they do connection. Ever mindful of conflicts of interest – actual or perceived – they hold themselves apart from influence and are wary of being swayed by sources or vocal readers. (Mayer, 2011, p. 12)

The editors of the four Mississippi weeklies in Cass's (2005) study all emphasized the importance of holding themselves apart from influence, took pride in their Fourth Estate role and provided examples of prize-winning investigative stories and series. Cass (2005, p. 23) said they regularly hold their local officials' 'feet to the fire', publish investigative stories, write hard-hitting editorials; demand public records, shape public policy and provide leadership at times of social and economic transition. Waid Prather of the *Cathaginian* discussed the importance of holding powerful figures and local authorities to account through frank and fearless reporting:

> The fact that you're a newspaper and cover a board meeting and write what happens has a Lysol effect. It's gonna kill some germs, whether you're spraying real good or not. (Cass, 2005, p. 23)

Hatcher (2005) has compared US community newspapers that have won the Pulitzer Prize. Varying types of data informed his analysis, including in-depth interviews and documents such as newspaper clippings, magazine articles and judges' comments, to discover how local journalists pursued these prize-winning stories. The findings suggest that the journalists had university degrees and worked for newspapers that were financially independent. They worked for, or were themselves, owners who were willing to take a stand on an issue whether or not it was one that was popular with readers, local leaders or advertisers. Hatcher (2005) found the journalists were willing to dedicate themselves to a story regardless of the hours and resources involved. They saw it as their primary role to take a stand on behalf of those who may not have a voice before those in power. In all but one example, they were also people who had formed some personal attachment to the community they served. And, on some level, at least two of them were people who had at times in their lives seen themselves as activists, who believed in the power that can come from small voices making themselves heard (see Chapter 5 for a discussion of advocacy journalism and community champions).

Hyperlocals: Doing community better?

The rise of hyperlocal news outlets can be understood as a backlash against commercial local media with traditional news and ethical values. Many hyperlocal news providers insist the focus should be less on crime and political controversy and more on figuring out how to help audiences 'do' community better. They aim to capture the wisdom of the crowd and collaborate with it. While digital platforms and social media are important tools for hyperlocal sites, there is also an emphasis on being out in the community and connecting people. In his report on UK hyperlocal media Radcliffe (2012) argues:

> Whilst new media tools can be a great means for both story gathering and story telling, word of mouth and visibility in your community are still valuable commodities which can play a key role in turning your hyperlocal site into a success. (Radcliffe 2012 p. 23)

In Australia, the owner of a Melbourne-based hyperlocal has described how tapping into the wisdom of the community helped the business find alternative streams of income through events and merchandise sales:

> ... we mined our traffic data, took notes on the stories most read and shared on our website, and listened to the topics that generated the most conversations on social media to find out what was most important to the community and how we could serve their needs. (Poh, 2013, p. 50)

This proprietor gives voice to a dilemma many journalists working at the hyperlocal level might experience at some stage. There is a discomfort in knowing people and feeling compromised, but can journalists afford to stand back from the community as relationships with audiences evolve, and it can be argued that this relationship is as important as content?

Tapping into community and facilitating conversations among audiences

Community management is clearly connected to technical skills, as it requires the intensive use of social media. Relations will be at least as important as content in years to come. New media, and especially social media forms, are inherently collaborative, which has compelled news organizations to find ways for audiences to participate in making and sharing news. Before the advent of participatory media, news processes were dominated by a top-down approach where audiences were the passive receptors of news. Today, audiences are growing accustomed to being part of the conversation and newsgathering process (Robinson, 2011; Singer et al., 2011; Hermida, 2012). As a result, news organizations are moving away from the traditional notion that news is solely determined by what news staffers think is important to the public and delivered as a unidirectional stream of authoritative information (Gillmor, 2004; Sylvie et al., 2004). Reporters are now utilizing Twitter, Facebook and blogs in an effort to connect with audiences. In essence, digital media has transformed the relationship between the journalist and the audience.

A more audience-centric approach to newsgathering and distribution has forced journalists to rethink their roles and job responsibilities. Integrating audience-generated content into traditional platforms is one practice impacting journalists' responsibilities. Cable News Network's (CNN's) iReport, launched in 2006, is a well-known example of this concept, referred to as 'citizen journalism' or 'participatory journalism' (Robinson, 2011; Singer et al., 2011; Hermida, 2012). Citizens have turned into roving reporters, recording videos and taking photos of newsworthy events and sending them to CNN for distribution online and/or on air.

More recently, people are sharing photos and other information about breaking news on social media. Reporters are relying on these firsthand accounts to 'fulfill a need for information from a location until professional journalists arrive on the scene' (Hermida, 2012, p. 664).

At the hyperlocal level, social media is recognized for its ability not only to connect with the audience, but also to help community members to be in touch with one another. For example, Niall Norbury from the British hyperlocal *AltReading*, which focuses mainly on entertainment and culture, says while *AltReading* has its website, as well as Twitter and Instagram accounts, it's the Facebook page that is the 'biggest driver of conversations' through people sharing links, seeing things on their feed and contributing a comment.

Commercial skills and entrepreneurial journalism

Journalists have always had to know a lot about the news but not much about the complexities of the news business. This is changing as the old business models stutter and fail, resulting in job losses, mergers and shutdowns. As Baines and Kennedy (2010) point out, the careers on which journalism graduates are embarking are increasingly likely to feature periods of unemployment, short-term contracts, self-employment and temporary work on specific projects. They could even find their journalism skill set is more employable outside media, news, and communication altogether. While many local news outlets have shrunk dramatically or closed their doors in recent years, especially in the UK, it's arguably at the local level where most opportunities exist for those who have the skills, knowledge, determination and flexibility to forge their careers. By moving towards self-sufficiency, journalists become less dependent on large media employers. Digital media provides opportunities for independent creators of media products, media start-ups or freelance work. In the sections that follow we explore some of the key skills and attributes needed by local journalists working for themselves and for others.

Business acumen

As the traditional business models and ways of sustaining local news are challenged, many journalists continue to put their heads in the sand. They don't want to know, because to be a 'pure', true journalist means to resist being 'tainted' by advertising and the business side of an operation. Traditional journalists are taught there is a line between editorial and advertising that they should never cross. Especially on local mainstream newspapers, reporters soon learn to loathe the advertorial round and the enthusiastic advertising salesperson trying to sell them stories about her or his clients. Martinelli (2012) contends that within the journalism academy there is an idealized separation of the newsroom where journalists produce the news and are disengaged from the advertising and marketing departments within a news organization.

The reality that news is a business is often given short shrift in journalism school curricula when advertising makes news dissemination possible (Martinelli, 2012, p. 159). News produced by journalists remains at the heart of the business, and the push for profits and the commercial nature of news are seen to compromise its integrity and autonomy. However, Lauterer (2006) argues that no matter how altruistic one's views may be, we cannot escape the fact that most news is a business and when its viability is threatened it is because of lack of advertising: 'When a paper succeeds though the (editorial) side may want to take all the credit, it is a business success and advertising makes the news possible' (Lauterer, 2006, p. 287).

While local journalists know advertising pays their wages and they understand the business on an abstract level, they are for the most part shielded from the complex realities involved in running the show.

However, there is an argument to say journalists and journalism studies scholars can no longer afford to occupy this high ground. Every advertising dollar is important to sustaining quality journalism. In the digital era audiences may expect content to be free, but it is certainly not cost-free to produce. Furthermore, in difficult economic times for news, being locked out of commercial decisions means journalists are being locked out of power.

For journalists at the local level, having the business skills to run their own enterprise, whether it's a blog, podcast or their own independent news site, is increasingly valuable. Local media entrepreneurs and journalists will have to be creative enough to harness streams of income in addition to advertising revenue. In Australia, the founder and editor-in-chief of Melbourne hyperlocal *Meld Magazine* Karen Poh makes a link between community management and business acumen: 'Tapping into the wisdom of the community has helped us to find alternative streams of income through events and merchandise sales' (Poh, 2013, p. 50).

Networking

A journalist cannot begin to write a story unless they know where to find it and have some idea of who to speak to. Knowing how to build a network and use it is a beneficial skill for journalists at all times (Bakker, 2014, pp. 603–604). In traditional journalism, the idea of networking means establishing and maintaining a strong bank of contacts that can provide story ideas and reliable and credible comment when needed. This involves getting away from the office and into the spaces where people meet, converse or where the news happens. An Australian journalist working in a regional area lamented that staff cutbacks at the newspaper where he worked meant there were only two fleet cars to be shared by a staff of 15 photographers and reporters. This resulted in journalists remaining close to the office and engaging with people online as they no longer had transport to get out into the community. He felt this was to the detriment of the newspaper's visibility and legitimacy in the town.

In this media environment some journalists and hyperlocal media operators are rethinking what 'networking' means in complex and varied ways. For example, Pamela Pinksi from Birmingham's *Digbeth is Good* says on one level networking is about sharing ideas with the audience. However, she also draws on a background in marketing to describe networking as finding different ways to amplify what is happening on her hyperlocal news site, using social media and also local mainstream media to promote stories and sponsored events (www.digbeth.org). It is worth considering that for local journalists working in the mainstream, hyperlocals in their area can be a great source of local news to tap into. Journalists also may find some benefit in engaging in practices of public journalism or advocacy journalism (as outlined in Chapter 5) to generate stories and network with both horizontal and vertical ties. For local media entrepreneurs, 'networking' can also involve assessing their own skills, identifying any shortfalls and ensuring they have connections with people who can help, or ask for help on any and all aspects of their business.

Opportunity identification

Identifying gaps in audiences' need for news has inspired many people to set up hyperlocal publications around the world. In Reading in the UK, *AltReading* was started in 2012 when its founder, Niall Norbury, realized the mainstream local news provider *Get Reading* provided only basic entertainment and culture news. Part of the strategy is to provide detailed news and information before events happen, rather than afterwards. It also involves finding interesting and different ways of covering topics to the other five news outlets that serve the region. As well as specialized entertainment news, Norbury said, 'we try to find hooks where the general public can get into topics they don't usually get into' (online-journalismblog.org). He gave the example of a feature article about the cultural life of Reading during the Cold War that spawned a lot of general interest. Pinski from *Digbeth is Good* urges says thinking about starting their own hyperlocal need to develop a unique selling point:

> Do something different. Don't try to replicate something that someone else in the local area is doing. What can you do to increase the impact of your story or publication? Use your connections, be current, be contactable; be friendly, be adaptable. (Pinksi, 2015)

Once opportunities have been identified other attributes are needed to convert them into realities. Small media entrepreneurs need skills in creative problem solving and strategic thinking. For example, Poh of *Meld Magazine* explained the importance of monitoring and marketing site traffic to attract advertisers:

> Targeted advertising obviously provides far better returns than simply serving Google ads, but you will need to reach critical mass before

advertisers are willing to commit. Businesses really only started paying attention once we had readership figures. (Poh, 2013, p. 50)

Media entrepreneurship

The stereotypical image of the entrepreneur is someone who skilfully employs other people's money to create a fast-growing business that sells lots of merchandise or services to make lots of money. However, many people have motives other than profit in mind when they establish a hyperlocal news site.

According to Tim van Gelder of *yourview.org.au* there is a broader notion of entrepreneurship that involves the marshalling of resources to develop a new, sustainable enterprise in pursuit of certain goals. The primary goal could be making lots of money, but it might instead be providing some kind of public good. The business plan might be a market analysis, strategic plan and spreadsheet, or it might be little more than 'let's get up and running as quickly and affordably as we can, and then adapt or "pivot" to meet challenges or exploit opportunities as they arise' (Van Gelder, 2013, p. 34).

Entrepreneurship is therefore best understood as an attitude, 'a mind-set rather than a skill-set', according to Mark Harrison, Head of Digital Production at the BBC (in Baines & Kennedy 2010, p. 101). However, there is a practical side. Media entrepreneurs require a suite of skills to succeed, whatever their goal (Ferrier, 2013). They need knowledge in business, people management, IT, sales, finance and law – but it's next to impossible for one person, or even two, to have all of these. This means being able to call upon on others with the necessary expertise. In community-based models this might mean recruiting suitable friends and volunteers. For-profits face the challenge of finding and maintaining the economic and human resources to meet their needs.

The reality is that while it is possible to attract a loyal following for relevant and interesting news content, resources are probably limited when it comes to support services such as human resources, training and developing a dedicated sales team to reach advertisers. The need for critical mass can also make it hard to attract ad revenues sufficient to establish and build sustainable businesses. Poh says a peak body is needed to help these typically lean outfits with training, sharing resources and other back-end services and to achieve economies of scale in the job market (Poh, 2013, p. 51). It is interesting to note that more than 100 years ago proprietors of Australia's small country newspapers came to the same conclusion and established country press associations in each state as clearing houses for advertisers. This meant when a company or organization wanted to advertise in country newspapers they only had to deal with one organization that represented its members (Kirkpatrick, 2010).

Summary

Local journalists have always worn many hats. Traditionally, this has meant being able to report on anything and everything that occurs in the area, from politics, industry, crime and courts through health, education and social justice to sport and grassroots community events. It has also meant being able to take photos, shoot vision, design a graphic or produce your own radio segment, on top of gathering the news. Advertising and the business side of things was the province of 'management' and the advertising department (or in very small operations the proprietor/editor). This chapter has considered the complexities that come with new hats: multiple platforms; information technology; interpretative and curatorial journalism; digital community roles; and entrepreneurial skills needed for the new economies of local news.

It began by considering how multimedia and information technology are more than changing sets of tools for doing the same old work of reporting and producing news. Technological change has been interwoven with organizational and social change, with news production becoming more team-oriented and planned as a result.

The local journalist's role has changed significantly in response to the way technologies are being used by their sources and audiences. Research suggests fewer journalists are performing more tasks than ever before. Rather than spending most of their time out of the office, attending events and meeting people, they now do much more of their research, including interviews, from their desks in the newsroom. There are legitimate concerns about the desk-bound intensification of work and shrinking opportunities for face-to-face contact with the community. On the other hand, there is also strong evidence to suggest the use of the Internet and social media for sourcing stories and finding contacts has broadened the range of sources of information used, thereby enhancing the participatory nature of local journalism practice. The change extends to journalists taking on more of a role as curators and interpreters of information from myriad online sources.

Curators of news are not on the front lines, covering a particular round, or filing exclusives. Instead they are responding to an audience need for guidance and interpretation as a torrent of content flows from innumerable sources. These include but are not limited to blogs, mainstream media and social networks. This torrent has created a vacuum where having a trusted editor to help sort out all this information has become as necessary as those who file the initial reports. Curators help audiences navigate through the vast ocean of content found online, and while doing so create a following based on several factors: trust, taste and tools. According to Becker (2009), curators are needed to assist people to filter through the news noise that blares through the pipes every day, curators we trust to show us what we need to know and make it easy to find. As journalism continues to evolve and adapt to advances in technology and the influence of social media, the role of the curator will continue to grow and the need for interpretation of big data and complex issues as they relate to local areas will increase.

City-based reporters have always had a greater degree of anonymity than their country cousins, who become most recognizable members of the communities in which they work and live. There are both advantages and disadvantages attached to a public profile and a high degree of familiarity with locals. Advantages include having a strong rapport and easy access to community leaders. Disadvantages include the dilemmas associated with news that could damage the reputation of someone the reporter considers a friend or important contact. Responsibilities attached to reflecting the community's agendas have multiplied with greater participation in public affairs via comments sections, online community forums hosted by news outlets and journalists' own use of social media such as Twitter, Facebook and Instagram. This can be understood as a changed familiarity with audiences that entails fresh understandings of such fundamental questions as 'What is news?'. Integrating audience-generated content into traditional platforms is one of the key practices shaping many journalists' work today. The next chapter explores in detail how the business of local news is changing and offers a range of perspectives on ways local journalists and media organizations can find their niche in the market for digital news.

In this chapter we have begun our discussion of media economics by considering the entrepreneurial know-how needed to start up a local news operation. While some of these ventures will fall by the wayside, it is worth remembering that the lucrative business of news has always had its winners and losers. In 2014 Australian journalist and historian Rachel Buchanan launched the *Melbourne Sirius*, a one-off obituary newspaper for the city of Melbourne's 525 defunct newspapers. As well as compiling the names, dates of existence and mastheads of newspapers, she also wrote footnotes on their 'lives'. They tell stories like that of *The Argus* (1846–1957), which was the first paper in the world to publish a colour photograph on the front page – the effort sent it bankrupt. Then there's *The Daily Truth* (1975), a newspaper Rupert Murdoch staffed with strike breakers as the regular staff of *The Age, Sun* and *Melbourne Herald* went on strike. It lasted three editions. Buchanan also tells of the subversive *Australasian Weed* (1977–1978), a series of pro-marijuana legalization newspapers. Its proprietor started papers called *Australasian Greed, Australasian Need, Australasian Seed, Australasian Weed* and *Australasian Plead*. They all featured a marijuana leaf in the masthead, and the first three carried the tagline 'All the dope on dope' (Robin, 2014).

It goes against the grain of traditional journalism to place responsibility for the financial side of news on the shoulders of those tasked with gathering and producing news. However, the reality is that to succeed with a hyperlocal requires funds and flair, whether the aim is to make a profit or do some good. Therefore local media entrepreneurs and journalists have to think and act creatively in order to generate streams of income in addition to advertising revenue.

7 Subsidize or Commercialize? The Economics of Local Journalism

Introduction

In 2015 an Australian journalist working for a small daily newspaper started a national petition to 'save local journalism'. One of the country's biggest media players, Fairfax Media, had just announced plans to drastically reduce the number of editorial staff, including photographers, in some of its bigger regional newspaper offices. It followed a decision months earlier by the nation's public broadcaster to cut 400 positions and close five regional radio posts in response to major government funding cuts.

The Australian situation mirrors other parts of the world where the wrecking ball has been taken to established local news providers as major media companies grapple with ways to retain their profit share. Since 2005, hundreds of newspapers have closed their doors in the United Kingdom and the United States – many at the local level. The fourth largest newspaper publisher in Britain, Northcliffe Media, cut staff numbers by at least 50 per cent and its competitors such as Johnston Press, Newsquest and Trinity all followed suit (as cited in Canter, 2013, p. 1092). In Canada, long-serving publications such as the *Kamloops Daily News* folded, and newspaper revenue fell 13 per cent between 2009 and 2014 (see Bailey, 2014; see also Chapter 3 for full discussion). The press in Venezuela, meanwhile, reported dealing with other crippling economic issues. For example, a shortage of paper forced some local newspapers to stop printing their editions and others to scale down publications (Bamat, 2014). At the same time there has been major consolidations – in the US, newspaper publishers Gannet and Tribune sought to position themselves in the digital world. The Tribune Company purchased Local TV LLC for $2.275 billion in 2014, adding 19 television stations in 16 markets to its portfolio (State of the Media white paper, 2014). It then spun off its TV division into a different company, TEGNA, in 2015.

At a time of such tumultuous change the future for local news is not all bad from an economic perspective. New ventures, often dubbed as 'start-up' or 'hyperlocal' media, have emerged where traditional newspapers no longer exist. The State of the Media 2014 white paper outlined a phoenix-like scenario in the global media landscape:

> There will always be cuts, layoffs and closures, but there also always will be new stories and new blood emerging from an old industry ... long-struggling media entities may have to give up the fight, but new ideas and innovation will rise from the ashes. (State of the Media white paper, 2014)

There are big-time investors who argue that in discussions about the future of news, local content is king. For example, one of the world's richest men, Warren Buffett, purchased 28 small-town newspapers across the United States in 2012 at a cost of $344 million. He was upbeat about their future and stated in his annual report to shareholders:

> Newspapers continue to reign supreme ... in the delivery of local news. If you want to know what's going on in your town ... there is no substitute for a local newspaper that is doing its job ... Wherever there is a pervasive sense of community, a paper that serves the special informational needs of that community will remain indispensable to a significant portion of its residents. (As cited in Badkar, 2013)

Warren Buffett might be optimistic, but the question still remains: how do local news operators make money in a fragmented media landscape and what business models are best to fund local journalism? This chapter examines the 'top-down' (professional media organizations and elites such as government) and 'bottom-up' (participatory journalism, the people formerly known as the audience) approaches to funding local media.

We begin by examining the role big media corporations have played in commercializing local content and what we term 'centralizing and dispersing' news production. The discussion then moves to the changing nature of advertising, paywalls, the role of social media juggernauts such as Facebook, and how governments support the circulation of news in communities. We then focus on demystifying the entrepreneurial landscape and start-up culture gathering traction at the local level by outlining some of the 'bottom-up' economic models that are often blended with 'top-down' approaches to help sustain local news. We explore what Deuze and colleagues (2007) refer to as a 'third space' – the convergence of big media with the people formerly known as the audience. While it is relatively easy to set up a hyperlocal site, providing one has a computer and access to the Internet, many start-ups have struggled to maintain viability, as witnessed by the spectacular rise and decline of *Patch* in the US. The chapter concludes by returning to a cultural studies approach that provides new insights into the sustainability of local news.

Funding models: 'Top-down' approaches

Advertising

The traditional advertiser model has been a goldmine for local media for centuries because of their niche geographic markets. The typical layout of a newspaper in the UK from the 19th century consisted of advertisements on the front and back pages, with editorial columns and news reports in between (Rubury, 2009, p. 14). UK media baron Lord Northcliffe refused to move advertisements from the front page of *The Times* newspaper in London as late as 1908:

> Advertisements? They are the most important news. And where would you have it if not on the front page. (As cited in Rubury, 2009, p. 50)

The importance of advertising to the future of local news across all media platforms, from newspapers, radio and television to online, is at the forefront of discussions about the industry. A barrage of Internet competitors now vie for a share of classified advertising, sometimes referred to as 'rivers of gold', which were once the domain of the traditional newspaper. Since advertising represents a major source of revenue in both print and online formats, a decline in advertising volume and value has a serious impact on profitability (Krüger & Swatman, 2002). It should also be noted that not only has there been a gradual shift of advertising to online, but also to non-news channels (Deuze, 2010, p. 270).

The global financial crisis that began in 2008 crystallized the sense of crisis in the media industry and highlighted the perennial issue of how the democratic role of journalism is sustained by private sector revenues and the need to align profit-seeking activities of individual businesses with the public interest (Tiffen, 2009). Until then, it could be argued that advertising had been given 'short shrift' in scholarship about the news and journalism, largely because of an idealized separation between editorial and advertising, where journalists produced the 'news' and were encouraged to disengage from the advertising and marketing departments within their organizations to protect journalistic integrity and autonomy. But no matter how altruistic one's views about journalism, there is no escape from the fact that news is a business that relies on advertising revenue to fund editorial activity.

Advertisements such as personals, real estate, items for sale and motoring have been the target of intense competition for local media in the digital environment. The Advertising Association in Britain predicts that the print advertising market is likely to shrink by a further £700m to £1.6bn by 2019, with the regional press taking most of the impact (Fenton et al., 2010). The Pew Research Institute in the US says traditional advertising from print and television still accounts for more than half of the total revenue supporting news, even though print ad revenues are falling rapidly (Mitchell, 2014). In many small communities, classified advertising has dropped by as much as 80 per cent since the year 2000 (Abernathy, 2014). As we highlighted in Chapter 4, however, classifieds – especially births, deaths and marriage columns – are a powerful point of distinction for local newspapers and there are many examples of news outlets that generate healthy revenue from these sections. Governments are also often required under legislation to advertise public notices in local media classifieds which serve as an important, often unexamined source of revenue (see Greenslade, 2012; Hess, 2015b, 2016; Radcliffe, 2015). Lacy (2011) argues if a local news provider is meeting a community's demands for news, information and connectedness, people who sell products and services to that community will advertise with them because they see value in being identified with that trusted and popular news platform (Lacy, 2011, p. 176).

Some of the advertising strategies now being deployed by media companies include 'native advertising' – a trendy way to advertise by allowing ads to stand as editorial content, while being clearly labelled as sponsors. US media researcher for magazine and online content Tayne Kim says native advertising, which is similar to the traditional advertorial recast in digital space, is an indication of the barrier eroding between advertising and editorial. He says there is a push towards buyers' guides and online shopping platforms, especially across magazine platforms (State of the Media white paper, 2014). *The Charlotte Observer* in North Carolina, for example, has experimented with how to help local advertisers become storytellers and is benefiting from sharing this expertise. The editor Ted Williams outlined several examples where the newspaper has worked with people from conveners of golf tournaments to an orthopaedic practice to co-create content. He gives the distinction between the traditional 'advertorial' and native advertising by approaching potential advertisers and asking them to consider:

> what are some really interesting stories that you can tell about Charlotte that meet your brand goals...what can you share with Charlotte that will also meet your marketing objectives as brands rather than write an advertorial on how you have to try this new particular product. (see Petulla, 2014)

Meanwhile, Johnston Press, a local newspaper publisher in the UK, created an initiative – Voice Local – to create branded content for advertisers, staffed by a team of commercial editors and product managers. Johnston Press said its native content had delivered high levels of engagement. Examples include a national supermarket discussion about cooking tips for salmon and a local vet writing about how pet owners can keep their animals safe during celebrations featuring fireworks (see Oakes, 2015).

Paywalls

Given the amount of free content available on the Internet, local news media organizations face challenges over how to manage access to, and the pricing of, their content. One of the strategies trialled and implemented by news outlets across the globe is the paywall. A paywall refers to any type of 'digital mechanism that separates free content from paid content on a website' (Chiou & Tucker, 2013, p. 62). It effectively serves as a barrier between Internet users and a news organization's online content (Pickard & Williams, 2014). News sites can construct paywalls in different ways. They can be content based, frequency based, micro-payment or app based (Chiou & Tucker, 2013). Typically, news sites will erect a content-based paywall under which certain types of information (for example, breaking news, reporter blogs) are freely accessible while other premium content can only be accessed via subscription. Chiou and Tucker (2013) studied paywalls at three local newspapers controlled by the Gannet Company (which owned at least 100 US newspapers and TV station websites). They found that paywall sites experienced a steep decline in visits after their introduction, especially among young readers.

They also raised concerns that local media had presumably fewer substitutes and paywalls might lead to less local news consumption overall (Chiou & Tucker, 2013). Myllylahti (2014) argues that online news paywalls create additional income for news companies, but at the current revenue levels they do not offer a viable business model in the short term. There is a further issue with paywalls: they are easy to bypass and articles are often available for free via search engines and social media. Myllylahti (2014) recommends that news sites consider abolishing paywalls for major events, as there have been instances of sites crashing due to public demand. This indicates that this type of news coverage should be seen as providing a community service (Myllylahti, 2014, p. 187).

German research shows consumers are critical of news sites that charge online customers for the same content in the print edition instead of offering new products that live up to the full potential of digital journalism (Wagenknecht, 2014). Pickard and Williams (2014) draw on examples from three American newspapers hailed as pioneers and success stories in the paywall debate and show they have experienced mixed success. Ultimately, they argue that paywalls are unable to offset steep losses in advertising revenue. They cite media economist Robert Picard who warns that although the idea of erecting a paywall is attractive, 'there's a fallacy in that decision' because readers have traditionally mostly paid for distribution costs, not the news (Picard, 2013, as cited in Pickard & Williams, 2014). As Picard points out, 'to suddenly think that they're going to start paying a lot of money to have it in digital ... [and] suddenly make the organizations wealthy again just doesn't make sense' (p. 207). Many publishers see online subscription models as a last resort for survival. Chyl's 2005 survey of Hong Kong residents found very few users actually responded to paid content and most had no intent to pay in the future (Chyl, 2005). British academic Tom Felle says local newspapers have little or no prospect of introducing successful paywall models. 'Economies of scale mean their potential audiences are too small to monetise via digital advertising and most are clinging to their print editions and using websites to build brands and market share' (Felle, 2016). In Australia, media, marketing and entertainment group Mumbrella argues there is enough data being trickled down from major media companies to indicate that digital subscriptions will not save the newspaper business model, including at the local level. They claim that subscription data from companies shows that 'the pattern is beginning to look like an initial surge of loyal subscribers when a paywall is first activated, but then growth quickly stalls' (Burrowes, 2014). It suggests the market size is far smaller than publishers would have hoped.

A nationwide study in the US found that only 5 per cent of Americans paid for local online news content (Rosenstiel, 2011), while research by the Oxford Reuters Institute for the Study of Journalism (2014) found that the number of people paying for any news hovers at about 10 per cent of online users, and in some cases less than that (Newman, 2014). Pickard and Williams (2014) contend paywalls tend to defy the Internet principle of openness, they disenfranchise people unable to afford the digital subscription cost and further inscribe commercial values into the newsgathering processes (Picard & Williams, 2014, p. 195).

Social Media: Friend or foe

Social media companies are not suffering the same misfortunes as traditional news providers over advertising, and they have not erected paywalls around content. Mark Zuckerberg's Facebook creation, with its slogan 'connects you with the people around you', has become a billion-dollar empire with more than one billion active users worldwide (www.facebook.com). There is no mistaking that the widespread use of social media such as Facebook and Twitter is transforming the way news is produced, disseminated and discussed (Hermida et al., 2012; Nielsen & Schroder, 2014). In 2013 the Pew Research Centre reported that 64 per cent of American adults used Facebook, and almost half of these used Facebook for news (Matsa & Mitchell, 2014). So is social media such as Facebook a friend or a foe to local media in the battle to retain audiences and find a suitable business model for news? The battle to preserve the notion of community and close ties is evident in Australia's regional press as it shifts into online spaces (Hess & Bowd, 2015). These newspapers are becoming increasingly reliant on tools such as Facebook to create a 'community' of identifiable members within which to generate discussion, promote stories and draw likes and friends. It has also become an important database for accessing sources and information.

The triumph of Facebook (in commercial terms) is its free membership base that enables people to connect with one another, and provides clear, rich data about audiences from which to generate advertising revenue. Senior Facebook engineer Karel Baloun explains that Facebook makes money largely from two strategies: advertisements that target people based on the information users enter into the site about themselves; and sponsored groups, events and notifications (Baloun, 2007, p. 66). However, local news sites often adopt a different strategy, with increasing focus on paid access to content. In Australia, for example, many local newspapers are still considering the paywall option, or have plans to introduce an e-edition that attracts a subscription fee.

There are also indications that Facebook is proving to be a double-edged sword for newspapers, serving as a direct form of competition, especially in regards to advertising. Hess and Bowd's 2015 study found small businesses were considering dropping advertising with local newspapers and moving to Facebook as it has the technology to target the particular groups they aimed to reach in specific locations. Readers who were interviewed said they were no longer placing items for sale in the newspaper and were using Facebook to connect with potential buyers. This resonates with research on Facebook that found the more closed the network in terms of geographic area, the more potential there was for Facebook to generate advertising (Baloun, 2007, p. 68). This underlines the company's ability to compete with news outlets where geography is a defining feature. The idea of Facebook being a social network site rather than news provider might blind local news media from seeing it as a foe rather than a friend. The commercial nature of Facebook has at times been masked behind more private values of inclusive and largely unrestricted membership, communities and friendship (Sennett, 2012). In a bid to preserve profits, local media should be encouraged to redirect traffic from Facebook to their websites as often as possible. They need to use their own platforms to facilitate discussions, invite comments, build networks and attract advertisers. Alternatively, newspapers might adopt the Facebook model of encouraging users to sign up to a website 'free of charge' to obtain data about their audiences that may be of interest to advertisers, a point we shall return to later in this chapter.

Preserving profits via centralization and 'dispersion'

Proprietors of local news companies have always been motivated by profit as much as a desire to serve the interests of a given community. The temptation to expand news as a business has created some of the biggest international conglomerates on earth. Media mogul Rupert Murdoch took control of the Australian family company with just one newspaper and built it into the global empire News Corporation. During the 20th century, family enterprises and metropolitan media players around the world expanded in size and scope, purchasing small independent news operations at the local level. During the past several decades, media entities began listing on stock exchanges, thereby becoming answerable to shareholders as well as local audiences.

When the traditional business model began to crumble, many media companies with interests in local news started to rethink the way information could be produced to cut costs and preserve profits. This led to the rise of centralized production nodes for local news. This model involves gathering news from a local area and sending it to a central location outside the geographic space to be edited, produced and packaged for audiences. Hood (2014) highlights the practice of outsourcing local broadcast news (fuelled by technology and industry economics), which leads to news being produced at a great distance from the source. He analysed 1000 news items in the US to determine how 'local' outsourced broadcasts really were. His study shows differences between locally produced and remotely produced stories. Firstly, local stations ran a significantly higher percentage of local, state and regional stories than outsourced stations; there were more on-air misspellings during outsourced newscasts, and a greater use of 'stand-ups' in outsourced news.

In Australia, televised 'local' news bulletins are often broadcast from metropolitan locations where a presenter will use phrases such as 'our community' and 'local success story' depending on the geographic region to which they are broadcasting. British scholar Steven Barnett (2009) contends that for local media outlets owned by large conglomerates, the process of centralization, standardization of editorial approaches and homogeneity of output are part of the process of maximizing shareholder value. Sjøvaag (2014) outlines how Norwegian media company Schibsted imposed serious cost-cutting measures in 2012 including staff reductions, content syndication and centralization of core services. In Australia, Fairfax Media has standardized its online space, with almost all of its 200 or so regional newspapers sharing a similar template in which to upload news and information. Only the content and the name and font of the mastheads differ.

The process of centralization and standardization does not fully describe the way local media production has been sliced and diced to preserve profits across digital and physical spaces. As highlighted in Chapter 2, local news outlets are not confined to geographic territory alone; they are situated in a 'geo-social' context. This means they hold influential positions in certain social flows and movements and are nodes to the wider global media network, connected to news media conglomerates or dependent upon new media empires such as Facebook, Apple and Google to reach audiences. The outsourcing of the creation, production and distribution of local news is much more complex than centralizing labour costs alone. The digital world has led to the rise of what we describe as the 'dispersion' of local news.

Dispersion is a term used in mathematics, sciences, physics and biology. In its simplest form it means the process of distributing something over an area. In statistics it is synonymous with scatter or spread and contrasted with location or central tendency (NIST/SEMATECH, 2012). Dictionary.com defines it as the scattering of values of a variable around the mean or median. In biology, dispersal refers to the movement of individuals from their birth site to their breeding site, as well as the movement from one breeding site to the other (Bonte et al., 2012). We use the term dispersion to explain the changing nature of local news production in a globalized world. Dispersion is largely a cost-cutting mechanism when local news is taken from its natural habitat (a geographic area) and drawn into global power structures in order to be produced and reproduced across wide geographic and digital spaces. As discussed previously, audiences are also dispersed across the globe and do not have to be physically present within a community to engage with local news.

When a company expands in size and scope one might expect it to deflate or contract in tough times. However, in a globalized world companies are able to disperse costs outside a niche geographic location to save money, outsourcing to other corporate entities based beyond the geographic areas that news outlets serve. Take the *Warrnambool Standard* in Australia. The small daily newspaper is owned by media giant Fairfax, which has engaged in savage cost-cutting strategies across its network. The *Standard* has retained a handful of journalists to produce news within the geographic space it serves, but the editorial production process is undertaken from a centralized location hundreds of kilometres away. When people want to read a story online, they often rely on the search engine Google to find the website, or are required to download an app for their smart device. The newspaper is printed in another regional location, and when people want to place a birth, death or marriage notice over the telephone they are transferred to a call centre in the Philippines. In Canada, meanwhile, the *Toronto Star* outsourced its ad sales and cut 72 jobs in 2014 (Houpt, 2013). The *Star* shifted advertising sales operations to Metro English Canada, a joint venture with a Swedish publishing company.

Barnett (2009) argues these strategies might seem a sensible short-term approach to business but can sacrifice journalism that is rooted in local communities. It is very difficult to specify the financial return on good journalism, but very easy to quantify the outgoing cost of journalists' salaries and expenses (Barnett, 2009, p. 10).

Problems with centralizing and dispersing local news

The problems with centralizing and dispersing local news can be seen most clearly at the hyperlocal level. For example, some large media companies have tried and failed at establishing hyperlocal 'franchises' (such as Patch in the US). They have experienced frustration because the economies of scale don't work in the world of local and hyperlocal news. In the words of one hyperlocal publisher: 'You can't Amazon local news' (Rieder, 2013). Barnett and Townend (2014) found the most successful hyperlocal ventures have been independent. They cite a journalist disapproving of the 'cookie-cutter' version of hyperlocal news:

> ... products of hyperlocal journalism may have more chance of audience and advertising success if it is 'artisanal' rather than 'mass-produced', is based on a close relationship with a local audience, and is driven by residents' passion, rather than a 'cookie-cutter version stamped out by an assembly line'. (Barnett & Townend 2014)

Major media players have endured a tumultuous experiment with excessively local news, and there appears to be little evidence of success in attempts by media companies to roll out hyperlocal sites nationally (Barnett & Townend, 2014). Farhi (2007) highlights the rapid rise and fall of a series of local news websites called Backfence in the US; and perhaps one of the most well-known hyperlocal ventures, Patch, has also endured a rocky road in this space with questions raised over the local news network's future (see also Barnett & Townend, 2014). At one point more than 30 independent community news sites in the US 'fought back' against attempts to commodify hyperlocal news on a large scale, with well-known sites such as *baristanet, The Batavian* and *New Haven Independent* banding together to launch the 'authentically local campaign' which:

> seeks to illuminate the difference between authentic local business and those that are just cashing in – before every town in America becomes one giant strip mall. This is not just about us, the owned-and-operated sites that write about place. It's about place. (Kennedy, 2011)

Government funding/subsidies

Top-down approaches to the business model of news usually focus on commercial influences, but we extend this approach to consider the role and involvement of elites or powerful institutions such as governments.

Holding onto their Patch?

Patch is an independent US hyperlocal news and information site founded in 2007 by Tim Armstrong in response to a shortage of online information about his hometown in Connecticut (Miller & Stone, 2009). Patch was acquired by Internet giant AOL in 2009 and announced plans to invest $50 million by constructing a national network of 'patchers' – one-person bureaus dedicated to hyperlocal coverage in a network of affluent metropolitan suburbs across America. The journalists recruited were reportedly earning between $38,000 and $45,000 annually and generally worked from home (Saleh, 2013, p. 235). By 2011 the cracks were beginning to show. The limited experience of most of its writers put them in direct competition with local news bloggers and by 2013 patch had begun consolidating its network (Kelly, 2015). At its height, the division employed more than 1000 people. Keeping traffic up with fewer staff presented a challenge. In 2013 the company announced it was cutting the number of local news sites from 900 to 600 (Saleh, 2013). The focus shifted to producing local content with fewer staff and Patch attempted to boost audiences by identifying stories with viral potential and running them across the sites. This move proved almost catastrophic for the company because their audiences were craving local content (Moses, 2015). AOL turned over majority ownership to investment company Hale Global in early 2014. Patch relies on a combination of local and national advertising to support locally sourced information and human interest stories (From, Hall & Manfull, 2015, p. 274).

During the past few decades, government subsidies, both direct and indirect, have been utilized to achieve a broad range of policy goals, including but not limited to supporting a vibrant news media sector (Hess et al., 2014).

In recent years, calls for government to intervene in the news media sector have grown louder as the commercial problems faced by news media organizations in the US and Britain, as well as Australia and elsewhere, have intensified. The exact nature, purpose and efficacy of any of the various subsidy proposals remain matters of widespread debate internationally (see Murschetz, 2013). The BBC and Australian

Broadcasting Corporation are examples of news providers wholly sub-sidized by governments; we will return to this in a moment. Zahariadis (2013) cites Nielsen and Linnebank (2011) to emphasize that subsidies can be subtle and not immediately obvious. For example, British news-papers enjoy the benefits of zero VAT per capita, which comes to an annual subsidy of £594 million (Zahariadis, 2013, p. 68). Public sup-port for media has remained unchanged for decades in six developed democracies – Finland, France, Germany, Italy, Britain and the US (Nielsen & Linnebank, 2011). It often takes the form of licence fee fund-ing going overwhelmingly to public service broadcasting; indirect sup-port for paid print media industry incumbents; and little support for online-only media organizations.

A Reuters Institute report (Nielson & Linnebank, 2011) also cites research in Scandinavia that shows various forms of indirect and direct support in the region has encouraged diversity in local media mar-kets by helping small- and medium-sized newspapers survive (see e.g. Gustafsson et al., 2009). In Canada, subsidies are provided by Newspaper Canada, which runs the Canada Periodical Fund, a subsidy programme for community newspapers and magazines (Murschetz, 2013). Other countries that provide some state aid (direct or indirect) for local media include Austria, Belgium, France (where subsidies to newspapers have come to be a raison d'être for the newspaper industry) and Sweden (see Murschetz, 2013). Denmark provides an innovation fund for restor-ing economically weak newspapers and bringing new publications to market. Meanwhile, in Italy where newspaper readership remains low compared to most of EU countries, an unhealthy dependence on state funding is created through a large amount going to publications linked to a political party or movement or an individual political figure (Zahariadis, 2013). Norway is reviewing its subsidy programme, offer-ing direct production grants especially to economically disadvantaged newspapers. A proposal in the US has been to increase support for local and regional non-profit news outlets (see Nee, 2014).

A US Federal Communications Commission taskforce on the future of media also lauded the digital non-profits for their public service, but did not recommend direct government support for them, despite acknowl-edging their economic vulnerability (Waldman, 2011). The report stated that the main focus of public policy should not be in providing funds, but rather in helping 'create conditions under which non-profit news operations can gain traction' (Waldman, 2011, p. 352). The only mon-etary support the taskforce recommended was in the form of targeting government advertising toward local news outlets instead of national entertainment media. Nee's (2014) research aimed to determine how leaders of these civic journalism start-ups viewed the government's role in ensuring their survival. Most were not open to direct government subsidies, but did not rule out assistance in the form of advertising, contracts for services and payments in kind. Meanwhile, the Knight Foundation's *Informing Communities: Sustaining Democracies* report called for increased support for public service media, as well as increasing the role of higher education and community and non-profit institutions as hubs of journalistic activity. It wanted to ensure local governments provide low-cost access to public records and make civic and social data available to the public. Finally, it identified a role for research to develop systematic quality measures of community information ecologies and study how they affect social outcomes. In the UK, Fenton and colleagues (2010) have called for the introduction of local news hubs, supported with funds from local authorities and foundations, which could bring together communities and professional journalists. The hubs would provide training, volunteer mentors and technical support for communities to engage in identifying, investigating and reporting local news. They suggest subsidies could come from local government advertising, guaranteeing that their information campaigns reach the target audience/s while supporting and nurturing local media.

Tory MP Louise Mensch has also called on the British government to subsidize the ailing local newspaper market, arguing that community-level coverage was more powerful than any 'Facebook campaign and a couple of tweets' (Sweney, 2012). In Australia, The Finkelstein Inquiry (2012) found that regional media could benefit from government funding to address the 'shortcomings in journalistic surveillance and the richness of the media environment felt most at local levels, outside the major cities' (2012, p. 331). Finkelstein noted:

> There is some evidence that both regional radio and television stations and newspapers have cut back substantially on their newsgathering, leaving some communities poorly served for local news. This may require particular support in the immediate future, and I recommend that this issue be investigated as a matter of some urgency. (Finkelstein & Ricketson, 2012, p. 11)

The issue of government subsidies is a prickly one. As Zahariadis (2013) argues, maintaining a business for private gain with public money raises

a host of 'thorny questions' that go to the heart of democratic governance. For example, subsidies can be used to create and perpetuate the
same actors in power, and undermine democratic efficacy and perceptions of accountability (Zahariadis, 2013, p. 69). In light of this, some
specific recent schemes deserve attention.

The BBC and local news

In 2013–2014, the BBC had a reported £2.7bn to spend in raised
licence fee money, on top of another £1.3bn in commercial and other
income (Kirk, 2016). About £23m is spent on local TV, while £150m
is dedicated to local radio from its £653m radio budget (ibid.). The
BBC has been criticized by commercial providers amid concern its vast
local news operation was putting traditional newspapers and other
independent providers out of business and using government funding to do so. The News Media Association representing independent
commercial news brands in the UK, for example, called on the BBC
to be more of a partner than a competitor and provide transparent
attribution to stories and linking to commercially funded sources, create a broader news syndication market for local providers and make
a greater proportion of news assets generated by the BBC available to
other UK news providers (News Media Association, 2015). Similarly
the Radio Centre, on behalf of commercial broadcasters, argued that it
was the role of the BBC to provide content that was not available elsewhere (Radio Centre, 2013). In 2015, the BBC outlined a series of proposals to support local news across Britain as part of its Charter Review
(BBC Charter Review, 2015). The BBC contended that in some local
communities it could soon become the only traditional news provider
and wanted to avoid this at all costs. It considered allocating licence
fee funding to invest in 100 public service reporters to cover councils, courts and public services in towns and cities across the UK. Any
news agenda, independent news provider or local paper including the
BBC could compete to win the contract to provide the reporting team
for each area. The BBC also proposed making its regional video and
local audio pieces available for immediate use on the Internet services
of local and regional news organizations to make local content easily searchable and retrievable. In 2013, the BBC began trialling Local
Live – an initiative that features stories published and researched by
external news providers linked to the BBC local news online sites (BBC
News, 2015).

Funding models: 'bottom-up' approaches

Since Rosen's declaration on 'the people formerly known as the audience' (2006), the mass audience which was once considered passive consumers of news is now being turned to for its capabilities of gathering news, editing, publishing and helping to pay for professionals to practice quality journalism. We look at some of the 'bottom-up' approaches to fund the circulation and production of local news and information in communities and the 'third space' that has led to a convergence culture between traditional and digital media players (Deuze et al., 2007). The role of the audience in discussions about the business of news has been given many names, including participatory journalism, produsage and crowd-sourced journalism, but these terms are ambiguous and have been applied inconsistently, making comparison of news systems difficult (Scott et al., 2015).

Citizen journalism and user-generated content

The role of user-generated content is largely adopted by top-down media players, which 'deliberately tap into participatory media culture and produce some kind of co-creative commons-based news platform' (Deuze, 2008, p. 110). User-generated content ranges from comments posted in response to stories to people contributing photographs of local events and natural disasters. It could be argued that local newspapers have always engaged in user-generated content – involving citizens in letters to the editor pages, providing football scores and fishing columns, but the term 'user-generated content' now largely refers to content created in digital space. Knight and Cook (2013) emphasize that social media, comments and discussions add to the traditional forms of content that individuals and organizations use to alert the newsroom to events and issues. They argue the closer a journalist is to their audience, the easier it is to link up and involve the community in finding and sharing stories.

The role of user-generated content is given specific attention in relation to hyperlocals, especially in discussions about who produces hyperlocal news (see Glaser, 2010), with the literature identifying and distinguishing between citizen journalists (Schaffer, 2005), user-generated content (Paulussen & D'heer, 2013; van Kerkhoven & Bakker, 2014) and professional journalists (Bunch, 2007; Williams et al., 2014). It is the hyperlocal phenomenon that arguably provides some of the most pure examples of the 'bottom-up approach' to local news.

A J-Lab survey of hyperlocals found that many do not need revenue to stay afloat thanks to self-funding and volunteer labour. The report states: 'When they talk about success, they are not talking about revenue. They are talking about the impact they've had on their communities' (as cited in Farhi, 2007, p. 42). Meanwhile, Kurpius and colleagues (2010, p. 366) reported that one of their study participants said the biggest expense at their hyperlocal was 'drinks at the coffee shop where he typically worked on the site'.

Third space – converged culture

Participatory news, also referred to as citizen or networked journalism (Jarvis, 2006), involves professionals and amateurs working together to get the story, focusing on the process more than the product (Deuze, 2010, p. 268). Volunteer sources provide a readily accessible database to supplement the old standbys. Singer (2010) sees it as a democratic vehicle, but also as a practical opportunity. Canter (2013) gives the example of *Citizen's Eye* in Britain, a non-professional independent news website serving Leicester. It is made up of agencies representing groups such as the elderly, homeless, former criminals, people with disabilities, and heritage and environment issues. It has 450 volunteers and regular contributors.

User-generated content is a potential resource lifeline for local British newspapers that have experienced a decline in revenue, according to Canter (2013). It means volunteers can take on more mundane parts of a journalist's job freeing the professionals to pursue more news. The model also brings new voices into journalists' work (Singer, 2010, p. 285). However, this raises concerns that collaborative journalism is market driven rather than civic oriented and audiences are being exploited for free content and labour so that news organizations can cut back on staff (see also Paulussen et al., 2007; Ornebring, 2008).

It is important to understand how community newspaper editors negotiate the professional complexities posed by citizen journalism – a phenomenon that, even in the abstract, would appear to undermine their gatekeeping control over content. Research in Texas found some support it or oppose it for philosophical reasons, while others have practical concerns (Lewis et al., 2010). Following this study, Lewis (2011) argues that journalists should be working with gifted amateurs to form a profitable cooperation of hybrid activity. Hermida and Thurman (2008) contend that user-generated content allows scope for different voices in news reporting and that the traditional gatekeeping approach to the integration of user-generated content may be a suitable model. Meanwhile, Jonsson and Ornebring (2011) emphasize the need to study user-generated content in terms of political economy because it is part of the context of consumption. Their research found that users tend to create popular culture-oriented content and personal/everyday life-oriented content rather than 'news'. Canter (2013) gives the example of local UK newspaper the *Leicester Mercury* engaging with user-generated content. She argues the key to its success is the creation of distinctive boundaries between low-level reporting carried out by community reporters and investigative journalism carried out by employed staff.

Crowdsourcing

Crowdsourcing is a term coined by the Internet trade press derived from the practice of outsourcing. It is also described as the 'worker-bee economy' for a situation in which both the so-called wisdom and also the labour of the crowd pollinates the beneficiary, often a Web 2.0 company or service (Rogers et al., 2013, p. 151). Crowdsourcing is the antithesis of Fordism, the assembly line mentality that dominated the industrial age (Howe, 2009, p. 14). It relies on the idea that we are all creators, artists, scientists, architects and designers who can share information with one another. Social media sites and tools such as YouTube and Wikipedia are undoubtedly two exemplary successes in crowdsourcing projects (Titangos, 2013, p. 186).

Crowdsourcing describes grassroots or citizen-led initiatives, whereby individuals are encouraged to share information that can be gathered for purposes of producing rigorous, comprehensive pieces of reporting. Zelizer and Allan (2010) describe how news organizations rely on crowdsourcing to produce large datasets, because when extensive official records are released to the public the challenge for journalists to sift through them alone is arduous. The involvement of the crowd means the dataset can be read by literally thousands of volunteers to help identify potentially newsworthy details (Zelizer & Allan, 2010, p. 28). Crowdsourcing has also been considered a way of resourcing investigative journalism, transforming the traditional idea of the investigative journalist 'as the solitary figure working from behind the scenes in great secrecy' to find out what has happened in controversial events (Hill & Lashmar, 2013).

Crowdsourcing can also be a simple way of tracking down unusual sources that a journalist may not know. If a reporter is working on a story and wants to get contacts, they can issue a plea via Twitter or Facebook.

There are also quick survey sites such as www.ask500people.com that allow users to ask a question and get answers that are geo-tagged to help ensure the feedback is as local as possible (Frost, 2010, p. 57).

In some contexts it is essential that the individuals forming the crowd be situated at a certain location to be able to perform a given task. Some of the compensations of crowdsourcing include cash bonuses, small monetary rewards, price incentives or exclusive information (Bauer & Strauss, 2014). There are also those without direct compensation where people are motivated to try something new, to share knowledge or accomplish common goals. Bauer and Strauss (2014) give the example of localmind. com, an application that allows users to direct questions about a specific location, such as a restaurant or club, to people who have checked in at this location. Users generally want to know what's happening at a particular place, how crowded a club is or whether there are good seats still available. Meanwhile, the American Public Media and Minnesota Public Radio has established the Public Insight Journalism initiative, which has drawn input from 30,000 sources and produced about 250 stories based on their collective insights (J-Lab/Knight Community News Network, 2014). The activities that come under the concept's umbrella are as diverse as the crowd itself, according to Howe (2009). He says while crowdsourcing tends to fall under the loose designation of user-generated content, it involves a range practices. He contends:

> User-generated content bears the unfortunate stigma of being amateurish or puerile or both....the essence of crowdsourcing lies in culling the brilliant from the banal. Crowdsourcing creative work usually involves cultivating a robust community composed of people with a deep and ongoing commitment to their craft and to one another. The social environment gives creative production a context in which the labour itself has meaning. The best ideas, regardless of the medium in which they're expressed, result in enhancing status of others. (Howe, 2009, pp. 178–180)

Establishing a community of content creators is key to success, but can be difficult to build and maintain. In lieu of regular payment, people want a sense of ownership over their contributions, and this often requires a company to offer royalty-sharing agreements or relinquish the rights to the work altogether. In Chapter 2 we explored the power of 'sense of place' and 'community' for those who live in or have a connection to the geographic locations that local news serves. Crowdsourcing has potential to tap into this sensibility for the viability of an organization.

Crowd funding

Crowd funding is an offshoot of crowdsourcing, which specifically targets the crowd for money. Examples include the San Francisco website spot.us, which began testing crowd funding at the local level in 2009. It allows freelance journalists to suggest stories and get funding from the public in the area (Dooley, 2009). Crowd funding can be defined as a means of financing projects through small individual donations – selling a concept to a large number of people (Fernandez-Sande, 2014, p. 182). Radio is possibly the first mass medium to use crowd funding. Fernandez-Sande (2014) describes how early radio programmes in many countries were underwritten by listener contributions until the fledgling market for broadcast advertising became firmly established. In some cases, fundraising took the form of subscription campaigns organized at the grassroots level by radio clubs and groups of listeners themselves in support of local radio programming.

In 2008, entrepreneur David Cohn founded spot.us with support of a Knight News Challenge grant. Spot.us is a platform that facilitated crowd funding, promotion, publishing and dissemination of journalism often by independent community news outlets and independent or citizen journalists (Gahran, 2015). The site was put on hold in 2014 after being sold to American Public Media in 2011. The company argued that most projects tended to be funded by friends and family, as opposed to community members with an interest or need for certain information. It also said people gave once and never returned. They argued that there were few successes, business wise, for scaling and sustaining a crowd funding platform (Gahran, 2015). Other sites that seek to support crowd funding projects at the local level include www.beaconreader.com, www. kickstart.com and www.pozible.com.

The cooperative approach: Blending subscription with crowd funding

There is also a funding model that blurs the boundaries between crowd funding and subscription. It might be described as a cooperative approach. The *Bristol Cable* in the UK runs as a cooperative news site (in print and online). It has about 500 members whose financial contributions raise approximately £1300 a month which is enough to meet day-to-day overheads and cover the costs of printing (Harris, 2015). Every working day, a small group of volunteers work there. They are motivated by aims of filling the vacuum left by a declining local and regional media, and investigating a tangle of ongoing issues in the city, from the treatment of refugees to the role of money in local politics (Harris, 2015).

Philanthropic funding

Newspapers as charitable organizations might offer a future model for local press. Greenslade and Barnett (2014) give the example of a newspaper in Maidenhead in the UK that transformed into a charitable trust to ensure its independence and foster community spirit. They argue it will take a few more similar initiatives before any kind of precedent is established:

> ... but it is just possible that [this] defining step might ... presage a new wave of journalism enterprises which are just as independent, just as dedicated to serving the local community, and maybe just as long-lived. (Greenslade & Barnett, 2014, p. 67)

Another initiative in the UK is Destination Local, driven by innovation charity Nesta with support from several partners including the Welsh Government, Creative Scotland and industry. The initiative has funded 22 new hyperlocal projects including: a reality app that allows people to view geo-located content about buildings and places of interest using a smartphone or tablet; a hyperlocal website in Kentish Town (www. kentishtowner.co.uk); and a community newspaper in Wales working with a television company and education college to create a Welsh-language mobile and digital service for hyperlocal news (Nesta, 2016). The Knight Foundation in the US embraces a 'hospital model of journalism'– the idea that news can be created by a collective, leveraging technologies and channels like social media (Scutari, 2015). It has developed a local media initiative that identifies promising new journalism outlets and provides them with the necessary funding to achieve long-term sustainability. The $US5 million initiative includes $US1 million in micro-grants to support non-profit online news outlets and public media across the US. As part of the programme $US3.5 million in grants were also awarded to 25 news organizations that have demonstrated potential for growth. A further $US500,000 went towards strengthening back-office editorial collaboration; business training and technology support for non-profit news outlets focused on producing investigative and public service journalism. Beneficiaries of this programme include the Wisconsin Centre for Investigative Journalism, NJ Spotlight in New Jersey and Investigate West in Seattle.

Other models include the Media Development Investment Fund (MDIF), which is a New York-based not-for-profit corporation started in 1995 as an investment fund for independent news outlets in countries with a history of media oppression. It provides low-cost loans to news outlets in Africa, Asia, Latin America, south-eastern Europe and the countries of the former Soviet Union. The foundation gives the example of Breeze FM in Zambia as a model for rural radio (www.mdif. org). Supporting investigative journalism at both the local and national level can be fraught with controversy, according to the MDIF's report on global investigative journalism. It says groups in places such as South Africa and Serbia are wary of raising money online through micro financing because they fear powerful interests will seek to sway or tarnish their work through large donations. They give the example of a Montenegrin watchdog group that sponsors investigative reporting returning some 300 euros from an online fundraising effort after learning the money came from a notorious Balkan mafia figure blacklisted by the US government (Kaplan, 2013).

Local news as a 'niche product'

We have argued elsewhere (Hess & Waller, 2016a) that a cultural studies approach might provide new insights into reviving the business model of local news in a digital environment. Creating free group membership much like the Facebook model (where users sign up for free to access information) can reinforce a sense of community and belonging among audiences in this fragmented media world. There is also a need to study the news habits or media-related practices of local audiences much more closely (see Bird, 2010a; Couldry, 2012) to better utilize online spaces for advertising. For example, the time slots in which advertisements appear on local news sites have received little attention in scholarship to date. In following people's media-related practices there might be scope for businesses to package advertising to online readers of local news at certain times of day. This is not new in the world of traditional news broadcasting, but it is for newspapers moving into online spaces. Peak times for local radio listening are during commuter rush hours and commercial television has a history of shaping advertising around prime time content. There are obvious 'rush' hours in which audiences might access online news platforms in metropolitan areas, especially while travelling on public transport to and from work. In many small towns and cities, however, residents might rely much more heavily on their own vehicles to get to and from work. Reading and driving is not compatible. Therefore, local news platforms will have to think more creatively about how they study, exploit, even create their own 'rush hours' for news online.

Focusing much more intently on how long people access local news online, where they are accessing it from and why they choose certain times of day can be valuable information in the pursuit of advertising revenue.

Investing in the forms of capital

In discussions about the value of news it is important to consider other advantages (all of which are rooted in economics) that come with being the 'go-to source' for local information. Bourdieu argues that in any social space there are forms of capital that individuals jostle for to gain advantage over others – economic, social, cultural and symbolic (Bourdieu, 1986). The café that organizes to print a hyperlocal news-letter in a tiny Canadian town might benefit economically from being perceived as the centre of local information and as a result generate more revenue from customers coming in to buy coffee. Consider also the apartment block superintendent in New York City who might start up a hyperlocal within his complex to generate community social capi-tal, instilling a sense of belonging among tenants to help them feel more secure, as though they are part of something 'bigger' beyond the four walls of their own apartment.

We must also acknowledge that not everyone who engages in local news necessarily sees themselves as a local, but that they are in some way eager to 'tap into' local knowledge about a place for one reason or another for their own benefit. Consider the British traveller backpacking around Germany for several weeks. They might be interested in finding our more about a given place, seeing where to go and what to do, and as a result seek out and read hyperlocal content.

Chapter 2 argued that local news media need to invest in local knowl-edge that manifests as a form of cultural capital to journalists working in this space. We have highlighted how knowing what makes a place 'tick' is vital to news outlets' success at this level. Further, local news outlets need to recognize and invest where possible in establishing or reinforcing their perceived power as being central to the social in any given geo-social space. To be seen as the centre of a given 'community' imbues news outlets with symbolic capital that can translate into eco-nomic capital (see Chapter 4). But it takes time. Local news media need to recognize the power of 'mediated social capital' to connect people with each other. This comes from constructing a sense of community, actively connecting people with one another, enacting forms of public journalism (see Chapter 5) and acknowledging the social and economic worth of a news outlet's births, deaths and marriages column. We sug-gest investments in the forms of capital are instrumental to the future economic viability of the local news media.

Some readers, sources of news and contributors interviewed for our research in Australia have also suggested that local news sites need to see themselves much more like a 'compendium' – a one-stop-shop of information from telephone and business directory to breaking news stories. As one reader and regular contributor to a local news outlet suggested:

> ...the news website could have the ability to tell me what's happening on any given day across the town, where I could go to eat and drink, events. It could have constant information about the community that might not necessarily be news, like how I could be engaged in the community and contributing to council planning and certain environmental schemes ... The potential for the digital is huge. Newspapers ignore it at their risk and unless they change they will become increasingly less relevant.

Finally, if local news is to be understood as a niche product, it's important to consider what business experts say about developing niche markets in online spaces. Business specialist Bijoor (2008) argues that the niche is a slice of marketing space that brands aspire to occupy for the sake of image, not volumes. Sometimes it can be a variation of a product commonly available in the market, or a new product or service, but it is almost always a variation of what is not being covered adequately by the mainstream. To be seen as central to news and information in a given locale is powerful for any major news media brand, but it requires investment, even if the returns are not on a grand scale. Other business strategists argue that niche products make no attempt to challenge the whole market and require a local rather than global view of doing business, something that larger players have tended to overlook in favour of the 'centralize and disperse model' discussed earlier. Bijoor (2008) says a niche strategy can fail due to lack of understanding of what a niche is, unaffordable pricing, defective product/market orientation or lack of preparation of the product and people selling the niche products. Other reasons for failure include being disconnected from market trends and insensitivity to shifts in the niche, its contents, and its customers and what it takes to appeal to them.

Summary

Seismic changes in the media industry mean that journalists working at the local level cannot afford to ignore the economics of news any longer. As the industrial model shrinks and changes an entrepreneurial culture is emerging, where journalists run their own news operations, or their jobs involve finding new ways to source income and editorial resources, as well as story ideas and contacts. Despite talk of a business model crisis (see Franklin, 2014), leading media economist Robert Picard says the digital age is a time for optimism:

> What is clear is that news providers are becoming less dependent on any one form of funding than they have been for about 150 years. Multiple revenue streams from readers and advertisers, from events and e-commerce, from foundations and sponsors, and from related commercial services such as web hosting and advertising services are all contributing income. It is too early to assess fully the efficacy and sustainability of these sources, but they provide reason to believe that workable new business models are appearing in news provision. (Picard, 2014, as cited in Franklin, 2014, p. 470)

In this chapter we have conceptualized the economics of local news in terms of 'top-down' and 'bottom-up' approaches to explore the different kinds of funding for local news. 'Top-down' approaches describe how traditional print and broadcast media make money from selling their products and conserving their resources. We have seen how rivers of advertising gold used to flow into the coffers of news companies, but these are drying up. We have explored other 'top-down' approaches designed to offset the advertising crisis. These include the introduction of paywalls and cost cutting through what we have termed the 'centralization and dispersion' of advertising, editorial and production. We have also revealed how in some countries government provides subsidies for commercial media. These strategies might generate revenue and save money in the short term, but could also cost in terms of credibility with audiences, and therefore impact on long-term viability. We have also seen how social media can be a two-edged sword for traditional media and looked at ways these can be used effectively by savvy news operators.

'Bottom-up' approaches describe ways of working with citizens to fund and produce news. Traditional media are employing some of these strategies, and we have seen how they work for start-ups and hyperlocal news outlets as well. We have defined and explained user-generated content and citizen journalism, explored crowdsourcing and crowd funding. Philanthropic funding through foundations, trusts and public institutions, including universities, are providing the means for many different forms of local media to survive and thrive.

Finally, we have offered a cultural studies approach to generate insights into reviving the business model of local news in a digital environment. These include looking to people's news habits for advertising strategies and recognizing the value of building social and cultural capital that can translate into economic capital for small media outlets. We have also suggested that ideas related to 'niche' journalism offer new ways to sell advertising, gain a special place in the hearts and minds of audiences and capitalize on local ways of doing business.

Conclusion

There's a new phenomenon emerging on Facebook that's generating plenty of 'friends' and 'likes' in local communities around the world. 'Buy, sell and swap' pages are probably serving a town or city somewhere near you. They provide a platform for people linked to a specific geographic area to sell and exchange their wares. Take, for example, the 'Long Island buy sell/swap' page in the United States where member Jeff is selling a new Xbox and Lynne has some designer handbags up for grabs. In Warrnambool, Australia, a theatre buff is seeking some lighting for a stage production, while the Leeds-Bamford page in the UK has lots of goodies available to its 2700 plus members. New and interesting practices are also emerging on these pages outside their intended scope. On one page, a woman has put a call out for her lost dog, someone wants to find the person who hit his car outside the supermarket and there's also a desperate plea to help find a missing engagement ring lost at a local swimming pool.

This is an exchange of news and information in its grassroots form, or in French sociologist Émile Durkheim's terms, an exemplar of organic solidarity that we outlined in Chapter 2. And it's making social media sites like Facebook immensely powerful as they increasingly become central to our social lives. Facebook's 'buy, sell and swap' pages serve much like snazzy, digital versions of the 18th-century newspaper – an era when shipping notices, properties for lease and goods for sale dominated front pages. People's appetite for this 'basic' type of information should not be overlooked in any discussion about the future of local media. As we have demonstrated throughout this book, there is a need to rethink the notion of what is news and look towards how local media connect people across business, economic, social, cultural, political and apolitical levels. We have highlighted that in a complex, globalized web of information flows there remains a basic need for human order. The ability to help generate the rules, direct the traffic or serve as a shining beacon in digital information flows and nodes generates immense power. In other words, the ability to be perceived as the legitimate source of all things 'local' to a given audience is arguably the most powerful influence of all.

Different angles on local news

A key component of this book has been to broadly outline the various theoretical approaches to studying local media. For example, if we adopt a democratic theoretical lens to explore local media in digital space, we might celebrate the plethora of voices that now have the opportunity to communicate from anywhere, any time, or what has been termed the democratization of the Internet. A deliberative democratic approach might inspire local journalists to utilize social media and digital technology to help audiences discuss and navigate issues of public concern. However, political economy scholars remind us that social media has created a new dynasty of media moguls (think Mark Zuckerburg with Facebook, or the creators of Google). News sites now depend increasingly on just a few digital platforms to disseminate content and engage with their audiences. A political economy focus highlights that Google and Facebook should never be perceived as neutral players in the media world, including in discussions about local media (see for example Picard, 2014; Hess & Bowd, 2015). Social media platforms might be viewed as 'tools' that hyperlocal entrepreneurs can exploit for 'free' information, or use to develop their own network of users. This could be viewed as a form of 'information subsidy' (Gandy, 1982; Davies, 2008) where already depleted newsrooms utilize social media content to fill their own content requirements. We can also think about employing convergence theory to discuss social media as a coming together of user and producer to create content for the benefit of a community in a marketplace of ideas and creativity.

All of these theoretical approaches present fruitful and valid areas of enquiry and we have drawn on them all throughout this book to sharpen our understanding of different aspects of media power. Chapter 1 discussed media power in detail, following Couldry (2012) to define it broadly as the symbolic power of media to construct reality and to control the social. It fuses cultural studies and political economy to suggest the power of 'local' media operates in and through people's everyday experiences and interactions. It is unmasked by studying people's media-related practices (Couldry, 2012) – what they say, do and think about media at all levels of society. The very idea of religiously tuning in to a local radio or television broadcast, the morning scroll through local news on an i-device, or placing a death notice in a local newspaper, for example, can be thought about as being more than banal practices that bring about order – but as a way of engaging in community and sense of place.

A media power approach helps us to consider important concepts such as 'community', 'local' and 'sense of place' in nuanced ways. We have developed the construct of 'geo-social' news as a theoretical shape ball that ideas of community and place can be pushed or pulled through. This perspective offers understanding of these key factors as powerful beliefs that are perpetuated through interacting with certain institutions in society. Geo-social news emphasizes a local news outlet's solid link to geographic territory while acknowledging the wider social space in which it plays a role, both in holding an influential position in certain social flows and movements and as a node to wider global news media and communication networks.

Studying local journalism

As we have ascertained, 'local' means different things in different contexts and so it needs to be studied in specific circumstances. A media power approach reminds us that there are those who play an influential role in defining and helping to construct meaning around the local. It also implores us to position journalists as part of society or the 'communities' they represent, not as objective bystanders positioned outside of social space. As we highlighted in Chapter 5, the public journalism movement of the 1990s began the task of positioning journalism as an active participant in the communities it serves. Shattering the myth of objectivity (something public journalism scholars rarely declare) is, in our view, central to rethinking the practice of local journalism. As Christians (1999) highlights, local journalists may be better to contextualize and make meaning of events, stories and information in the best interests of the communities they represent.

Beyond rose-tinted views

Overwhelmingly, the democratic function of the press continues to be idealized and reinforced by practitioners, policymakers and educators alike at global, national and local levels. Popular culture, from Hollywood films to novels by the likes of Evelyn Waugh and Graham Greene have helped to create an image of the hard-nosed reporter who will stop at nothing to uncover the truth. We do not discount the democratic function of the press. We have celebrated and acknowledged the important role local journalists play in their communities in holding the powerful to account. There are spectacular examples of local journalists exposing corruption and performing valuable investigative journalism. It is at the local level, after all, that people experience government decision making from agriculture to welfare policies, tax and economy, as well as the power of the state through the courts and police. There is no shortage of important issues for local reporters to investigate, from government and corporate corruption to human rights abuses.

At the same time, we have lamented how resources are being stripped out of newsrooms, and acknowledged that journalists are becoming more deskbound. Research in a range of different countries shows reporters are spending less of their days getting out and about to meet people and witness events. While information might be easier (and cheaper) to find and access online, there are fewer and fewer staff in mainstream newsrooms to sift through the torrents of information and work out what it is the public needs to know.

American scholar Barbie Zelizer (2012) has pointed out that democratic theory may have passed its shelf life in terms of how we understand journalism in this new era. A sole emphasis on media and democracy can deflect attention from journalism's own considerable power, and also the way it affects our lives beyond the public sphere.

For too long, local media has been considered the 'poor cousin' in scholarly literature about journalism, when it has much to offer our understandings of this relationship. Local media has at times been accused of being too myopic and narrow, but the same allegation might be levelled against journalism scholarship, which at times forgets its relationship to wider social space and instead perpetuates the traditional norms and conventions that are so influential in the field.

There is equally a need to explore the dark side of media power at the local level, especially the dangers of exclusionary treatment of 'outsiders' (such as ethnic minorities and people living with disabilities). The flipside is that local journalists can play a powerful role in educating audiences, preventing and bridging social divides and celebrating diversity within communities.

The emphasis on 'objectivity', meanwhile, has prevented journalism from breaking boundaries and playing a much more active role in bringing people together – from the important practice of public journalism to facilitating conversations online between 'communities within communities' and advocating much more strongly for the interests of its locality.

Specificity and diversity

Diversity has been a quiet but constant theme throughout the book, so it is important to shine a light on its importance in the practice and study of local journalism. In Chapter 3 we embarked on a journey across the globe to consider the key scholarly themes shaping research into the sector. We encountered different concerns and some sharp contrasts across topics including government regulation, business models, what mediums work best for certain cultures, and journalism practice. However, one thing became abundantly clear: no matter where you stand in the world, local journalism matters to people and gets expressed in ways that reflect the places and people within the geo-social spaces it serves.

Many industry practitioners and scholars who research hyperlocal news have been in the pursuit of the 'holy grail' – the formula for how to make serious money from news at the local level. The focus has been on a variety of funding models, from advertising to philanthropy and crowd sourcing. Such models are important and helpful to maintain diversity and a vibrant media sector, but the pursuit of profit has limited understandings of journalism's overall value at the excessively local level. The struggles endured by large-scale media enterprises such as Patch in the US suggest 'local' news might not be suitable for massification. The evidence presented throughout this book suggests it thrives best in niche environments. Centralization and dispersion are concepts we used in Chapter 7 to demonstrate how local commercial news is being sucked into globalized, corporate information flows. This means that at times newsmakers lose sight of ensuring their roots stay firmly embedded in the geographic soil where understandings of the 'local' are nurtured through media.

Economic success is important and explains why the business model of news has become such a dominant part of the conversation. But this is putting the cart before the horse. Our emphasis has been on how local media generate legitimacy rather than profits alone. While ultimately this may be rooted in economics, legitimacy requires other forms of capital (cultural, social and symbolic) and takes time to generate. Local knowledge is a powerful form of cultural capital when transferred into the journalistic field.

We have seen that ongoing changes in newsgathering and news consumption are creating strong demand for journalists with diverse digital and technical skills. Chapter 6 considered some emerging trends for 'doing local journalism' and how these are being interwoven with old ideas about the role. We set out to show that journalists working at the local level are not only using different tools: they are doing different things, including curating user-generated content and setting up, managing and generating revenue sources for their own hyperlocal news outlets. All the while, concerns remain about maintaining ethical relationships with community members and traditional skills and practices such as investigative journalism.

Local news and everyday digital practices

The shift to digital space has been the greatest social change since the Industrial Revolution. Media researchers and practitioners should always be mindful that this seismic shift has not just affected journalism: it has changed the way people go about their daily lives. This means we must explore closely what is happening at the everyday level to help find answers and drive innovation. We have argued that the way journalism is practised at the local level needs some rethinking, with concepts such as meaning-making, curating, filtering and contextualizing now co-existing with terms such as accuracy, objectivity and civic conduit.

Studying local journalism in the 21st century is no easy feat, and as we highlighted in the Introduction the formula for successful journalism at the local level cannot be bottled and measured in a test tube. This book has drawn on current research from around the work and used extensive qualitative interviews and exemplars to flesh out key ideas. We urge scholars interested in researching this area to look to media anthropology for methodological inspiration. Bird (2010b) says that in addition to asking how journalists make news, and how people use news, an important question is: what are the stories that people in any given society are being offered as tools to make meaning? (p. 8). It is our contention that until journalism scholars ask more of these kinds of questions, local media will not be understood well.

Excessively local news is often produced in informal spaces that are more challenging for journalism scholars to learn about and access, including private homes, community centres, schools and pubs. Wahl-Jorgensen (2010) proposes a multi-sited, multi-method approach to fill gaps in our knowledge. She says this is all the more important as a pedagogical intervention because many scholars teach present and future newsmakers from areas where journalistic work is so different that they find little to recognize in the current literature (Wahl-Jorgensen 2010, p. 29).

What we can say with some certainty is that news media providers viewed as central to the social in a given 'local' setting will survive, if not thrive. This is no easy feat, but we are certain this is the key to the future of local journalism in a digital world.

Endnotes

1 Couldry makes the point that the idea of the natural centre may be perceived as being different depending on where we live but that the media is considered to have a privileged position to that centre (Couldry, 2003a, p. 45).

2 Carey (1969) suggests journalists are 'brokers in symbols' who translate the attitudes, knowledge and concerns of one speech community into alternative but persuasive and understandable terms for another community – a role that operates in two directions, 'vertically, professional communicators link elites in any organization or community with general audiences, and horizontally, they link two differentiated speech communities at the same level of social structure' (p. 26). Carey highlights that the messages, ideas and purposes of any given source of news can be converted into a symbolic strategy designed to inform or persuade an audience, placing journalists in a position of advantage in social networks and information flow, while journalists perform the role of translating information from elites in a way that is understandable to the masses (Carey, 1969). Hess's idea of linking under a mediated social capital framework suggests there is value in journalists facilitating direct engagement or serving as a 'broker' between these elites and wider audiences.

3 Thanks to Cardiff University's affiliated Centre of Community Journalism. The work of *The Lincolnite* was showcased as part of a special conference event organized by the centre. See www.communityjournalism.co.uk.

4 The masthead won the Pulitzer Prize in 2014 for a series of editorials that explained the complex issue of rising pension costs, engaging readers and 'driving home the link between necessary solutions and their impact on everyday lives'. See www.pulitzer.org/bycat/Editorial-Writing.

5 Personal communication with author, 13 November 2014.

6 Anecdotal evidence based on interviews with authors and correspondence with the Country Press Australia incorporation.

References

Abernathy, P. 2014, *Saving community journalism: The path to profitability*, University of North Carolina Press, Chapel Hill, NC.

Adornato, A. 2014, 'A digital juggling act: New media's impact on the responsibilities of local television reporters', *Electronic News*, vol. 8, no. 1, pp. 3–29.

Agosta, D. E. 2007, 'Constructing civil society, supporting local development: A case study of community radio in postwar El Salvador', *Democratic Communiqué*, vol. 21, no. 1, pp. 4–26.

Aldridge, M. 2003, 'The ties that divide: Regional press campaigns, community and populism', *Media Culture and Society*, vol. 25, pp. 491–509.

Alexander, M. 2010, 10 May, 'When in Rome, but actually we are still stuck in Ireland', *The Standard*. Retrieved 21 June 2016 online from www.standard. net.au/blogs/plainly-speaking/when-in-rome-but-actually-were-stuck-in-ireland/1825686.aspx

Algan, E. 2005, 'The role of Turkish local radio in the construction of a youth community', *Radio Journal: International Studies in Broadcast & Audio Media*, vol. 3, no. 2, pp. 75–92.

Anderson, B. 1983, *Imagined communities: Reflections on the origin and spread of nationalism*, Verso, London.

Andersen, R., Dardenne, R. & Killenberg, G. M. 1994, *The conversation of journalism: Communication, community and news*. Praeger Publishers, Westport.

Applegate, E. 2009, *Advocacy journalists: A biographical dictionary of writers and editors*, Scarecrow Press, Lanham, Maryland.

Armando, A. 2014, 'The greedy giants: Centralized television in post-authoritarian Indonesia', *International Communication Gazette*, vol. 76, no. 4, pp. 390–406.

Artz, L. 2012, '21st century socialism: Making a state for revolution, *TripleC (Cognition, Communication, Co-Operation): Open Access Journal for a Global Sustainable Information Society*', vol. 10, no. 2, pp. 537–554.

Ash, E., Peeling, A. & Hettinga, K. 2010, 'Does content matter? The effects of type and number of user-generated comments on news stories'. Paper presented at the AEJMC annual conference, Denver.

Austin, L. 2014, 'Faith-based community radio and development in the South Pacific Islands', *Media International Australia*, No. 150, pp. 114–121.

Aviles, J. & Carvajal, M. 2008, 'Integrated and cross-media newsroom convergence: Two models of multimedia news production – the cases of Novotecnica and La Verdad Multimedia in Spain', *Convergence*, vol. 14, no. 2, pp. 221–239.

Aziz, R. 2014, 4 March, 'Letter from Newtown: A community newspaper covers a national tragedy', *New Yorker*, Retrieved 21 June 2016 online from www.newyorker.com.

Badkar, M. 2013, 2 March 'Buffett explains why he paid $334 million for 28 newspapers, and thinks the industry still has a future', *Business Insider Australia*. Retrieved 23 June 2016 online from www.businessinsider.com.au/warren-buffett-buying-newspapers-2013-3.

Bagdikian, B. H. 1997, *The media monopoly*, Beacon Press, Boston.

Bailey, I. 2014, 9 January, 'Kamloops newspaper to close doors after more than 80 years', *The Globe and Mail*. Retrieved 23 June 2016 online from www.theglobeandmail.com/news/british-columbia/the-kamloops-daily-news-to-stop-publishing/article16260187/.

Bainbridge, J., Goc, N. & Tynan, E. 2008, *Media and journalism: New approaches to theory and practice*, Oxford University Press, South Melbourne, Victoria.

Baines, D. 2013, United Kingdom: Subsidies and democratic deficits in local news, in P. Murschetz (ed.) *State aid for newspapers: Theories, cases, actions*, Springer, Berlin, pp. 337–356.

Baines, D. & Kennedy, C. 2010, 'An education for independence; should entrepreneurial skills be an essential part of journalist's toolbox?', *Journalism Practice*, vol. 4, no. 1, pp. 97–113.

Baker, M. 2010, 'Selling a state to the nation: Boosterism and Utah's first national park', *Journalism History*, vol. 36, no. 3, pp. 169–176.

Bakker, P. 2014, 'Mr. Gates returns: Curation, community management and other new roles for journalists', *Journalism Studies*, vol. 15 no. 5, pp. 596–606.

Bala-Ndi, Marie M. 2013, 'Questioning public interest journalism in New Caledonia', *Pacific Journalism Review*, vol. 19 no. 1, pp. 73–83.

Baloun, K. M. 2007 *Inside Facebook, life work and vision of greatness*, Karl Baloun Inc.

Bamat, J. 2014, 9 January, 'Paper shortage threatens closure of Venezuela dailies', *France24*. Retrieved 23 June 2016 online from www.france24.com/en/20140128-venezuela-media-protests-paper-shortage-newspapers-closures-foreign-currency/.

Banjade, A. 2007, *Community radio in Nepal: A case study of community radio Madanpokhara*. Unpublished PhD thesis, Ohio, Ohio University.

Barnes, T. 1991, 'Metaphors and conversations in economic geography: Richard Rorty and the gravity model', *Human Geography*, vol. 73, no. 2, pp. 110–120.

Barnett, S. 2009, *Journalism, democracy and the public interest: Rethinking media pluralism for the digital age*, Reuters Institute for the Study of Journalism, Working Paper.

Barnett, S. and Townend, J. 2014, 'Plurality, policy and the local: Can hyperlocals fill the gap?', *Journalism Practice*, vol. 9, no. 3, pp. 332–349.

Baudrillard, J. 1983, *Simulations*, Scmiotexte, New York.

Bauer, M. A. & Strauss, C. 2014, 'Fostering collaboration by location-based crowdsourcing', in Y. Yuo (ed.) *Cooperative design, visualisation and engineering lecture notes in computer science* 8686, pp. 88–95.

BBC. *United States of America Country Profile*. Retrieved 30 June online from http://news.bbc.co.uk/2/hi/americas/country_profiles/1217752.stm#media.

BBC Charter Review 2015. Retrieved 23 June 2016 online from http://downloads.bbc.co.uk/aboutthebbc/reports/pdf/futureofthebbc2015.pdf.

BBC News. 2009, April 23, 'Shark "dumped" on Australian paper'. Retrieved 23 June 2016 online from http://news.bbc.co.uk/1/hi/8015205.stm.

BBC News. 2015, 9 February, 'Local Live – giving users access to BBC newsrooms'. Retrieved 26 June 2016 online from www.bbc.com/news/uk-england-21045859.

Beaudesert Times. 2014, 10 October, 'Beaudesert Times hosts volunteer forum'. Retrieved 25 June 2016 online from www.beaudeserttimes.com.au/story/2617179/spotlight-on-volunteering-at-forum/.

Becker, M. 2009, 'The hubris of the paid news curator', *Hypercrit.net*. Retrieved 27 June 2016 online from www.hypercrit.net/2009/07/04/the-hubris-of-the-paid-news-curator/

Benson, R. 2004, 'Bringing the sociology of media back in', *Political Communication*, vol. 21 no. 3, pp. 275–292.

Benson, R. 2008, 'Normative theories of journalism', in W. Donsbach (ed.) *The Blackwell international encyclopaedia of communication*, Wiley-Blackwell, Cambridge, pp. 2591–2597.

Benson, R. & Neveu, E. 2005, *Bourdieu and the journalistic field*, Polity, London.

Bergés S. L. 2012, 'Spain: An information society without traditional offline community media?', *Journal of Radio & Audio Media*, vol. 19 no. 2, pp. 134–151.

Berkowitz, D. 2008, 'Reporters and their sources', in K. Wahl-Jorgensen & T. Hanitzsch (eds) *Handbook of journalism studies*, Routledge, New York, pp. 102–115.

Berkowitz, D & TerKeurst, J. V. 1999, 'Community as interpretive community: Rethinking the journalist-source relationship', *Journal of Communication*, vol. 49 no. 3, pp. 125–136.

Beyer, A. & Figenschou, T. 2014, 'Human-interest fatigue: Audience evaluations of a massive emotional story', *International Journal of Communication*, vol. 8, pp. 1944–1963.

Birks, J. 2010, 'The democratic role of campaign journalism', *Journalism Practice*, vol. 4, no. 2, pp. 208–223.

Bijoor, H. 2008, 'They're on their own trip', *Outlook Business*, pp. 74–75.

Björkroth, T & Grönlund, M 2014 'The growth of leading regional newspapers', *Nordicom Review*, vol. 35, no. 1, pp. 115–133.

Bird, E. 2010a, 'From fan practice to mediated moments: The value of practice theory in the understanding of media audiences', in B. Brauchler and P. J. (eds) *Theorising media and practice*, Berhahn Books, pp. 85–105.

Bird, E. 2010b 'Introduction: The anthropology of news and journalism, why now?', in E. Bird (ed.) *The anthropology of news and journalism*, Indiana University Press, Indianapolis, pp. 1–20.

Bishara, A. 2010, 'New media and political change in the occupied Palestinian territories: Assembling media worlds and cultivating networks of care', *Middle East Journal of Culture & Communication*, vol. 3, no. 1, pp. 63–81.

Bollinger, L. C. 1991, *Images of a free press*, University of Chicago Press, Chicago.

Booker, C. 2004, *The seven basic plots: Why we tell stories*, Continuum, London.

Bonte, D. et al. 2012, 'Costs of dispersal', *Biological Reviews*, vol. 87, no.2, pp. 290–312.

Bosch, T. 2010, 'Digital journalism and online public spheres in South Africa', *Communication: South African Journal for Communication Theory & Research*, vol. 36, no. 2, pp. 265–275.

Bourdieu, P. 1977, *Outline of a theory of practice*, Cambridge University Press, Cambridge.

Bourdieu P. 1984, *Distinction: A social critique of the judgement of taste*, Harvard University Press, Cambridge, MA.

Bourdieu, P. 1986, 'The forms of capital', in J. G. Richardson (ed.) *Handbook of theory and research for the sociology of education*, Greenwood Press, New York, pp. 241–58.

Bourdieu, P. 1989, Social space and symbolic power, *Sociological Theory* vol. 7, pp. 14–25.

Bourdieu, P. 1990, *The logic of practice*, Polity Press, Cambridge.

Bourdieu, P. 1991, *Language and symbolic power*, Polity Press, Cambridge.

Bourdieu, P. 1992, *An invitation to reflexive sociology*, University of Chicago Press, Chicago.

Bourdieu, P. 1998, *On television*, The New Press, New York.

Bourdieu, P. 1999, *The weight of the world – social suffering in contemporary society*, Polity Press, Oxford.

Bourdieu, P. 2005a, 'The political field, the social science field, and the journalistic field', in R. Benson and E. Neveu (eds) *Bourdieu and the journalistic field*, Polity, London, pp. 29–47.

Bourdieu, P. 2005b, *The social structures of the economy*, Polity Press, Cambridge.

Bourdieu, P. 2006, 'The forms of capital', in H. Lauder, P. Brown, J. A. Dillabough and A. H. Halsey (eds) *Education, globalisation and social change*, Oxford University Press, Oxford, pp. 105–118.

Bourdieu, P. & Wacquant, L. 1992, *An invitation to reflexive sociology*, University of Chicago Press, Chicago.

Bowd, K. 2003, 'How different is "different"? Australian country newspapers and development journalism', *Asia Pasific Media Educator*, vol. 14, pp. 117–130.

Bowd, K. 2007, 'A voice for the community: Local newspaper as local campaigner', *Australian Journalism Review*, vol. 29, no. 2, pp. 77–89.

Bowd, K. 2009, 'Did you see that in the paper?: Country newspapers and perceptions of local ownership', *Australian Journalism Review*, vol. 31, no. 1, pp. 49–61.

Bowd, K. 2010, 'Local voice, local choice: Australian country newspapers and notions of community', PhD thesis, University of South Australia, Adelaide, UniSA research archive.

Bowd, K. 2012, 'Reflecting regional life: Localness and social capital in Australian country newspapers', *Pacific Journalism Review*, vol. 17, no. 2, pp. 72–91.

Brighton, P. & Foy, D. 2007, *News values*, Sage, London.

Brisset-Foucault, F. 2011, 'Peace-making, power configurations and media practices in northern Uganda: A case study of Mega FM', *Journal of African Media Studies*, vol. 3, no.2, pp. 205–225.

Brownsville Herald. 2015, 8 July, 'Annual ritual calls for safe, bountiful shrimp season'. Retrieved 16 June 2016 online from www.brownsvilleherald.com/news/local/article_a5a7cd28-2515-11e5-a0e2-932e19844a31.html.

Bruns, A., Burgess, J., Crawford, K. & Shaw, F. 2012, '#qldfloods and @QPSMedia: Crisis communication on Twitter in the 2011 South Wat Queensland Floods, Research Report, ARC Centre of Excellence for Creative Industries and Innovation. Retrieved 15 September 2015 online from www.mappingonlinepublics.net/dev/wp-content/uploads/2012/01/qldfloods-and-@QPSMedia.pdf.

Buchanan, C. 2009, 'Sense of place in the daily newspaper', *The Journal of Media Geography*, vol. Spring, pp. 62–82.

Bunch, W. 2007, 'Forgetting why reporters choose the work they do.' *Nieman Reports*, vol. 61, no. 4, pp. 28–30.

Burns, L. 2002, *Understanding journalism*, Sage, London.

Burns, L. S. 2012, *Understanding journalism* (2nd edn) Sage, London.

Burrowes, T. 2014, 'The data is finally in, newspapers aren't going to get enough digital subscribers'. *Mumberella*. Retrieved 27 June 2016 online from http://mumbrella.com.au/data-finally-newspapers-arent-going-get-enough-digital-subscribers-206839.

Burt, R. S. 2001, 'Structural holes versus network closure as social capital', in N. Lin, K. Cook & R. Burt (eds) *Social capital: Theory and research*, Sociology and Economic Controversy and Integration Series, Aldine de Gruter, New York, pp. 31–56.

Burt, R. S. 2005, *Brokerage and closure: An introduction to social capital*, Oxford University Press, New York.

Bustillos, M. 2016, 'How the Las Vegas Review-Journal unmasked its owners, *The New Yorker*. Retrieved 28 June 2016 online from www.newyorker.com/business/currency/how-the-las-vegas-review-journal-unmasked-its-owners.

Butz, D. & Eyles, J. 1997, 'Reconceptualising senses of place: Social relations ideology and ecology', *Geografiska Annaler*, vol. 79, pp. 1–25.

Byerly, K. 1961, *Community journalism*, Chilton Company, Philadelphia.

Canter, L. 2013, 'The source, the resource and the collaborator: The role of citizen journalism in local UK newspapers', *Journalism: Theory Practice Criticism*, vol. 14, no. 8, pp.1091–1109.

Carey, J. 1969, 'The communications revolution and the professional communicator', *Sociological Review Monograph*, vol. 13, pp. 23–38.

Carey, J. 1989, *Communication as culture*, Unwin Hyman, Boston.

Carey, J. 1997a, 'The communications revolution and the professional communicator. Afterword: The culture in question', in E. S. Munson & C. A. Warren (eds) *James Carey: A critical reader*, University of Minnesota Press, Minneapolis, pp. 128–143.

Carey, J. 1997b, 'Community, public and journalism', in E. Black (ed) Mixed news: The public/civic/communitarian journalism debate. Lawrence Erlbaum, Mahway, NO. pp 1–15.

Carey, J. 1999, 'In defence of public journalism', in T. Glasser (ed.) *The idea of public journalism.* Guildford, New York, pp. 49–66.

Carlson, M. & Franklin B., 2011, *Journalists, sources and credibility: New perspectives.* Routledge, Abingdon, Oxon.

Carper, A. 1997, 'Marketing news' in P. Norris (ed.) *Politics and the press: The news media and their influences,* Lynne Rienner Publishers, Boulder, CO, pp. 45–66.

Carroll, J. 2001, *The western dreaming: The western world is dying for want of a story.* HarperCollins, Sydney.

Cass, P. 1999, 'Tuning into the coconut wireless', *British Journalism Review,* vol. 10, pp. 55–59.

Cass, J. 2005, 'Wonderful weeklies', *American Journalism Review,* vol. 27, no. 6, pp. 21–29.

Castells, M. 2010, *The rise of the network society: With a new preface,* Vol. 1, 2nd edn, Wiley-Blackwell, Oxford.

Chandrasekhar, P. 2010, 'A study of community radio in Andhra Pradesh', *Global Media Journal: Indian Edition,* pp. 1–31.

Chantier, P. & Stewart, P. 2009, *Essential radio journalism: How to produce and present radio news,* A & C Black, London.

Charity, A. 1996, 'What is public journalism: Five communities, five examples', *National Civic Review,* vol. 85, no. 1, pp. 14–17.

Cheng, H. L. 2005, 'Constructing a transnational, multilocal sense of belonging: An analysis of Ming Pao (West Canadian Edition)', *Journal of Communication Inquiry,* vol. 29, pp.141–159.

China Daily. 2009, 4 April, 'Shark dumped on Australian newspaper's doorstep'. Retrieved 12 April 2012 online from www.chinadaily.com.cn/world/2009-04/24/content_7710943.htm.

Chiou, L. & Tucker, C. 2013, 'Paywalls and the demand for news', *Information Economics and Policy,* vol. 25, no. 2, pp. 61–69.

Chiumbu, S. & Ligaga, D. 2013, 'Communities of strangerhoods?: Internet, mobile phones and the changing nature of radio cultures in South Africa', *Telematics & Informatics,* vol. 30, no. 3, pp. 242–251.

Christians, C. 1999, 'The common good as first principle', in T. Glasser (ed.) *The idea of public journalism,* The Guilford Press, New York, pp. 67–84.

Christians, C., Glasser, T., McQuail, D., Nordenstreng, K. & White, R. 2009, *Normative theories of the media: Journalism in democratic societies,* University of llinois Press, Illinois.

Chyl, H. 2005, 'Willingness to pay for online news: An empirical study on the viability of the subscription model', *Journal of Media Economics,* vol.18, no. 2, pp.131–142.

Collins, P. 2010, 20 April, 'Volcano flight bans hurt tourism', *The Standard.* Retrieved 30 June 2016 online from www.standard.net.au/news/local/news/general/volcano-flight-bans-hurt-tourism/1808182.aspxash.

Conrad, D. 2014, 'Deconstructing the community radio model: Applying practice to theory in East Africa', *Journalism*, vol. 15, no. 6, pp. 773–789.

Costera Meijer, I. 2010, 'Democratizing journalism?', *Journalism Studies*, vol. 11, no. 3, pp. 327–342.

Cottle, S. 2003, *Media organization and production*, Sage, London.

Couldry, N. 2000, *The place of media power: Pilgrims and witnesses of the media age*, Routledge, London.

Couldry, N. 2003a, *Media rituals: A critical approach*, Routledge, London.

Couldry, N. 2003b, 'Media meta-capital: Extending Bourdieu's field theory', *Theory and Society*, vol. 32, no. 5/6, pp. 653–677.

Couldry, N. 2004, 'Theorising media as practice', *Social Semiotics*, vol. 14, no. 2, pp. 115–32.

Couldry, N. 2005, 'Media rituals: Beyond functionalism', in E. W. Rothenbuhler & M. Coman (eds) *Media anthropology*, Sage, London, pp. 59–69.

Couldry, N. 2012, *Media, society world: Social theory and digital media practice*, Polity Press, Cambridge.

Couldry, N. & Curran, J. 2003, 'The paradox of media power' in N. Couldry & J. Curran (eds) *Contesting media power: Alternative media in a networked world*, Rowman & Littlefield Publishers, Oxford, pp.3–17.

Couldry, N. & Dreher, T. 2007, 'Globalisation and the public sphere', *Global Media and Communication*, vol. 3, no. 1, pp. 79–100.

Craig, G. 2004, *The media, politics and public life*, Allen and Unwin, Crows Nest, NSW.

Cremedas, M. & Lysak, S. 2011, 'New media skills competency expected of TV reporters and producers: A survey', *Electronic News*, no. 5, pp. 41–59.

Curran, J. 2002, *Media and power*, Routledge, London.

Das, R. 2010, 'Scope of revitalizing rural development through community radio', *Global Media Journal: Indian Edition*, pp. 1–14.

Davies, N. 2008, *Flat Earth News: An award-winning reporter exposes falsehood, distortion and propaganda in the global media*, Chatto and Windus, London.

Davis, A. 2003, 'Public relations and news sources', in S. Cottle (ed.) *News, public relations and power*, Sage, London, pp. 27–43.

Davis, A. 2007, *The mediatisation of power*, Routledge, London.

Dayan, D. & Katz, E. 1992, *Media events: The live broadcasting of history*, Harvard University Press, Cambridge, MA.

de Tocqueville, A. 1945, *Democracy in America*, Knopf, New York.

Deuze, M. 2004, 'What is multimedia journalism?', *Journalism Studies*, vol. 5, pp. 139–152.

Deuze, M. 2007a, *Media work*, Polity Press, Cambridge.

Deuze, M. 2007b, 'Journalism in liquid modern times', *Journalism Studies*, vol. 8, no.4, pp. 671–679.

Deuze, M. 2008, 'The professional identity of journalists in the context of convergence culture', *Observatorio*, vol. 2 no. 4, pp. 103–117.

Deuze, M. 2010, 'Journalism and convergence culture', in S. Allan (ed.) *The Routledge companion to news and journalism*, Routledge, Abingdon, Oxon, pp. 267–276.

Deuze, M. 2011, *Managing media work*, London, Sage.

Deuze, M., Bruns A., & Neuberger, C., 2007, 'Preparing for an age of participatory news', *Journalism Practice*, vol. 1 no. 3, pp. 322–338.

Doctor, K. 2013, 'The newsonomics of the surprisingly persistent appeal of newsprint.' Niemanlab.org. Retrieved 23 June 2016 online from http://nie.mn/I11y7H.

Donohue, G., Tichenor, P. & Olien, C. 1995, 'A guard dog perspective on the role of media', *Journal of Communication*, vol. 45, no. 2, pp. 115–132.

Dooley, P. 2009, 'History of journalism: 1930–1995', in C. Sterling (ed.) *Encyclopedia of journalism*, Sage, Thousand Oaks, CA, pp. 708–714.

Downie Jr., L. & Schudson, M. 2009, 'The reconstruction of American journalism', *Columbia Journalism Review*, vol. 48, no. 4, pp. 28–51.

Duhé, S., Mortimer, M., & Chow, S. 2004, 'Convergence in North American TV newsrooms: A nationwide look', *Convergence: The International Journal of Research into New Media Technologies*, vol. 10, pp. 81–104.

Durham, M. 1998, 'On the relevance of standpoint epistemology to the practice of journalism: The case for strong objectivity', *Communication Theory*, vol. 8, no. 2, pp. 117–140.

Durkheim, É. 1995 [1912], *The Elementary Forms of Religious Life* tr. K. Fields. Free Press, Glencoe.

DW. 2012, 16 May 'Freedom of Indonesian journalists under threat', *DW Made for Minds*. Retrieved 16 June 2016 online from www.dw.com/en/freedom-of-indonesian-journalists-under-threat/a-15954119.

Eggins, J. 2008, 'Community development and church-based radio broadcasting', in E. Papoutsaki & U. Harris (eds) *South Pacific Islands communication: Regional perspectives, local issues*, Asian Media Information and Communication Centre, Singapore: Nanyang Technological University, pp. 206–218.

Entman, R. 2010, 'Framing media power', in P. D'Angelo & J. Kuypers (eds) *Doing news framing analysis: Empirical and theoretical perspectives*, Routledge, New York, pp. 331–355.

Ericson, R. 1999, 'How journalists visualize fact', *The Annals of the American Academy of Political and Social Science*, vol. 560, no. 1, pp. 83–95.

Eriksen, T. & Nielsen, F. 2001, *A history of anthropology*, Pluto Press, London.

Erzikova, E. & Lowrey, W. 2014, 'Preventive journalism as a means of controlling regional media in Russia', *Global Media & Communication*, vol. 10, no. 1, pp. 35–52.

Ewart, J. 2010, *Reporting Diversity Talkback report*. Retrieved 23 June 2016 online from www.reportingdiversity.org.au/docs/Talkbackradioreport.pdf

Ewart, J. 2014, 'Local people, local places, local voices and local spaces: How talkback radio in Australia provides hyper-local news through mini-narrative sharing'. *Journalism: Theory, Practice and Criticism*, vol. 15, no. 6, pp. 709–807.

Ewart, J. & Massey, B. L. 2005, '"Local (people) mean the world to us": Australia's regional newspapers and the closer to readers assumption', *Media International Australia*, no. 115, pp. 94–108.

Evensen, B. 2008, *The responsible reporter* (3rd edition), Peter Lang, New York.

Eyles, J. 1985, *Sense of place*, Silverbrook Press, Warrington.

Farhi, P. 2007, 'Rolling the dice', *American Journalism Review*, vol. 29, no. 3, pp. 40–43.

Felle, T. 2013, 'From boom to bust: Irish local newspapers post the Celtic Tiger', in J. Mair, N. Fowler& I. Reeves (eds) *What do we mean by local? Grassroots journalism and its death and rebirth.* Abramis, Bury St Edmunds, pp. 41–50.

Felle, T. 2016, 'Are paywalls saving journalism?', *The Conversation*, Feb 22. Retrieved 25 June 2016 online from www.theguardian.com/media/greenslade/2012/jul/19/advertising-local-newspapers.

Fenton, N. 2006, 'Bridging the mythical divide: Political economy and cultural studies approaches to the analysis of the media', in E. Devereux (ed.) *Issues and key debate in the media studies*, Sage, London, pp. 7–27.

Fenton, N., Metykova, M., Schloseberg, J. & Freeman, D. 2010, *Meeting the needs of local Communities*, Media Trust, London.

Fernandez-Sande, M. 2014, 'Radio ambulante: Narrative radio journalism in an age of crowdfunding', in T. Bonini & B. Monclus (eds) *Radio audiences and participation in the age of the networked society*, Routledge, New York, pp. 176–194.

Ferree, M. M. 2002, *Shaping abortion discourse: Democracy and the public sphere in Germany and the United States*, Cambridge University Press, Cambridge.

Ferrier, M., 2013, 'Media entrepreneurship', *Journalism & Mass Communication Educator*, vol. 68, no. 3, pp. 222–241.

Filho, A. 2009, 'Brazilian community communication initiatives in radio and TV digital switchover', *International Journal of Media & Cultural Politics*, vol. 5, no. 1/2, pp. 55–68.

Fine, B. 2001, *Social capital versus social theory: Political economy and social science at the turn of the millennium*, Contemporary political economy series, Routledge, London.

Finkelstein, R. & Ricketson, M. 2012, 'Report of the Independent Inquiry Into Media and Media Regulation', Department of Broadband, Communications and the Digital Economy. Retrieved 20 June 2016 online from www.dbcde.gov.au/__data/assets/pdf_file/0006/146994/Report-of-the-Independent-Inquiry-into-the-Media-and-Media-Regulation-web.pdf.

Firmstone, J. & Coleman, S. 2015, 'Rethinking local communicative spaces: Implications of digital media and citizen journalism for the role of local journalism in engaging citizens', in R. K. Nielsen (ed.) *Local journalism: The decline of newspapers and the rise of digital media.* Reuters Institute for the Study of Journalism, Oxford, pp. 117–140.

Forde, S. 2011, *Challenging the news: The journalism of alternative and independent media*, Palgrave Macmillan, London.

Forde, S., Foxwell, K. & Meadows, M. 2009, *Developing dialogues: Indigenous and ethnic community broadcasting in Australia*, Intellect, Bristol.

Fourie, P. 2007, 'The role and function of the media in society', in P. Fourie (ed.) *Media studies: Media history, media and society*, Juta & Co, Capetown, pp. 184–207.

Fowler, R. 1991, *Language in the news*, Routledge, London.

Foxwell, K., Ewart, J., Forde, S. & Meadows, M. 2008, 'Sounds like a whisper: Australian community broadcasting hosts a quiet revolution', *Westminster Papers in Communication & Culture*, vol. 5, no. 1, pp. 5–24.

Franklin, B. 2006, *Local journalism and local media: Making the local news*, Routledge, London.

Franklin, B. 2008, 'The future of newspapers', *Journalism Studies*, vol. 9, pp. 630–641.

Franklin, B. 2014, 'The future of journalism: In an age of digital media and economic uncertainty', *Journalism Practice*, vol. 8, no. 5, pp. 469–487.

Freelon, D. 2015, 'Discourse architecture, ideology, and democratic norms in online political discussion', *New Media & Society*, vol. 5, pp. 772–791.

Friedland, L. 2004, 'Public journalism and communities', *National Civic Review*, vol. 93, no. 2, pp. 36–42.

Fraser, N. 1990, 'Rethinking the public sphere: A contribution to the critique of Actually Existing Democracy', *Social Text*, no. 25, pp. 56–80.

From, M., Hall, H. & Manfull, A. 2015, *Student journalism and media literacy*, Rosen Publishing Group, New York.

Frost, C. 2010, *Reporting for journalists*, Routledge, Abingdon, Oxon.

Fry, G. 1997, 'Framing the islands: Knowledge and power in changing Australian images of the 'South Pacific', *The Contemporary Pacific*, vol. 9, no. 2, pp. 305–344.

Gahran, A. 2015, 'As spot.us ends, insights on community news crowd funding', Knight Digital Media Center. Retrieved 27 June 2016 online from www.knightdigitalmediacenter.org/blogs/agahran/2015/02/spotus-ends-insights-community-news-crowdfunding

Galper, J. 2002, An exploration of social capital, giving and volunteering at the United States county level, Urban Institute. Retrieved 23 June 2016 online from www.urban.org/cnp/galper/galper.ht.

Galtung, J. & Ruge, M. 1965, 'The structure of foreign news', *Journal of Peace Research*, vol. 2, pp. 64–91.

Galtunge, J. & Ruge, M. 1981, 'Structuring and selecting news', in S. Cohen & J. Young (eds) *The manufacture of news: Social problems, deviance and the mass media* (rev. ed.), Sage, Beverly Hills, CA, pp. 52–63.

Gandy, O. 1982, *Beyond agenda setting: Information subsidies and public policy*. Ablex, Norwood, NJ.

Gans, H. J. 1979, *Deciding what's news*, Pantheon, New York.

Gans, H. 2011, Multiperspectival news revisited: Journalism and representative democracy, *Journalism*, vol. 12, no. 1, pp. 3–13.

Gatua, M., Patton, T. & Brown, M. 2010, 'Giving voice to invisible women: FIRE as a model of successful community radio in Africa', *The Howard Journal of Communications*, vol. 21 no.2, pp. 164–181.

Gaynor, N. & O'Brien, A. 2010, *Drivers of change? Community radio in Ireland*. Retrieved 27 June, 2016 online from www.doras.dcu.ie.

Gazali, E. 2002, 'The Suharto Regime and its fall through the eyes of the local media', *Gazette: International Journal for Communication Studies*, vol. 64, no. 2, pp. 121–140.

Gaziano, C. & McGrath, K. 1987, 'Newspaper credibility and relationships of newspaper journalists to communities', *Journalism Quarterly*, vol. 64, pp. 317–345.

Gehl, R. 2009. 'YouTube as archive: Who will curate this digital wunderkammer?', *International Journal of Cultural Studies*, vol. 12 no. 1, pp. 43–60.

Gilligan, E. 2012, 'The Minnesota team: Key studies of institutional power and community media', in B. Reader & J. Hatcher (eds) *Foundations of community journalism*, Sage, Los Angeles, pp. 59–64.

Gillmor, D. 2004, *We the media: Grassroots journalism by the people, for the people*, O'Reilly Media, Sebastopol, CA.

Giovannelli, M. 2012, 'A partnership too valuable to give up: Why the Miami Herald and WLRN are sticking together', Retrieved 22 June 2016 online from www.niemanlab.org/2012/02/a-partnership-too-valuable-to-give-up-why-the-miami-herald-and-wlrn-are-stickingtogether/

Gitlin, T. 1980, *The whole world is watching*, University of California Press, Berkeley, CA.

Glaser, M. 2010, 'Citizen journalism: Widening world views, extending democracy.', in S. Allan (ed.) *The Routledge companion to news and journalism*, Routledge, London and New York, pp. 578–590.

Glasser, T. & Craft, S. 1998, 'Public journalism and the search for democratic ideals', in T. Liebes & J. Curran (eds) *Media Ritual and Identity*, Routledge, London, pp. 203–218.

Golding, P. & Murdock, G. 1991, 'Culture, communication and political economy', in J. Curran & M. Gurevitch (eds) *Mass media and society*, Edward Arnold, London, pp. 70–92.

Goldstein, K. 2015, *Canada's digital divides: Technology, age, income, citizens, institutions*. Retrieved 23 June 2016 online from www.media-cxmi.com

Gordon, J. 2009, 'Community radio, funding and ethics: The UK and Australian models', in J. Gordon (ed.) *Notions of community: A collection of community media debates and dilemmas*, Peter Lang, Oxford, pp. 59–80.

Graber, D. 1988, *Processing the news: How people tame the information tide* (2nd ed.), Longman, New York.

Greenslade, R. 2012, 19 July, 'How newspapers already receive below-the-line government subsidies, *The Guardian*. Retrieved 25 June 2016 online from www.theguardian.com/media/greenslade/2012/jul/19/advertising-local-newspapers

Greenslade, R. 2014, 9 May, 'Which local newspaper has run the best campaign? You decide...', *The Guardian*. Retrieved 23 June 2016 online from www.theguardian.com/media/greenslade/2014/may/09/campaigning-journalism-local-newspapers.

Greenslade, R. & Barnett, S. 2014, 'Can charity save the local press?', *British Journalism Review*, vol. 25, no. 1, pp. 62–67.

Grenfell, M. 2008, *Pierre Bourdieu: Key concepts*, Acumen, Durham.

The Guardian. 2016, 24 February, 'Democracy warning as Canadian outlets merge and papers close', *The Guardian*. Retrieved 27 June 2016 online from www.theguardian.com/world/2016/feb/24/democracy-warning-as-canadian-media-outlets-merge-and-papers-close

Gupta, A., Paul, S., Jones, Q. & Borcea, C. 2007, 'Automatic identification of informal social groups and places for geo-social recommendations', *International Journal of Mobile Network Design and Innovation*, vol. 2, pp. 159–171.

Gustafsson, K., Örnebring, H. & Levy, D. 2009, 'Press subsidies and local news: The Swedish case', Reuters Institute for the Study of Journalism, Oxford.

Guth, D. 2015, 'Amber waves of change: Rural community journalism in areas of declining population', *Journal of Applied Journalism and Media Studies*, vol. 4, no. 2, pp. 259–275.

Gutsche, R. 2015, 'Boosterism as banishment: Identifying the power function of local, business news and coverage of city spaces', *Journalism Studies*, vol. 16, no. 4, pp. 497–512.

Haas, T. 2007, *The pursuit of public journalism*, Routledge, New York.

Haas, T. 2012, *The pursuit of public journalism: Theory, practice criticism* (2nd ed.), Routledge, Abingdon, Oxon.

Haas T. & Steiner, L. 2001, 'Public journalism as a journalism of publics: Implications of the Habermas-Fraser debate for public journalism', *Journalism: Theory Practice Criticism*, vol. 2, no. 2, pp.123–147.

Habermas, J. 1989, *The structural transformation of the public sphere: An inquiry into a category of bourgeois society*, Polity Press, Cambridge.

Habermas, J. 1996, *Between facts and norms*, Polity Press, Cambridge.

Hadland, A. & Thorne, K. 2004, *The people's voice: The development and current state of the South African small media sector*, HSRC Press, Cape Town.

Halbert, J. & McDowell, W. 2013, 'Sustaining local radio journalism: A case study of the WLRN/Miami Herald Strategic Alliance', *Journal of Radio and Audio Media*, vol. 20. no. 1, pp. 17–34.

Hall, S. 1973, 'The determination of news photographs', in S. Cohen & J. Young (eds) *The Manufacture of news: A reader*, Sage, Beverly Hills, pp. 176–190.

Hall, S., Critcher, C., Jefferson, T., Clarke, J. & Roberts, B. 1978, *Policing the crisis: Mugging, the state and law and order*, Palgrave, London.

Hanitzsch, T. 2007, 'Deconstructing journalism culture: Toward a universal theory', *Communication Theory*, vol. 17, no. 4, pp. 367–385.

Hanusch, F. 2015, 'A different breed altogether? Distinctions between local and metropolitan journalism cultures', *Journalism Studies*, vol. 16 no. 6, pp. 816–833.

Harber, A. 2011, *Diepsloot*, Jonathan Ball, Johannesburg.

Harcup, T. & O'Neill, D. 2001, 'What is news? Galtung and Ruge revisited', *Journalism Studies*, vol. 2, no. 2, pp. 261–280.

Harding, S. 1991, *Whose science? Whose knowledge? Thinking from women's lives*, Cornell University Press, Ithaca, NY.

Hardy, J. 2014, 'Critical political economy of communications: A mid-term review', *International Journal of Media and Cultural Politics*, vol. 10, no. 2, pp. 189–202.

Harris, J. 2015, 5 November, 'Cities: The Bristom conundrum', *The Guardian*. Retrieved 25 June 2016 online from www.theguardian.com/cities/2015/nov/05/bristol-conundrum-gentrification-danger-poor-really-stretched-stokes-croft-george-ferguson.

Harvey, D. 1989, *The condition of postmodernity: An inquiry into the origins of social change*, Blackwell, Cambridge.

Harwood, R. 2000, *Tapping Civic Life* (2nd edition), Pew Centre for Civic Journalism, Washington.

Hatcher, J. 2005, 'Small papers, big stories: A comparison of community newspapers that have won the Pulitzer Prize', *Grassroots Editor*, vol. 46, no. 1, pp. 1–10.

Hatcher, J. 2012a, 'Community journalism as an international phenonema', in B. Reader and J. Hatcher (eds) *Foundations of community journalism*, Sage, London, pp. 241–254.

Hatcher, J. 2012b, 'A view from the outside: What other social science disciplines can teach us about community journalism', in B. Reader and J. Hatcher (eds) *Foundations of community journalism*, Sage, London, pp. 129–149.

Hatcher, J. & Haavik, E. 2014, 'We write with our hearts', *Journalism Practice*, vol. 8, no. 2, pp. 149–163.

Hayes, M. 2010, *Reframing polynesian journalism: From Tusitala to liquid modernity*. Alfred Deakin Research Institute Working Paper No. 9. Geelong, Deakin University. Retrieved 25 June 2016 online from www.gwww.deakin.edu.au/research-services/forms/v/3090/adri-working-paper-09.pdf+mark+hayes+journalism.

Heider, D., McCombs, M. & Poindexter, P. 2005, 'What the public expects of local news: Views on public and traditional journalism', *Journalism and Mass Communication Quarterly*, vol. 82, no. 4, pp. 952–967.

Herbert-Cheshire, L. & Higgins, V. 2004, 'From risky to responsible: Expert knowledge and the governing of community-led rural development', *Journal of Rural Studies*, vol. 20, pp. 289–302.

Herman, E. & Chomsky, N. 1998, *Manufacturing consent: The political economy of the mass media*, The Bodley Head, London.

Hermans, L., Schaap, G. & Bardoel, J. 2014, 'Re-establishing the relationship with the public', *Journalism Studies*, vol. 15, no. 5, pp. 642–654.

Hermida, A. 2012, 'Tweets and truth: Journalism as a discipline of collaborative verification', *Journalism Practice*, vol. 6, no. 5–6, pp. 659–668.

Hermida, A., Fletcher, F., Korell, D. & Logan, D., 2012, 'Share, like, recommend: Decoding the social media news consumer', *Journalism Studies*, vol. 13, no. 5–6, pp. 815–824.

Hermida, A. & Thurman, N. 2008, 'A clash of cultures: The integration of user-generated content within professional journalistic frameworks at British newspaper websites', *Journalism Practice*, vol. 2, no. 3, pp. 343–356.

Hesmondhalgh, D. 2007, *The cultural industries* (2nd edn), Sage, London.

Hess, K. 2013a, 'Breaking boundaries: Recasting the small newspaper as geo-social news,' *Digital Journalism*, vol. 1, no. 1, pp. 45–60.

Hess, K. 2013b, 'Tertius tactics: Mediated social capital as a resource of power for traditional news media', *Communication Theory*, vol. 23, no. 2, pp. 112–130.

Hess, K. 2015a, 'Making connections: 'Mediated social capital and the small-town press', *Journalism Studies*, vol. 16, no. 4 pp. 482–496.

Hess, K. 2015b, 'Ritual power: Illunimating the births, deaths and marriages column in news media research', *Journalism: Theory, Practice Criticism*, doi: 10.1177/1464884915570419.

Hess, K. 2016, 'Shifting foundations: Journalism and the power of the common good', *Journalism: Theory Practice Criticism*, doi: 10:1177/1464884915627149.

Hess, K. & Bowd, K. 2015, 'Friend or foe? Regional newspapers and the power of Facebook', *Media International Australia*, no. 156, pp. 19–28.

Hess, K. & Waller, L. 2008, 'An exploratory study of relationships between local government media officers and journalists in regional Australia', *Asia Pacific Public Relations Journal*, vol. 9, pp. 287–302.

Hess, K. & Waller, L. 2009, 'Play it again, Sam: How journalists cashed in on YouTube's favourite koala', *Australian Journalism Review*, vol. 31, no. 2, pp. 75–84.

Hess, K. & Waller, L. 2011, 'Blockbusters for the YouTube generation: A new product of convergence culture', *Refractory*, vol. 19. Retrieved 24 June 2016 online from http://refractory.unimelb.edu.au/2011/08/01/blockbusters-for-the-youtube-generation-a-new-product-of-convergence-culture-%E2%80%93-kristy-hess-and-lisa-waller/.

Hess, K. & Waller, L. 2012, 'The Snowtown we know and love: Small newspapers and heinous crimes', *Rural Society Journal*, vol. 2, no. 12, pp.116–125.

Hess, K & Waller, L. 2013, News judgements: A critical examination of reporting non-convictions for minor crimes, *Australian Journalism Review*, vol. 35, no. 1, pp. 59–70.

Hess, K. & Waller, L. 2015, Community journalism in Australia: A media power perspective, *Community Journalism*, vol. 4, no. 1. Retrieved 29 June 2016 online from http://journal.community-journalism.net/volume-4-issue-1.

Hess, K. & Waller, L. 2014, 'Geo-social journalism: Reorienting the study of small commercial newspapers in a digital environment', *Journalism Practice*, vol. 8, no. 2, pp. 121–136.

Hess, K. & Waller, L. 2016a, 'Hip to be hyper: The subculture of excessively local news', *Digital Journalism*, vol. 4, no. 2, pp. 193–210.

Hess, K. & Waller, L. 2016b 'River flows and profit flows: The powerful logic driving local news', *Journalism Studies*. DOI.10.1080/1461670X.2014.981099.

Hess, K., Waller, L. & Ricketson, M. 2014, 'Are there news gaps in rural/regional Australia? Researching media plurality beyond Finkelstein', *Australian Journalism Review*, vol. 36, no. 2, pp. 157–169.

Hill, S. & Lashmar, P. 2013, *Online journalism: The essential guide*, Sage, London.

Hillary, G. A. 1955, 'Definitions of community: Areas of agreement', *Rural Sociology*, vol. 20, no. 2, pp. 111–123.

Hille, S. & Bakker, P. 2014, 'Engaging the social news user', *Journalism Practice*, vol. 8, no. 5, pp. 563–572.

Hirst, M. 2011, *News 2.0: Can journalism survive the internet?*, Allen and Unwin, Crows Nest, New South Wales.

Hollander, E., Hidayat, D. N. & D'Haenens, L. 2008, 'Community radio in Indonesia', *Javnost-The Public*, vol. 15, no. 3, pp. 59–74.

Hood, L. 2014, 'Remote delivery of local TV news: When local may be hundreds of miles away', *Electronic News*, vol. 8, no. 4, pp. 290–305.

Hopmann, D. N. & Shehata, A. 2011, 'The contingencies of ordinary citizen appearances in political television news', *Journalism Practice*, vol. 5, no. 6, pp. 657–671.

Houpt, S. 2013, 'Toronto Star outsources ad sales, cuts 72 jobs', *The Globe and Mail*. Retrieved 26 June 2016 online from www.theglobeandmail.com/report-on-business/torstar-outsources-ad-sales-cuts-72-jobs/article15449723/ .

Howarth, A. 2015, 'Exploring a curatorial turn in journalism', *M/C Journal*, vol. 18, no. 4. Retrieved 26 June 2016 online from www.journal.media-culture.org.au

Howe, J. 2009, *Crowdsourcing: How the power of the crowd is driving the future of business*, Random House, New York.

Howley, K. 2005, *Community media: People, places and communication technologies*, Cambridge University Press, Cambridge.

Howley, K. 2010, *Understanding community media*, Sage, Thousand Oaks, CA.

Huang, E., Rademakers, L., Fayemiwo, M. & Dunlap, L. 2004, 'Converged journalism and quality: A case study of The Tampa Tribune news stories', *Convergence: The International Journal of Research into New Media Technologies*, vol. 10, pp. 73–91.

Hutchins, B. 2004, 'Castells, regional news media and the information age', *Continuum: Journal of Media and Cultural Studies*, vol. 18, pp. 577–590.

Hutchins, R. 1947, *A free and responsible press: Report of the Commission on Freedom of the Press*, University of Chicago Press, Chicago.

Inglis, T. 2008, *Global Ireland: Same difference*, Routledge, New York.

Iroga, R., 2008, 'Local media's role in peace building in post-conflict Solomon Islands', in E. Papoutsaki, & U. Harris (eds) *South Pacific Islands communication: Regional perspectives, local issues*, Asian Media Information and Communication Centre, Singapore: Nanyang Technological University, pp. 152–174.

Jacobs, J. 1961, *The death and life of great American cities*, Penguin Books in association with Jonathan Cape, Harmondsworth Lauterer.

Janowitz, M. 1967, *The community press in an urban setting: The social elements of urbanism* (2nd ed.), University of Chicago Press, Chicago.

Jarvis, J. 2006, 'Networked journalism'. Buzzmachine weblog. Retrieved 27 June 2016 online from http://buzzmachine.com/2006/07/05/networked-journalism/.

Jeffres, L. W., Lee, J.-W., Neuendorf, K. & Atkin, D. 2007, 'Newspaper reading supports community involvement', *Newspaper Research Journal*, vol. 28, no. 1, pp. 6–23.

Jenkins, H. 2006, *Convergence culture: Where old and new media collide*, New York University Press, New York.

Jiang, F. & Huang, K. 2013, 'Community media in China: Communication, digitalization, and relocation', *Journal of International Communication*, vol. 19, no. 1, pp. 59–68.

Jiménez, NR and Scifo, S. 2010, Community media in the context of European media policies. Telematics and Informatics, vol.27, no. 2. pp. 131–140.

J-Lab/Knight Community News Network. 2014, 'A guide to crowdsourcing'. Retrieved 18 June 2016 online from http://kcnn.org/learning-modules/tools-for-citizen-journalists/a-guide-to-crowdsourcing/

Jolly, R. 2014, *Media of the people: Broadcasting community media in Australia*, Parliament of Australia, Canberra.

Jonsson, A. & Ornebring, H. 2011, 'User-generated content and the news: Empowerment of citizens with interactive illusion?', *Journalism Practice*, vol. 5, no. 2, pp. 127–144.

Jung, J. Y., Toriumi, K. & Mizukoshi, S. 2013, 'Neighborhood storytelling networks, Internet connectedness, and civic participation after the Great East Japan Earthquake', *Asian Journal of Communication*, vol. 23, no. 6, pp. 637–657.

Kaniss, P. 1991, *Making local news*, University of Chicago Press, Chicago.

Kang, S. 2013, 'The elderly population and community engagement in the Republic of Korea: The role of community storytelling network, *Asian Journal of Communication*', vol. 23, no. 3, pp. 302–321.

Kaplan, D. 2013, *Global investigative journalism: Strategies for support*, A report to the Centre for International Media Assistance. Retrieved 27 June 2016 online from www.cima.ned.org/wp-content/uploads/2015/01/CIMA-Investigative-Journalism-Dave-Kaplan.pdf.

Kaye, J. & Quinn, S. 2010, *Funding journalism in the digital age: Business models, strategies, issues and trends*, Peter Lang, New York.

Kelly, S. 2015, *The entrepreneurial journalists toolkit*, Focal Press, Abingdon, Oxon.

Kennedy, D. 2011, 'Indies fight back against Patch', Media Nation, May 11, retrieved 9 July, 2016 online from https://dankennedy.net/2011/05/13/indies-fight-back-against-patch/

Kerkhoven, M. & Bakker, P. 2015, 'Hyperlocal with a mission? Motivation, strategy, engagement', in R. K. Nielsen (ed.) *Local Journalism. The decline of newspapers and the rise of digital media*, Reuters Institute for the Study of Journalism, pp. 185–202.

Khan, S. U. 2010, 'Role of community radio in rural development, *Global Media Journal: Indian Edition*', Jun 2010, pp. 1–9.

Kies, R. 2010, *Promises and limits of web-deliberation*, Palgrave, New York.

Killenberg, G. M. & Dardenne, R. 1997, 'Instruction in news reporting as community-focused journalism', *Journalism & Mass Communication Educator*, vol. 52, no. 1, pp. 52–8.

Kilman, L. 2015 'A profound shift in the newspaper business model, evolving for years is finally here', World Association of Newspapers report. Retrieved 27 June 2016 online from www.wan-ifra.org/press-releases/2015/06/01/world-press-trends-newspaper-revenues-shift-to-new-sources

Kirk, A. 2016, 16 April. 'How does the BBC spend its £3.7b in licence fee money?', *The Telegraph*. Retrieved 2 June 2016 online from www.telegraph.co.uk/news/2016/04/14/how-does-the-bbc-spend-its-5bn-in-licence-fee-money/

Kirkpatrick, R. 1998, 'Shield of the people? The provincial press and the Fourth Estate', *Australian Journalism Review*, vol. 20, no. 2, pp. 82–103.

Kirkpatrick, R. 2010, *The bold type: A history of Victoria's country newspapers*, Country Press Association of Victoria, Ascot Vale, Vic.

Kitamura, Y. 2009, 'Chiho-shi', in J. Hamada, Y. Tajima & K. Katsura (eds) *Shinbungaku*, Nihon Hyoron-sha, Tokyo, pp. 50–59.

Kitch, C. & Hume J. 2008, *Journalism in a Culture of Grief*, Routledge, London.

Kivikuru, U. 2013, 'Upstairs downstairs: Communication contradictions around two African refugee camps', *Journal of African Media Studies*, vol. 5, no. 1, pp. 35–51.

Knight, M. & Cook, C. 2013, *Social media for journalists: Principles and practice*, Sage, London.

Knight Commission on the informational needs of community in a democracy 2009, *Informing communities: sustaining democracy in the digital age*. Washington: The Aspen Institute. Retrieved 16 June 2014 online from www.knightcomm. org/wpcontent/uploads/2010/02/Informing_Communities_Sustaining_ Democracy_in_the_Digital_Age.pdf.

Koch, T. 1991, *Journalism for the 21st century*. Praeger, New York.

Kolodzy, J. 2013, *Practicing convergence journalism*, Routledge, New York.

Kotilainen, S. & Rantala, L. 2009, 'From seekers to activists', *Information, Communication & Society*, vol. 12, no. 5, pp. 658–677.

Kovach, B. & Rosenstiel, T. 2007, *The elements of journalism: What newspeople should know and the public should expect*, 2nd edn. Crown, New York.

Krein, K. 2015, 'Young' talent: Northfield native becomes YouTube sensation, *Northfield News*. Retrieved 27 June 2016 online from www.southernminn.com/ northfield_news/arts_and_entertainment/article_af44e7ca-a813-5a2e-b459- b1dab1f147b6.html.

Kreuters, M., Young, L. & Lezin N. 1998, *Measuring social capital in small communities*. Atlanta, School of Public Health, St Louis University.

Kruger, F. 2011, 'News broadcasting on south African community radio: in search of new public spheres, Ecquid Nowi', *African Journalism studies*, vol. 32 no. 3, pp. 61–79.

Kruger, F. 2012, 'Fourth estate or fifth column? The media on the 2011 campaign trail', in S. Booysen (ed) *Local elections in south Africa, parties, people, politics*. Sub Press, Bloemfontein, pp. 229-244.

Krüger, C. & Swatman, P. M. C. 2002, 'Online regional newspapers: Paths to glory or the road to ruin?', Conference Proceedings 'BIT'2002' – the 12th Annual Business Information Technology Conference, Manchester, England, November 6–7.

Kurpius, D., Metzgar, E. & Rowley, K. 2010, 'Sustaining hyperlocal media', *Journalism Studies*, vol.11, no. 3, pp. 359–376.

Lacy, S. 2011, 'The economics of community newspapers', in J. Hatcher and B. Reader (eds) *Foundations of Community Journalism*, Sage, London, pp. 174–177.

Lang, G. E. & Lang, K. 1981, 'Watergate, an exploration of the agenda-building process', *Mass Communication Review Yearbook*, no. 2, pp. 447–468.

Lauterer, J 1995. *Community journalism: The personal approach.* Ames, IA: Iowa State University Press.

Lauterer, J. 2006, *Community journalism: relentlessly local,* University of North Carolina Press, Chapel Hill.

Lauterer, J. 2014 'In which Editor Li gets it right', *Blues Highway Journal,* Retrieved 26 June 2016 online from http://blogs.web.jomc.unc.edu/bluehighways/?cat=10

Layton, S. 1995, 'The demographics of diversity: Profile of Pacific Island journalists', *Australian Studies in Journalism,* vol. 4, pp. 123–143.

Lealand, G. & Hollings, J. 2012, 'Journalism in New Zealand'. In D. Weaver & L. Willnat (eds) *The global journalist in the 21st century,* Routledge, New York, pp. 126–138.

Lee, D. & Newby, H. 1983, *The Problem of Sociology: an introduction to the discipline,* Unwin Hyman, London.

Lev-On, A. 2012, 'Communication, community, crisis: Mapping uses and gratifications in the contemporary media environment', *New Media & Society,* vol. 14, no. 1, pp. 98–116.

Lewis, J., Williams, A. & Franklin B. 2008, 'A compromised Fourth Estate? UK news journalism, public relations and news sources', *Journalism Studies,* vol. 9, no. 1, pp. 1–20.

Lewis, S. 2011, 'The open source ethos of journalism innovation: Between participation and professional control', Future of Journalism Conference, Cardiff, Wales, 2011.

Lewis, S., Kaufhold, K. & Lasorsa, D. 2010, 'Thinking about citizen journalism: The philosophical and practical challenges of user-generated content for community newspapers', *Journalism Practice,* vol. 4, no. 2, pp. 193–179.

Lim, M. 2003, 'The Internet, Social Networks and Reform in Indonesia', in N. Couldry & J. Curran (eds) *Contesting Media Power,* Roman and Littlefield Publishers, Oxford, pp. 273–288.

Livingston S. & Bennett W. 2003, 'Gatekeeping, indexing and live-event news: Is technology altering the construction of news?', *Political Communication,* vol. 20, no. 4, pp. 363–380.

Lowrey, W., Brozana, A. & Mackay, J. B. 2008, 'Toward a measure of community journalism', *Mass Communication and Society,* vol. 11, pp. 275–299.

Lu, Y. & Chu, Y. 2012, 'Media use, social cohesion, and cultural citizenship: An analysis of a Chinese metropolis, *Chinese Journal of Communication',* vol. 5, no. 4, pp. 365–382.

Lu, V. 2016, 'Bleak times for local journalism in Canada'. Retrieved 26 June 2016 online from www.beta.thesatar.com

Lupton, D. 2015, *Digital Sociology,* Routledge, London.

Lynch, L. 2013, *Exploring Journalism and the Media,* 2nd edition, Mason, OH, South-Western Cengage Learning.

Lyons, M. 2008, *BBC trust rejects local video proposals.* BBC Trust media release, November 11. Retrieved 27 June 2016 online from www.bbc.co.uk/bbctrust/news/press_releases/2008/local_video_prov.html

Lysak, S., Cremedas, M. & Wolf, J. 2012, 'Facebook and Twitter in the newsroom: How and why local TV news is getting social with viewers', *Electronic News,* vol. 6. no. 4, pp. 187–207.

Madamombe, I. 2005, 'Community radio: A voice for the poor'. Retrieved 27 June 2016 online from www.un.org/africarenewal/magazine/july-2005/community-radio-voice-poor.

Maganaka, A., 2004, 'Development journalism coverage among community newspapers in the Philippines', *Journal of Development Communication,* vol.15, no. 1, pp. 1–13.

Magpanthong, C. & McDaniel, D. 2011, 'Media democratization at the crossroads: Community radio in Thailand and Malaysia', *Journal of Radio & Audio Media,* vol. 18, no. 1, pp. 116–128.

Maras, S. 2013, *Objectivity in journalism,* Polity Press, Cambridge.

Martin, J. 2011, 26 May, 'What's so wrong with "parachute journalism"?' *Columbia Journalism Review.*

Martinelli, D. 2012, 'Considering community journalism from the perspective of public relations and advertising', in B. Reader & J. Hatcher (eds), *Foundations of community journalism,* Sage, London, pp. 157–175.

Marymont, K. 2007, 'Mojo a Go-Go', *Quill, 2007 Supplement Journalist,* pp. 18–21.

Maslog, C. C. 2012, 'Asian and American perspectives on community journalism', in B. Reader and J. Hatcher (eds), *Foundations of Community Journalism,* Sage, London, pp. 125–127.

Massey, D. 1994, *Space, place and gender,* Polity Press, Cambridge.

Matbob, P. & Papoutsaki, E. 2008, 'Local media, regional sensitivities: Reporting West Papua's 'independence movement' in the Papua New Guinean press', in E. Papoutsaki & U. Harris, (eds) *South Pacific Islands communication: Regional perspectives, local issues,* Asian Media Information and Communication Centre, Singapore: Nanyang Technological University, pp. 235–253.

Matheson, D. 2007, 'In search of popular journalism in New Zealand', *Journalism Studies,* vol. 8, no. 1, pp. 28–41.

Matsa, K. & Mitchell, A. 2014, 'Eight key takeaways about social media and news'. Retrieved 26 June 2016 from www.journalism.org/2014/03/26/8-key-takeaways-about-social-media-and-news/.

Mayer, J. 2011, 'Engaging communities: Content and conversation', *Neiman Reports,* Summer 2011, pp. 12–14.

McAdams, M. & Berger, S. 2001, 'Hypertext', *The Journal of Electronic Publishing,* vol. 6, Retrieved 27 June 2016 online from www.press.umich.edu:80/jep/06-03/McAdams/pages/.

McChesney, R. 2015, *Rich media, poor democracy: Communication politics in dubious times,* The New Press, New York.

McLuhan, M. & Fiore, Q. 1967, *The medium is the massage,* Allen Lane, London.

McLuhan, M., Fiore, Q. & Agel, J. 2001, *The medium is the massage: An inventory of effects.* Ginko Press, Corte Madera, CA.

McLuhan, M. & Powers, B. 1989, <I>*The global village: Transformations in world life and media in the 21ˢᵗ century*, Oxford University Press, New York.

McManamey, R. 2005, 'Exploring community newspapers and social capital: the micro-giants of media and community – the quiet revolution', *New Community Quarterly*, vol. 3, pp. 3–14.

McNeill, L. 2005 'Writing lives in death: Canadian death notices as auto-biography', in J. Rak (ed.), *Auto/biography in Canada: Critical Directions*, Wilfred Laurier University Press, Waterloo, ON, pp. 187–206.

McQuail, D. 2003, *Media accountability and freedom of publication*, Oxford University Press, Oxford.

McQuail, D. 2013, *Journalism and society*, Sage, London.

Meadows, M., Forde, S., Ewart, J. & Foxwell, K. 2009, 'Making good sense: Transformative processes in community journalism', *Journalism*, vol. 10, no. 2, pp. 155–170.

Mencher, M. 2010, *News: Reporting and writing*, 12ᵗʰ edition, McGraw Hill, New York.

Mersey, R. D. 2009, 'Online news users sense of community', *Journalism Practice*, vol. 3, pp. 347–360.

Mersey, R. D. 2010, *Can journalism be saved? Rediscovering America's appetite for news*, ABC-CLIO, Santa Barbara, CA.

Merritt, D. 1995, *Public journalism and public life: Why telling the news is not enough*, Erlbaum, Hillsdale, NJ.

Merritt, D. 2009, *Public journalism and public life: Why telling the news is not enough*, 2nd edition, Routledge, New York.

Meyrowitz, J. 1985, *No sense of place: The impact of electronic media on social behavior*, Oxford University Press, Oxford.

Mhlanga, B. 2009, 'On the psychology of oppression: Blame me on history', *Critical Arts*, vol. 23, no. 1, pp. 106–112.

Mhiripiri, N. 2011, 'Zimbabwe's community radio "initiatives": Promoting alternative media in a restrictive legislative environment', *Radio Journal: International Studies in Broadcast & Audio Media*, vol. 9, no. 2, pp. 107–126.

Miller, S. 2014, 28 July, 'Beachside tribute from Bunbury family for MH17 victims', *Western Advocate*. Retrieved 27 June 2016 online from www.westernadvocate.com.au/story/2426477/beachside-tribute-from-bunbury-family-for-mh17-victims/

Miller, C. & Stone, B. 2009, 13 April, 'Hyperlocal website delivers news without newspapers', *The New York Times*. Retrieved 27 June 2016 online from http://www.nytimes.com/2009/04/13/technology/start-ups/13hyperlocal.html?_r=1and

Misajon, R. & Khoo, T. 2008, 'Pinoy TV: Imagining the Filipino Australian community', *Journal of Australian Studies*, vol. 32, no. 4, pp. 455–466.

Mitchell, A. 2014, 'State of the news media 2014'. Retrieved 26 June 2016 online from www.journalism.org/2014/03/26/state-of-the-news-media-2014-overview/

Molotch, H. & Lester, M. 1974, 'News as purposive behaviour', *American Sociological Review*, vol. 39, no. 6, pp. 101–112.

Moore, P. 2008, 'From the Bogside to Namibia: The place of community broadcasting in post-conflict cultural reconstruction', *Radio Journal: International Studies in Broadcast & Audio Media*, vol. 6, no.1, pp. 45–58.

Moore, R. 2008, 'Capital', in M. Grenfell (ed.) *Pierre Bourdieu: Key concepts*, Acumen, Durham, pp. 101–118.

Moores, S. 2000, *Media and everyday life in modern society*, Edinburgh University Press, Edinburgh.

Moores, S. 2005. *Media/Theory: Thinking about media and communications*, Routledge, London.

Moores, S. 2012, *Media, place and mobility*, Palgrave MacMillan, New York.

Moring, I. 2000, 'Scales of space, place and money: Discursive landscapes of regional inertia, identity and economical change', *NORDICOM Review*, vol. 21, no. 2, pp. 171–189.

Morley, D. 2000, *Home territories: media, mobility and identity*, Routledge, London.

Moses, L. 2015, 'Has Patch finally cracked the code on hyperlocal', *Digiday*. Retrieved 26 June 2016 from http://digiday.com/publishers/patch-finally-cracked-code-hyperlocal/

Murillo, M. A. 2003, 'Community radio in Colombia: Civil conflict, popular media and the construction of a public sphere', *Journal of Radio Studies*, vol. 10, no. 1, pp.120–140.

Murrell, C. 2015, *Foreign correspondents and international newsgathering: The role of fixers*. Routledge, London.

Murschetz, P. 2013, 'State aid for newspapers: First theoretical disputes', in P. Murschetz (ed.) *State Aid for newspapers: Theories, cases, actions*, Springer, London, pp. 21–48.

Myllylahti, M. 2014, 'Newspaper paywalls – the hype and the reality', *Digital Journalism*, vol.2, no.2, pp.179-194.

Nassanga, G. L., Manyozo, L. & Lopes, C. 2013, 'ICTs and radio in Africa: How the uptake of ICT has influenced the newsroom culture among community radio journalists', *Telematics & Informatics*, vol. 30, no. 3, pp. 258–266.

Ndela, N. 2010, 'Alternative media and the public sphere in Zimbabwe', in K. Howley (ed.), *Understanding Community Media*, Sage, Thousand Oaks, CA, pp. 87–95.

Nee, R. 2014, 'Social responsibility theory and the digital non-profits: Should the government aid online news startups?', *Journalism*, vol. 13, no. 3, pp. 326–343.

Nesta. 2016, 'Our projects'. Retrieved 18 June 2016 online from http://www.nesta.org.uk/project/destination-local

Nethercote, J. 2006, 8 June, The local paper that ignores local news, *Crikey*. Retrieved 23 June 2016 online from www.crikey.com.au/2006/06/08/the-local-paper-that-ignores-local-news/?wpmp_switcher=mobile.

Neveu, E. 2007, 'Pierre Bourdieu', *Journalism Studies*, vol. 8 no. 2, pp. 335–347.

Newman, N. 2014, 'Executive summary and key findings', in *Reuters Institute Digital News Report 2014*, Reuters Institute for the Study of Journalism, University of Oxford, Oxford. Retrieved 26 June 2016 online from https://

reutersinstitute.politics.ox.ac.uk/sites/default/files/Reuters%20Institute%20 Digital%20News%20Report%202014.pdf.

News Media Association 2015, *The BBC's role in the news media landscape: The publishers' view*, retrieved 23 June 2016 online from http://downloads.bbc.co.uk/ bbctrust/assets/files/pdf/our_work/local_radio_news/news_media_association.pdf

Newsmith, S. 2015, 15 September, 'How a Florida newspaper began advocating for better bike safety', *Columbian Journalism Review*. Retrieved 26 June 2016 online http://www.cjr.org/united_states_project/fort_myers_news_press_bicycle_ safety.php

New York Daily News. 2015, 6 July, 'Birds steal skinny-dippers' underwear to build nests in Scotland'. Retrieved 16 June 2016 online from www.nydailynews.com/news/ world/birds-steal-skinny-dippers-underwear-build-nests-article-1.2282696

Nielsen. 2011, *State of the media: Social media report Q3*. Retrieved 27 June 2016 online from www.nielsen.com/us/en/insights/.../2011/social-media-report-q3.html

Nielsen, R. 2015, 'Introduction: The uncertain future of Local Journalism', in R. K. Nielsen (ed.) *local journalism: The decline of newspapers and the rise of digital media*. Reuters Institute for the Study of Journalism, Oxford. pp 1–25.

Nielsen, R. & Linnebank, G. 2011, 'Public support for the media: A six country overview of direct and indirect subsidies', Reuters Institute for the Study of Journalism. Retrieved 27 June 2016 online from http://reutersinstitute.politics. ox.ac.uk/sites/default/files/Public%20support%20for%20Media.pdf.

Nielsen, R. & Schroder, K. C. 2015, 'The relative importance of social media for accessing, finding and engaging with news', *Digital Journalism*, vol. 2, no. 4, pp. 472–489.

Nip, J. 2008, 'The last days of civic journalism'. *Journalism Practice*, vol. 2, no. 2, pp 179–196.

NIST.SEMATECH (2012). *NIST/SEMATECH e-handbook of statistical methods*. Retrieved 27 June 2016 online from www.itl.nist.gov/div898/handbook/.

Noelle-Neumann, E. 1993, *The spiral of silence* (2nd edn), University of Chicago Press, Chicago.

Nord, D. 2015, 'The Victorian city and the urban newspaper' in R. John & J. Silberstein-Loeb (eds) *Making news: The political economy of journalism in Britain and America from the glorious revolution to the internet*, pp. 73–106. Oxford University Press, Oxford.

Nussbaum, M. 2004, *Hiding from humanity: Disgust, shame and the law*, Princetown University Press, Princetown.

Oakes, M. 2015, 17 November, 'Johnston Press launches native ads team', *Media week*. Retrieved 27 June 2016 online from www.mediaweek.co.uk/ article/1373023/johnston-press-launches-native-ads-team

Odine, M. 2013, 'Use of radio to promote culture in South Africa', *Journal of Radio & Audio Media*, vol. 20, no.1, pp. 181–196.

Olorunnisola, A. 2002, 'Community radio: Participatory communication in postapartheid South Africa', *Journal of Radio Studies*, vol. 9, no. 1, pp. 126–145.

O'Neill D. & O'Connor C. 2008, 'The passive journalist: How sources dominate local news', *Journalism Practice*, vol. 2, no. 3, pp. 487–500.

Ornebring, H. 2008, 'The consumer as producer – of what?' *Journalism Studies*, vol. 9, no. 5, pp. 771–785.

Paek, H., So-Hyang Y. & Shah, D. V. 2005, 'Local news, social integration, and community participation: Hierarchical linear modeling of contextual and cross-level effects', *Journalism & Mass Communication Quarterly*, vol. 82, no. 3, pp. 587–606.

Papoutsaki, E. & Harris, U. 2008, Unpacking 'islandness' in South Pacific Islands communication', in E. Papoutsaki & U. Harris (eds) *South Pacific Islands communication: Regional perspectives, local issues*, Asian Media Information and Communication Centre, Singapore: Nanyang Technological University, pp. 1–12.

Park, R. 1922, *The immigrant press and its control*, Harper and Brothers, New York.

Patterson, T. 2000, 'The United States: News in a free-market society', in R. Gunther & A. Mughan (eds) *Democracy and the media: A comparative perspective*, Cambridge University Press, New York, pp. 241–265.

Patton, L. 2015, 'Commercialization and competition in the media sector'. Retrieved 27 June 2016 online from www.valuepartners.com/downloads/PDF.../commercialisation_and_competition.pdf.

Paul, S. 2015, 21 April, 'Survey on media use in Middle East sows return to the local, *Media Shift*. Retrieved 27 June 2016 online from http://mediashift.org/2015/04/survey-on-media-use-in-middle-east-shows-a-return-to-the-local/

Paulussen, S. & D'heer, E. 2013, 'Using citizens for community journalism: Findings from a hyperlocal media project', *Journalism Practice*, vol. 7, no. 5, pp. 588–603.

Paulussen, S., Heinonen, A., Domingo, D. & Quant, T. 2007, 'Doing it together: Citizen participation in the news making process', *Observatorio*, vol. 1, no. 3.

Pauly, J. & Eckert M. 2002, 'The myth of the local', *Journalism & Mass Communication Quarterly*, vol. 79, pp. 310–326.

Pavlik, J. 2000, 'The impact of technology on journalism', *Journalism Studies*, vol. 1, pp. 229–237.

Peters, C. & Broersma, M. 2013, *Rethinking journalism: Trust and participation in a transformed news landscape*, Routledge, London.

Peters, C. & Witschge, T. 2014, From grand narratives of democracy to small expectations of participation. *Journalism Practice*, vol. 9, no. 1, pp. 19–34.

Petley, J. 2013, *Media and public shaming: Drawing the boundaries of disclosure*, Reuters Institute for the Study of Journalism, Oxford University, Oxford.

Petulla, S. 2014, 15 May, 'The Charlotte Observer takes native advertising local', *The Content Strategist*. Retrieved 27 June 2016 online from https://contently.com/strategist/2014/05/15/the-charlotte-observer-takes-native-advertising-local/

Pew Research Centre. 2012, *State of the news media 2012: New devices, platforms spur more news consumption*. Retrieved 27 June 2016 online from www.pewresearch.org/2012/03/19/state-of-the-news-media-2012/

Pew Research Centre. 2013, *State of the News Media 2013*. Retrieved 26 June 2016 online from www.stateofthemedia.org/2013/overview-5/.

Pew Research Centre. 2015, *State of the News Media 2015*. Retrieved 26 June 2016 online from www.journalism.org/2015/04/29/state-of-the-news-media-2015/.

Phillips, A. 2010, 'Old sources new bottles', in N. Fenton (ed.) *New media, old news: Journalism and democracy in the digital age*, Sage, London, pp. 87–101.

Phillips, A. 2015, *Journalism in context: Practice and theory for the digital age*, Routledge, London.

Picard, R. 2014, 'Twilight or new dawn of journalism?', *Digital Journalism*, vol. 2, pp. 1–11.

Picard, R. 2015, 'The humanisation of media? Social media and the reformation of communication', *Communication Research and Practice*, vol. 1, no. 1, pp. 32–41.

Pickard, V. 2015, *America's battle for media democracy*, Cambridge University Press, Cambridge.

Pickard, V. & Williams, A. 2014, 'Salvation or folly? The promises and perils of digital paywalls', *Digital Journalism*, vol. 2, no.2, pp. 195–213.

Picone, I. 2007, 'Conceptualising online news use', *Observatorio Journal*, vol. 3, pp. 93–114.

Pinski, P. 2015, Pamela Pinksi from Digbeth is Good. *Creative Citizens*. Retrieved 26 June 2016 online from https://youtu.be/4i4E9NxjCMA.

Podber, J. 2012, 'Interactive community radio: An examination of community radio in central Mexico', *Intercultural Communication Studies*, vol. 21, no. 1, pp. 131–139.

Poh, K. 2013, *Meld Magazine*, in M Simmons (ed.) *What's next in journalism: Media entrepreneurs tell their story*, Scribe, Brunswick, Vic, pp. 43–51.

Poindexter, P. M., Heider, D. & McCombs, M. 2006, 'Watchdog or Good Neighbor?', *The Harvard International Journal of Press/Politics*, vol. 11, no. 1, pp. 77–88.

Postill, J. 2010, 'Introduction: Theorising media and practice', in J. Postill (ed.) *Theorising media and practice*. Berghahn Books, New York, pp. 1–34.

Powers, M., Zambrano, S. & Baisnee, O. 2015, 'The news crisis compared: The impact of the journalism crisis on local news ecosystems in Toulouse (France) and Seattle (US)', in R. K. Nielsen (ed.) *Local journalism: The decline of newspapers and the rise of digital media*. JB Taurus, London, pp. 31–50.

Poynting, S. 2006, 'What caused the Cronulla riot?' *Race & Class*, vol. 48, no 1, pp. 85–92.

Price, V., Tewksbury, D. & Powers, E. 1997, 'Switching trains of thought: The importance of readers' cognitive responses', *Communication Research*, vol. 24, no. 5, pp. 481–506.

Prochazka, F., Weber, P. & Schwieger, W. 2016, 'Effects of civility and reasoning in user comments on perceived journalistic quality', *Journalism Studies*, doi: 10.1080/1461670X.2016.1161497.

Propp, V. 1975, *Morphology of the folktale*. University of Texas, Austin.

Putnam, R. 2000, *Bowling alone: The collapse and revival of American community*, Simon & Schuster, New York.

Radcliffe, D. 2012, *Here and now: UK hyperlocal media today*. Retrieved 23 June 2016 online from www.nesta.org.uk.

Radcliffe, D. 2015, 'Where are we now? UK hyperlocal media and community journalism in 2015', Cardiff University and Nesta. Retrieved 24 June 2016 online from www.communityjournalism.co.uk/wp-content/uploads/2015/09/C4CJ-Report-for-Screen.pdf.

Radio Centre. 2013, 'Radio Centre response to BBC Trust service review of BBC news and current affairs'. Retrieved 24 June 2016 online from www.radiocentre. org/files/radiocentre_response_to_trust_review_of_bbc_news_and_current_affairs.pdf

Radojković, M. 2009. 'Why can't civil society media grow in Serbia?' *International Journal of Media & Cultural Politics*, vol. 5, no.1–2, pp. 88–101.

Rancho Santa Margarita Patch. 2015, 1 July, 'Dolphin jumps on boat, crashing wedding anniversary'. Retrieved 16 June 2016 online from http://patch. com/california/ranchosantamargarita/dolphin-jumps-boat-crashing-wedding-anniversary

Rausch, A. 2012, *Japan's local newspapers: Chihoshi and revitalization journalism*, Routledge, Abingdon, Oxon.

Reader, B. 2012, 'Drawing from the critical cultural well', in B. Reader and J. Hatcher (eds) *Foundations of community journalism*. Sage, London, pp. 109–123.

Reader, B. & Hatcher, J. 2012, *Foundations of Community Journalism*, Sage, Thousand Oaks, CA.

Reich, Z. 2015, 'Why citizens still rarely serve as news sources: Validating a tripartite model of circumstantial, logistical and evaluative barriers', *International Journal of Communication*, vol. 9, pp. 773–795.

Reider, R. 2013, 21 August, 'Small independent local news makes headlines', *USA Today*. Retrieved 27 June 2016 online from www.usatoday.com/story/ money/columnist/rieder/2013/08/20/small-independent-hyperlocal-news-websites/2676515/

Reporters Without Borders. 2015. *World Press Freedom Index 2015*. Retrieved on 27 June 2016 https://index.rsf.org

Richards, I. 2013, 'Beyond city limits: Regional journalism and social capital', *Journalism*, vol. 14, no. 5, pp. 627–642.

Robie, D. 2004, *Mekim Nuis – South Pacific media, politics and education*. Suva, University of the South Pacific Book Centre.

Robie, D. 2008, 'South Pacific notions of the Fourth Estate: A collision of media models, culture and values', *Media Asia*, vol. 32, no. 2, pp. 86–94.

Robie, D. 2009, 'Diversity reportage in Aotearoa: Demographics and the rise of the ethnic media', *Pacific Journalism Review*, vol. 15, no. 1, pp. 67–91.

Robie, D. 2013, 'Coups, conflicts and human rights: Pacific media paradigms and challenges', *Australian Pacific Media Educator*, vol. 22, no. 2, pp. 217–229.

Robin, M. 2014, 'Modern, subversive and short-lived: A newspaper eulogy', *Crikey*. Retrieved 26 June 2016 online from www.crikey.com.au/2014/02/28/ modern-subversive-and-short-lived-a-newspaper-eulogy/.

Robinson, S. 2009, '"If you had been with us": Mainstream press and citizen journalists jockey for authority over the collective memory of Hurricane Katrina', *New Media and Society*, vol. 11, no. 5, pp. 795–814.

Robinson, S. 2011, 'Anyone can know: Citizen journalism and the interpretive community of the mainstream press'. *Journalism*, vol. 12, no. 8, pp. 963–982.

Robinson, S. 2014, 'Introduction', in S. Robinson (ed.) *Community journalism midst media Revolution*, Routledge, London. pp. 1–9.

Rodríguez, J. M. 2005, 'Indigenous radio stations in Mexico: A catalyst for social cohesion and cultural strength', *Radio Journal: International Studies in Broadcast & Audio Media*, vol. 3, no. 3, pp. 155–169.

Rodríguez, C., Ferron, B. & Shamas, K. 2014, 'Four challenges in the field of alternative, radical and citizens' media research', *Media, Culture & Society*, vol. 36, no. 2, pp. 150–166.

Rorty, R. 1979, *Philosphy and the mirror of nature*, Princeton University Press, Princeton, NJ.

Rose, N. 1996, 'The death of the social? Re-figuring the territory of government', *Economy and Society*, vol. 25, no. 3, pp. 327–356.

Rosen, J. 1997, 'Introduction: "We'll have that conversation" journalism and democracy in the thought of James W. Carey', in E. Stryker-Munson & C. Warren (eds), *James Carey: A critical reader*, University of Minnesota Press, Minneapolis, pp. 191–206.

Rosen, J. 1999, *What are journalists for?*, Vail-Ballou Press, New York.

Rosen, J. 2006, 'The people formerly known as the audience'. *Press Think: Ghost of Democracy in the Media Machine*. Retrieved 23 June 2016 online from http://archive.pressthink.org/2006/06/27/ppl_frmr.html.

Rosenberry, J. 2012, 'Some connections between journalism and community', in B. Reader & J. Hatcher (eds) *Foundations of Community Journalism*, Sage, Los Angeles, pp. 25–42.

Rosenberry, J. 2014, Classic elements engagement in the US apply to Irish online community news sites', *Community Journalism*, vol. 4, no. 1. Retrieved 26 June 2016 online from http://journal.community-journalism.net/articles/classic-elements-engagement-us-journalism-apply-irish-online-community-news-sites

Rogers, R., Weltevrede E., Borra E. & Niederer S. 2013, 'National web studies' in J. Hartley, J. Burgess & A. Bruns (eds) *A Companion to new media dynamics*, Wiley-Blackwell, Oxford, pp. 142–166.

Rosenstiel, T., Mitchell, A., Rainie, L. & Purcell, K. 2011, 'Survey: Mobile news and paying online', in *The State of the News Media 2011: An annual report on American journalism*. Pew Research Center's Project for Excellence in Journalism.

Rothenbuhler, E. W. 1998, *Ritual communication: from everyday conversation to mediated ceremony*. Sage, Thousand Oaks.

Rothenbuhler, E. W. 2006, 'Communication as ritual', in G. J. Shepherd, J. St John & T. Striphas (eds) *Communication as -; Perspective on Theory*, Sage, London, pp. 13–21.

Rubury, M. 2009, *The novelty of newspapers: Victorian fiction after the invention of the news*, Oxford University Press, New York.

Ruggiero, T. 2004, 'Paradigm repair and changing journalism perceptions of the internet as an objective news source', *Convergence*, vol. 10, no. 4, pp. 92-106.

Saleem, N. & Hanan, M. 2014, 'Media and conflict resolution: Toward building a relationship model', *Journal of Political Studies*, vol. 21, no. 1, pp. 179–198.

Saleh, N. 2013, *The complete guide to article writing*, Writers Digest Books, Cincinnati, OH.

Salgado, S. & Strömbäck, J. 2012, 'Interpretive journalism: A review of concepts, operationalizations and key findings', *Journalism*, vol. 13, no. 2, pp. 144–161.

Savage, M., Bagnall, G. & Longhurst, B. J. 2005, 'Local habitus and working class culture', in F. Devine, M. Savage, J. Scott & R. Crompton (eds), *Rethinking class: Culture, identities and lifestyle*, Palgrave, London, pp. 95–122.

Schudson, M. 1995, *The power of news*, Harvard University Press, Cambridge, MA.

Schudson, M. 2001, 'The objectivity norm in American journalism', *Journalism*, vol. 2, pp. 149–170.

Schudson, M. 2013, 'Would journalism please hold still!', in C. Peters & M. Broersma (eds) *Rethinking journalism*. Routledge, Abingdon, Oxon, pp. 191–205.

Schulhofer-Wohl, S. & Garrido, M. 2013, 'Do newspapers matter? Short-run and long-run evidence from the closure of The Cincinnati Post,' Journal of Media Economics, vol. 26, no. 2, pp. 60–81.

Schultz, I. 2007, 'The journalistic gut feeling', *Journalism Practice*, vol. 1, no. 2, pp 190–207.

Schultz, J. 1998, *Reviving the fourth estate: Democracy, accountability and the media*. Cambridge University Press, Cambridge.

Scott, J., Millard D. & Leonard P. 2015, 'Citizen participation in news: Do online news users choose sites that match their interests and preferences', *Digital Journalism*, vol. 3, no. 5, pp 737–758.

Scotton, J. & Hatchen, W. 2010, *New media for a new China*, Wiley-Blackwell, West Sussex.

Scutari, M. 2015, 'A closer look at the Knight Foundation's "venture capital" fund for local news outlets', *Inside Philanthropy*..Retrieved 26 June 2016 online from www.insidephilanthropy.com/journalism/2015/1/8/a-closer-look-at-the-knight-foundations-venture-capital-fund.html.

Selvin, B. 2015, 'The status of editorial writing in Australian, Canadian and US weekly newspapers', *Community Journalism*, vol. 4, no. 1. Retrieved 23 June 2016 online from http://journal.community-journalism.net/articles/status-editorial-writing-australian-canadian-and-us-weekly-newspapers.

Sennett, R. 2012, *Together: The rituals, pleasures and politics of cooperation*, Yale University Press, Boston.

Shah, D. V., McLeod, J. M. & Yoon, S. H. 2001, 'Communication, context and community', *Communication Research*, vol. 28, no. 4, pp. 464–506.

Sharma, A. 2011, 'Emergence of community radio: Harnessing potential role for rural development', *Journal of Development Communication*, vol. 22, no. 2, pp. 29–50.

Shoemaker, P., Lee, J. H., Gang, K. & Cohen, A. 2007, 'Proximity and scope as news values', in E. Devereaux (ed.) *Media studies: Key issues and debates*, Sage, London, pp. 231–248.

Shoemaker, P. & Reese, S. 2014, *Mediating the message in the 21st century*. Routledge, New York.

Siebert, F., Peterson, T. & Schramm, Q. 1956, *Four theories of the press: The authoritarian, libertarian, social responsibility and soviet communist concepts of what the press should be and do*, University of Illinois Press, Urbana.

Sigelman, L. 1973, 'Reporting the news: An organisational analysis', *American Journal of Sociology*, vol. 79, pp. 132–150.

Singer, J. 2004, 'Strange bedfellows? The diffusion of convergence in four news organizations', *Journalism Studies*, vol. 5, no. 1, pp. 3–18.

Singer, J. 2010, 'Journalism in the network' in S. Allan (ed.), *Routledge companion to news and journalism*, Routledge, London, pp. 277–286.

Singer, J., Domingo, D. & Heinonen, A. 2011. *Participatory journalism: Guarding open gates at online newspapers*, Oxford, Wiley-Blackwell.

Singh, S. & Prakash, S. 2008, 'Storms in the Pacific: The volatile mix of democracy, politics and media in three island states', in E. Papoutsaki & U. Harris (eds) *South Pacific Islands communication: Regional perspectives, local issues*, Asian Media Information and Communication Centre, Singapore, Nanyang Technological University, pp. 117–134.

Sirianni, C. & Friedland, L. 2001, *Civic innovation in America: Community empowerment, public policy and the movement for civic renewal*, University of California Press, Berkeley.

Sissons, H. 2006, *Practical journalism: How to write news*, Sage, London.

Sjøvaag, H. 2014, 'Homogenisation or differentiation? The effects of consolidation in regional newspaper market', *Journalism Studies*, vol. 15, no. 5, pp. 511–521.

Smith, L., Tanner, A. & Duhé, S. F. 2007, 'Convergence concerns in local television', *Journal of Broadcasting & Electronic Media*, vol. 51, pp. 555–573.

Smyrnaios, N., Marty, E. & Bousquet, F. 2015, 'Between journalistic diversity and economic constraints: Local pure players in Southern France', in R. K. Nielsen (ed.) *Local journalism: The decline of newspapers and the rise of digital media*. JB Taurus, London, pp. 165–184.

Society of Professional Journalists. 2000, *SPJ Code of Ethics*. Retrieved 26 June 2016 online from www.spj.org/ethicscode.asp.

Soeffer, H. 1997, *The order of rituals: The interpretation of everyday life*, Transaction Publishers, New Jersey.

Song, Y. & Chang, T. K., 2013, 'The news and local production of the global: Regional press revisited in post-WTO China', *International Communication Gazette*, vol. 75, no. 7, pp. 619–635.

Sparks, C., 2000, 'Dead trees to live wires', in J. Curran & M. Gurevitch (eds), *Mass media and society*, Oxford University Press, New York. pp 268–292.

Stamm, K. R. 1988, 'Community ties and media use', *Critical Studies in Mass Communication*, vol. 5, no. 4, pp. 357–361.

Standring, S. 2008, *The Art of Column Writing*, Illinois, Marion Street Press.

Starck, N. 2006, *Life after death. The art of the obituary*, Melbourne, Melbourne University Press.

Starkey, G. 2011, *Local radio, going global*. Palgrave Macmillan, Basingstoke.

State of the Media white paper, 2014, Retrieved 27 June 2016 online from http://www.cision.com/us/resources/white-papers/state-of-the-media-report-2014/

Stassen, W. 2010, 'Your news in 140 characters: Exploring the role of social media in journalism', *Global Media Journal: African Edition*, vol. 4, no. 1, pp. 1–16.

Sun, W. 2012, 'Localizing Chinese media: A geographic turn in media and communication research', in W. Sun, and J. Chio (eds), *Mapping media in China: Region, province, locality*, Routledge, New York. pp. 13–28.

Sweney, M. 2012, 'Louise Mensch calls for subsidies for local newspapers', *The Guardian*. Retrieved 27 June 2016 online from www.theguardian.com/media/2012/apr/25/louise-mensch-subsidies-local-newspapers.

Swidler A. 2001, 'What anchors cultural practices', in T. Schatzki, C. Knorr & E. Von Savigny (eds) *The practice turn in contemporary theory*, Routledge, London, pp. 74–92.

Sylvie, G., Wicks, J., Hollifield, C., Lacy, S. & Sohn, A. 2004, *Media management: A casebook approach* (4th edn), Lawrence Erlbaum, Mahwah, NJ.

Tacchi, J. & Grubb, B. 2007, 'The case of the e-tuktuk', *Media International Australia Incorporating Culture & Policy*, no. 125, pp. 71–82.

Tate, C. D. & Taylor, S. A. 2014, *Scholastic journalism*, 12th edn, Wiley-Blackwell.

Tezon, A. 2003, 'Cheerleaders, watchdogs and community builders: How rural weekly newspaper publishers in the Midwest view their roles', Newspapers & Community-Building Symposium IX. Kansas City, Mo., 25–26 September.

Tiffen, R. 2009, 'Australian journalism', *Journalism*, vol. 10, no. 3, pp. 384–386.

Titangos H., 2013, *Local community in the era of social media technologies: A global approach*, Chandos Publishing, Oxford.

Thomas, J. 2006, 'The regional and local media in Wales', in B. Franklin (ed.), *Local journalism and local media: making the local news*, Routledge, London, pp. 49–65.

Thurman, N. & Lupton, B. 2008, 'Convergence calls: Multimedia storytelling at British news websites', *Convergence: The International Journal of Research into New Media Technologies*, vol. 14, no. 4, pp. 439–455.

Tonnies, F. 1957, *Community and Society (Gemeinschaft and Gesellschaft, 1887)* trans. by Charles P. Loomis, Michigan State University Press, East Lansing.

Townend, J. 2015, 'Hyperlocal media and the news marketplace', in S. Barnett and J. Townend (eds) *Media power and plurality: From hyperlocal to high-level policy*, Palgrave Macmillan, London, pp. 83–98.

Tsfati, Y. & Livio, O. 2008, 'Exploring journalists' perceptions of media impact', *Journalism & Mass Communication Quarterly*, vol. 85, no. 1, pp. 113–130.

Tuan, Y. 1977, *Space and place: The perspective of experience*, University of Minnesota Press, Minneapolis.

Tuchman, G. 1978, *Making news*. Free Press, New York.

Tuchman, G. 2002, 'The production of news', in K. Jensen (ed.) *A handbook of media and communication research*, Routledge, London, pp. 78–97.

Tumber, H. & Prentoulis, M. 2005, 'Journalism and the making of a profession' in H. de Burgh (ed.), *Making Journalists*, Routledge, New York, pp. 58–74.

Turner, G. 2003, *British Cultural Studies: An Introduction*, 3rd ed, Routledge, London.

Ullah, M. S. & Chowdhury, M. A. 2006, 'Community radio movement in Bangladesh: In search of lobbying strategies', *Journal of Development Communication*, vol. 17, no.2, pp. 20–32.

Ullah, M.S. 2014, 'De-westernization of media and journalism education in South Asia: In search of a new strategy', *China Media Research*, vol. 10, no. 2, pp. 15–23.

University of Sussex. 2014, 22 August, 'Sussex computer scientists help innovation centre to "make media local"', *Sussex University Staff Bulletin*. Retrieved 26 June 2016 online from www.sussex.ac.uk/internal/bulletin/staff/201314/22082014/innovation_centre_project_makes_media_local

Ursell, G. 2001, 'Dumbing down or shaping up? New technologies, new media, new journalism', *Journalism*, vol. 2, pp. 175–196.

Van Gelder, T. 2013, 'Your view', in M. Simmons (ed.) *What's next in journalism: Media entrepreneurs tell their story*, Scribe, Brunswick, Vic, pp. 28–35.

Van Kerkhoven, M. & Bakker, P. 2014, 'The hyperlocal in practice: Innovation, creativity and diversity', *Digital Journalism*, vol. 2, no.3, pp. 296–309.

van Vuuren, K. 2007, 'Contours of community: The independent community press in South-East Queensland', *Media International Australia*, no. 124, pp. 96–107.

Vicente, C., Freni, D., Bettini, C. & Jenson, C. 2011, 'Location-related privacy in geo-social networks', *IEEE Internet Computing*, vol. 15, no. 3, pp. 20–27.

Voakes, P. 2004, 'A brief history of public journalism', *National Civic Review* (fall issue 2), pp. 24–36.

Voltmer, K. & Wasserman, H. 2014, 'Journalistic norms between universality and domestication: Journalists' interpretations of press freedom in six new democracies', *Global Media and Communication*, vol. 10, no. 2, pp. 1–16.

Wagenknecht, 2014, 'Can the wall pay out? Selected research results on the theory and practice of newspaper paywalls'. Accessed 27 June 2016 online from www.grin.com/en/e-book/272924/can-the-wall-pay-out-selected-research-results-on-the-theory-and-practise

Wahl-Jorgensen, K. 2005, 'Threats to local journalism in Britain: The market vs. the right to communicate', *Javnost-The Public*, vol. 12, no. 3, pp. 79–93.

Wahl-Jorgensen, K. 2010. 'News production, ethnography and power: On the challenges of newsroom-centricity', in S. Elizabeth Bird (ed.) *The anthropology of news and journalism: Global perspectives*, Indiana University Press, Bloomington, pp 21–34.

Waisbord, S. 2009, 'Advocacy journalism in a global context', in K. Wahl-Jorgensen & T. Hanitzsch (eds), *The handbook of journalism studies*, Routledge, New York, pp. 371–385.

Waisbord, S. 2013, *Reinvesting professionalism: Journalism and news in global perspective*, Wiley, Cambridge.

Waldman, S. 2011, 'Information needs of communities: The changing media landscape in a broadband age'. Retrieved 27 June 2016 online from www.fcc.gov/infoneedsreport.

Waller, L. & Hess, K. 2015, 9 July, 'The myths big media peddle to demand deregulation', *The Conversation*. Retrieved 27 June 2016 online from http://theconversation.com/the-myths-big-media-peddle-to-demand-deregulation-

Wasko, J. 2014, 'The study of the political economy of the media in the twenty-first century', *International Journal of Media and Cultural Politics*, vol. 10, no. 3, pp. 259–271.

Watson, J. & Hill, A. 2000, *A dictionary of communication and media studies*, 4th edition, Arnold, London.

Weaver D. H. and Willnat L. (eds), 2012 *The global journalist in the 21st century*, Routledge, New York.

Webb, J., Schirato, T. & Danaher, G. 2002, *Understanding Bourdieu*, Allen and Unwin, Crows Nest, New South Wales.

Weiss, D. 2009, 'Journalism and theories of the press', in S. Littlejohn (ed) *Encyclopedia of communication theory*, Sage, London, pp. 574–579.

Wicked Local Plymouth 2015, 'Our view: We're looking for followers', *Wicked Local Plymouth*, 15 July 2015. Retrieved 27 June 2016 from http://plymouth.wickedlocal.com/article/20150715/NEWS/150718351/?Start=1

Williams, A., Harte, D. & Turner, J. 2014, 'The value of UK hyperlocal community news: Findings from a content analysis, an online survey and interviews with producers', *Digital Journalism*, vol. 3, no. 5, pp. 680–703.

Williams, A., Wardle, C. & Wahl-Jorgensen, K. 2011, 'Have they got news for us?', *Journalism Practice*, vol. 5, no. 1, pp. 85–99.

Willnat, L., Weaver, D. & Choi, J. 2013, 'The global journalist in the 21st century: A cross-national study of journalistic competencies. *Journalism Practice*, vol. 7, no. 2, pp. 163–183.

Witschge, T. & Nygren, G. 2009, 'Journalism: A profession under pressure?', *Journal of Media Business Studies*, vol. 6, no. 1, pp. 37–59.

Wotanis, L. 2012, 'When the weekly leaves town: The impact of one news-room's relocation on sense of community', *Community Journalism*, vol. 1 no. 1, pp. 11–28.

Wylie, F. 2015, 'Are we biased? You bet!', *Oolagah Lake Leader*, October 8, p. 4.

Yu, R. 2015, 29 June, 'TEGNA, Gannett go separate ways as print spin off is completed, *USA Today*. Retrieved 27 June 2016 online from www.usatoday.com/story/money/2015/06/29/tegna-gannett-split-completed/29455687/

Zahariadis, N. 2013, 'Industrial subsidies: Surveying macroeconomic policy approaches', in P. Murschetz (ed.), *State Aid for newspapers: Theories, cases, actions*, Springer, London, pp. 59–72.

Zelizer, B. 2004, *Taking journalism seriously: News and the academy*. Sage, Thousand Oaks, CA.

Zelizer, B. 2012, 'On the shelf life of democracy in journalism scholarship.' *Journalism*, vol. 14, no. 4, pp. 459–473.

Zelizer, B. & Allan, S. 2010, *Keywords in news and journalism studies*, Open University Press, New York.

Zhang, S. 2014, *Impact of globalisation on the press in China*, Lexington Books, Plymouth.

Index

Abernathy, Penny, 62
Aceh Nias Reconstruction Radio
  Network, 70
activism and local media, 66–7
Adornato, Anthony, 139, 140
advertising, 164–6
  for sale, 165
  native advertising, 165
  personal ads, 165
  real estate, 165
advocacy, 8–9, 95, 111–34
advocacy journalism, 9, 112, 121–7
  difference from public journalism,
    121–2
  fundraising, 125
  local examples, 125
  role of local media, 123–5
Africa
  activism and local media, 66–7
  community radio, 66–7
  humanitarian aid, 67
  role of community radio, 5
Africa Renewal Project, 65–6
Aldridge, Meryl, 132
Algan, Ece, 74
Allan, Stuart, 179
alternative media, 53–4, 122–3
  existence outside power structures,
    53–4
AltReading, 157
Anderson, Benedict, 27, 54
Anderson, Rob, 108
Applegate, Edd, 122
Arab Spring, 73–4
audience
  conversation with, 153–4
  journalism's relationship with, 13
  opinion, 130–1
  role and motivation, 28
Austin, Paige, 94–5

Australian Broadcasting Corporation
  (ABC), 75, 173–4
Aviles, Jose, 82
Aziz, R., 103–4

Backfence, 172
Baines, David, 154–5
Bakker, Piet, 137, 147
Baloun, Karel, 168
Barnett, Steven, 169, 171, 172, 182
Barton Wood, Robb, 74
Bauer, Christine, 180
BBC, 158, 24, 63, 105, 173
  local news, 24, 176–7
Berger, Stephanie, 147–8
Berkowitz, Dan, 97, 105
Bijoor, Harish, 185
Bird, Elizabeth, 193
Birks, Jen, 126
Birmingham School, 26
births, deaths and marriages, 106–7
Bolivarian Revolution, 73
Bollinger, Lee C., 86
bonding, 114
Booker, Christopher, 92
Boorstin, Daniel, J., 127
boosterism, 126–7, 128, 131–2
Bourdieu, Pierre, 29–30, 31–4, 36, 45,
  49, 53, 86, 98–9, 112–13, 120–1,
  184
Bowd, Kathryn, 52, 169
Boyle, Susan, 21, 149
Breeze FM (Zambia), 183
bridging, 114
bridging social capital, 115–21
Brisset-Foucault, Florence, 67
Bristol Cable, 181
Broadcasting Act 1996 (UK), 63
Brozana, Amanda, 39
Bruns, Axel, 102

Buchanan, Carrie, 56
Buffett, Warren, 163
Burke, Edmund, 14
Burns, Lynette Sheridan, 85
business models of local news, 50,
    162–87
  economies of scale, 167
  paywalls, 166–8
  see also funding models for local
    media; government funding for
    media; subsidies
business of news, 154–9
  acumen of journalists, 155–6

Caerphilly Observer, 141
campaign journalism, 112, 122–3
  Scotland, 126
Canadian Association of Journalists,
    61
Canadian Broadcasting Corporation,
    60–1
Canter, Lily, 178, 179
capital, 31, 32, 33–4, 46, 184–5
  see also bridging social capital;
    cultural capital; mediated social
    capital; symbolic capital
Carey, James, 18, 26, 115, 116
Carlson, Matt, 95
Carlyle, Thomas, 14
Carroll, John, 93
Carthaginian, 151–2
Carvajal, Miguel, 82
Cass, J., 63, 87, 151–2
Castells, Manuel, 40–1
centralization of newsrooms, 169–71,
    192
  problems, 172
Centre for Community Journalism,
    Cardiff University, 63–4
Chandrasekhar, P., 72
Chang Tsan-Kuo, 69
Chaoyang TV, 25
Charlotte Observer, 165–6
Chicago School, 3
China
  great Internet firewall, 67
  grey zones, 68
  local media, 68–70
  party newspaper, 69
  state control of media, 5, 24–5, 68
Chiou, Lesley, 166
Chiumbu, Sarah, 67
Chomsky, Noam, 21–2
Chowdhury, Badrul Haider, 72
Christians, Clifford, 87–8, 190
Chu Yajie, 69
churnalism, 100
circulation figures: drop in, 39–40
citizen journalism, 19, 177–8
Citizen's Eye, 178
City Talking (Leeds), 141
civic involvement, 3
  see also community
civic journalism, 114
  facilitating conversations, 116–18
  see also public journalism
civic mapping, 117
civic republicanism, 18
Clark, Curtiss, 103–4
click bait, 42–3
climate change, 59
co-creation, 20
Cohn, David, 181
Coleman, Stephen, 17
commodification of news, 23–5
Communications Act 2003 (UK), 63
community, 6, 7, 37, 51–5, 180
  dark side, 54–5
  integration, 3
  involvement, 87
  management, 153–4
  rural, 52
  sense of, 60
  symbolic power and, 54
  ties, 3–4, 16
  see also local
community journalism, 61
  responsibilities to community and
    society, 150–4
community media, 53–4
  existence outside power structures,
    53–4
  regional Australian, 75–6
community radio
  Africa, 5, 65–7
  Australia, 76–7

community radio – *continued*
  El Salvador, 73
  Indonesia, 71
  Ireland, 65
  South Africa, 65–6
  South America, 73
conflict resolution, 91–2
  journalists as de-escalation agents, 91
Conrad, David, 67
contact book, 96
convergence journalism, 19, 20–1,
  138
  United Kingdom, 21
  United States, 21
convergence theory, 19–21
Costera Meijer, Irene, 81
Couldry, Nick, 28, 29–30, 45, 189
Country Press Australia/Deakin
  University cadet journalism
  course, 117
Country Women's Association of
  Australia (CWA), 8–9
Craft, Stephanie, 116
Craig, Geoffrey, 108
credibility
  local habitus and, 49–51
Cremedas, Michael, 139
critical cultural well, 27
critical political economy of communication, 22, 29
  divergence from cultural studies
    approach, 28–31
crowd funding, 181
  subscription combined with, 181
crowdsourcing, 179–80
cultural capital, 48–9, 184–5
cultural codes, 85
cultural studies approach, 26–8, 29
  divergence from political economy
    approach, 28–31
curatorial journalism, 144, 146–7
  digital curation, 146
  hyperlinking, 147–8
  image curation, 149
  local news, 149–50
  social media, 148–9

D'heer, Evelien, 82
Danaher, Geoff, 37

Das, Rajesh, 72
Davies, Nick, 100
Davis, Aeron, 99–100
de Tocqueville, Alexis, 16
  theory of democracy, 16
de-professionalization of journalism,
  23
democracy, 8–9
  deliberative, 15
  democratic theory, 8, 13–19, 189
  grassroots, 9
  radical, 16
  role of journalism in, 13–14
Deuze, Mark, 23, 55
development journalism, 72, 126
Dewey, John, 26
Digbeth, 156–7
digital curation, 146
  hyperlinking, 147–8
digital media, 2
digital revolution, 1, 2, 59, 139
disaster journalism, 101–4
  ethical responsibility, 103
  role of local media, 102, 103, 104
  sense of community, 101
  situational information, 102
dispersion of newsrooms, 169–71, 192
  problems, 172
diversification of media, 25
diversity, 191–3
Doctor, Ken, 141
Donohue, George A., 98
Durkheim, Émile, 52, 188

e-tuktuk, 72
Eckert, Melissa, 44
editorials, 128–30
elite sources, 96–100, 116
  agents of power elite, 98
  influence on news, 93
  local identities, 98–9
  power elite, 97–100
  prominent individuals, 93, 98–9
embodied knowledge, 46
  see also habitus; local
Engels, Frederick, 21
entrepreneurial journalism, 154–9
entrepreneurship, 158–9
Erzikova, Elina, 81

ethnic
  broadcasting, 76–7
  press, 3
Eyjafjallajokull volcano eruption,
    41–2

Facebook, 30, 61, 104, 130–1, 168–9
Fairfax Digital Media, 42
faith-based broadcasting, 79
Federation of Red Cross and Red
    Crescent Societies, 102
Felle, Tom, 64–5
Fenton, Natalie, 28, 63
field, 46
  in journalism, 31, 32–3
Filho, Adilson, 73
Finkelstein inquiry, 76
Firmstone, Julie, 17
fixers, 75
flow, 40–1
  space of, 40, 41
Forde, Susan, 77, 123
Fourth Estate function, 10, 13, 14, 59,
    62–3, 116, 118
Frankfurt School, 21
Franklin, Bob, 43, 95, 100
Freelon, Deen, 131
Friedland, Lewis, 117, 119
funding models for local media,
    164–76
  see also crowd funding; crowdsourc-
    ing; government funding for
    media; philanthropic funding

Galtung, Johan, 85, 88–95
Gannett Company, 25, 162, 166
gatekeeping role of journalists, 130–1
Gatua, M.W., 66
Gaziano, Cecile, 151
Gehl, Robert, 21, 148–9
Gemeinschaft, 52
geo-social
  context, 36–58, 56, 170
  model, 36–7
  news, 6
  social dimension, 40–3
  see also proximity
geography: media boundaries, 38–9
Gesellschaft, 52

Get Reading, 157
Glasser, Theodore, 116
global
  financial crisis, 164–5
  local production of, 69
  village, 40
globalization
  impact on media, 6
Golding, Peter, 21
Goldstein, Ken, 60
Google, 30
government funding for media, 172–6
  Europe, 174
  United States, 174–5
Graber, Doris, 93
Greene, Graham, 190
Greenslade, Roy, 182
Grubb, Ben, 72
Gurner, Richard, 141
Guth, David, 127
Gutsche, Ted, 131–2

Haas, Tanni, 118, 120
Habermas, Jürgen, 15, 16–17, 18
habitus, 31, 32, 33
  local, 46–9
Halbert, John, 143–4
Hanan, Mian, 91
Hanusch, Folker, 77
Harcup, Tony, 92, 94, 95
Hardy, Jonathan, 22
Harris, Usha, 79
Harrison, Mark, 158
Hatcher, John, 16, 152
Heider, Don, 115, 116
Hermida, Alf, 178
Hess, Kristy, 27, 47, 54–5, 113, 169
Hillary, George, 53
Hollander, Ed, 71
Hood, Lee, 170
Howarth, Anita, 146
Howley, Kevin, 53, 123
Huang Kuo, 68
Huang, Edgar, 138
human interest, 93–4
humanitarian aid, 67
Hume, Janice, 104, 106
Hurricane Katrina, 104
Hutchins, Robert Maynard, 14–15

Hynds, Ernest C., 122
hyperlocal enclaves, 55
hyperlocal media, 2, 3, 43, 63–4, 112, 139, 153
  Belgium, 82
  start-ups, 5

imagined community, 27
Indian Ocean tsunami, 70
Indonesian envelope journalism, 70
industrialized model of news, 86
infotainment, 92
Inglis, Tom, 46
integration of media, 25–6
International Society of Weekly Newspapers (US), 125
interpretive journalism, 144, 145–6
Ionescu, Daniel, 118

Janowitz, Morris, 3
Japan earthquake, 70
Japan Local Newspaper Association, 70
Jenkins, Henry, 19–20
Jiang Fei, 68
Johnston Press, 166
Jönsson, Anna Maria, 179
journalism, *see* local journalism, journalistic practices
journalistic *doxa*, 86–7
journalistic practices
  changing job opportunities, 137
  changing skill requirements, 135–62
  changing work practices, 138–9
  curatorial skills, 154–50
  entrepreneurial skills, 154, 158–9
  identifying opportunities, 157–8
  interpretation skills, 144–50
  maintaining correct distance, 151–2
  multimedia skills, 137–44
  networking, 156–7
  role convergence, 138
  technological change, 136, 137–44
  working conditions, 155
  see also de-professionalization of journalism

Kaniss, Phyllis, 44
Kennedy, Ciara, 154–5

Khan, Saad Ullah, 72
Kilman, Larry, 141
Kim, Tayne, 165
Kirkpatrick, Rod, 122
Kitamura, Yukiya, 117
Kitch, Carolyn, 104, 106
Kivikuru, Ullamaija, 67
Kolodzy, Janet, 19

labour conditions, 23
Lang, Gladys, 90
Lang, Kurt, 90
Las Vegas Review-Journal, 23
Lauterer, Jock, 69–70, 130, 155
Lee, David, 53
Leicester Mercury, 179
letters to the editor, 130–1
Lev-On, Azi, 74
Lewis, Justin, 100
Lewis, Seth, 178
Li Guo Chen, 69
Ligaga, Dina, 67
linking, 14–15
Livio, Oren, 74
local media
  Africa, 5, 65–7
  Aotearoa New Zealand, 77–8
  Asia, 67–73
  Australia, 75–7
  Bangladesh, 72
  Brazil, 73
  Canada, 60–1
  centralization of news, 4, 163, 169–71
  China, 67, 68–70
  as community champions, 111–34
  decline in daily press, 61
  declining newsrooms, 4
  economics, 162–87
  Europe, 80–2
  geography of, 38–9
  Germany, 80
  historical ties, 38–9
  India, 72
  Indonesia, 67, 70–1
  Ireland, 64–5
  Israel, 74–5
  Japan, 70
  Korea, 70

maintenance of traditions, 5, 105–7
Malaysia, 71
Middle East, 73–5
Nepal, 72
Netherlands, 81
nominal nature of, 4, 5
North America, 60–3
Oceania, 75–80
Palestine, 74–5
premises, 1
regional differences, 59–83
role, 1
Rwanda, 67
Scandinavia, 81
Serbia, 81
South Africa, 65–6
South America, 73
South Pacific, 78–80
Sri Lanka, 72
staff cuts, 162
Thailand, 71
Turkey, 74
United Kingdom, 63–4
United States, 61–3
local news
    challenges, 2
    changing views of, 9–10
    community responsibility, 150–4
    defining, 85
    democratic theory and, 16–19
    digital form, 5
    diverse styles, 5
    embracing change, 10–11
    importance to people, 59
    as niche product, 183
    as practice, 5
    as product, 5
    shaping, 84–110
    studying, 190–1
    see also local media
local
    connections, 50–1
    embodiment of, 45–6
    in geo-social context, 43–4
    identity, 44–5
    knowledge, 48–9, 50–1
    meaning, 4–5, 6–7, 36–58
    practical, 45–6
    status of journalists, 49

theoretical perspectives, 44–5
local public sphere, 8
local-global network, 40–1
localmind.com, 180
Lowrey, Wilson, 39, 81, 87
Lu Ye, 69
Lupton, Ben, 20
Lynch, Lorrie, 128
Lysak, Suzanne, 139

Mackay, Jenn, 39
Madamombe, Itai, 65–6
Maganaka, Albert, 126
Magpanthong, Chalisa, 71
Mandela, Nelson, 65
Marx, Karl, 21
Massey, Doreen, 57
Matbob, Patrick, 80
Matheson, Donald, 77
McAdams, Mindy, 147–8
McChesney, Robert, 21
McCombs, Maxwell, 115, 116
McDaniel, Drew, 71
McDowell, Walter, 143–4
McGrath, Kristin, 151
McLuhan, Marshall, 40
McQuail, Denis, 136–7
media concentration, 24
Media Development Investment
    Fund, 182–3
media ownership, 22–3
    see also media power
media power, 29–31
    dark side, 131–2
    lens, 12–13, 54
    local, 6
    myth of mediated centre, 29–31
mediated social capital, 112–15, 121
    collective, 113
    community newspaper content as,
    113
    forms of, 114–15
mediation, journalism as, 14
Meld Magazine, 156
Mencher, Melvin, 85, 91
Mensch, Louise, 175
Merritt, Davis 'Buzz', 92, 115, 118–19
Mersey, Rachel, 39
meta-capital, 29–30

Meyrowitz, Joshua, 38
Miami Herald, 143–4
Mojo Movement, 109–10
Moores, Shaun, 45, 54
Morley, David, 38
multimedia skills for journalism, 137–44
Murdoch, Rupert, 22, 95
Murdock, Graham, 21
Murrell, Colleen, 75

naming and shaming, 132–3
narrative appeal, 92–3
    archetypes, 93
    rites of passage, 105–6
    traditional news themes, 92–3, 105–7
National Newspaper Association (US), 61–2
Near You Now, 150
Nee, Rebecca Coates, 175
Nepal earthquake, 90
network society, 40
networking, 156–7
Neumann, Noelle, 89
Newby, Howard, 53
News Corporation, 22, 169
news industries
    organisation of, 5
    regulation of, 5
News Media Association (UK), 176
news production
    outsourcing, 170
    see also centralization of news-rooms; dispersion of newsrooms
news sources, 95–110
    crisis and disaster, 101–4
    events, 100–1
    ordinary people, 108–10
    public relations professionals, 99–100
    social media, 104–5
news values, 88–95
    diversity of, 88–9
newspapers, local *see* local newspapers
Next Door, 62
Nielsen, Rasmus Kleis, 9, 17, 109
Norbury, Niall, 157
Nord, David, 23
Nygren, Gunnar, 137–9

O'Connor, Catherine, 64, 109
O'Neill, Deirdre, 64, 92, 94, 95, 109
obituaries, 106
objectivity, 6, 86–7
    myth of, 85–8
    in public journalism, 118–19
Olivia magazine, 20
    MyOwnOlivia project, 20–1
Örnebring, Henrik, 179
Otago Daily Times, 77
owner-operator model, 10

Pacific Islands News Association, 79
Pacific Media Watch, 79
Pacnews, 79
Papoutsaki, Evangelia, 79, 80
parish pump, 84
Park, Robert, 10
participatory news, 178
    see also citizen journalism
Patch, 62, 94–5, 172, 173, 192
Paulussen, Steve, 82
Pauly, John, 44
Pavlik, John, 139
paywalls, 166–8
    social media and, 168–9
philanthropic funding of media, 182–3
Picard, Robert, 30–1, 147, 167
Pinski, Pamela, 156–7
place-based news, 6
place, 40, 47
    see also belonging; sense of place
Podber, Jacob, 73
Poh, Karen, 156, 157–8
Poindexter, Paula, 115, 116
political economy, 21–6
Powers, Elizabeth, 93
Powers, Matthew, 80
Prather, Waid, 151–2
precariousness, 55
Prentoulis, Marina, 144
Price, Vincent, 93
print news, 140–1
Prochazka, Fabian, 131
Project on Public Life and the Press, 115

propaganda model, 22
Propp, Vladimir, 92
Provincial China Project, 69
proximity, 39, 41, 57, 89–90, 144
    see also sense of place
public, 6
Public Insight Journalism, 180
public journalism, 61, 87, 112, 114,
    115–21, 190
    community responsibility, 150–4
    education in Australia, 117
    Japanese newspapers, 117
    as journalistic practice, 116, 117
    legitimacy of sources, 120
    motivation to perform, 120–1
    as multifaceted phenomenon,
        115
    objectivity in, 118–19
    power issues, 119–21
    public meetings, 118
    reporting positive enterprise stories,
        118
    United Kingdom, 118
    use of ordinary people, 18
    see also advocacy journalism
public relations
    as source of news, 96, 98–100
public sphere, 15–17
    see also local public sphere
Pulitzer Prize, 152
Putnam, Robert, 17, 113

radio journalism, 142–4
    immediacy of local radio, 142
    see also community radio
Radojković, Miroljub, 81
Reader, Bill, 27–8
readers
    relationship with community
        newspapers, 87
    see also audience
refugees, 59
Reich, Zvi, 97, 108
Richards, Ian, 113
Robie, David, 78, 79
Rosen, Jay, 115, 116, 177
Rosenberry, Jack, 3
Ruge, Mari Homboe, 85,
    88–95

Saleem, Noshina, 91
Salgado, Susana, 145
Schirato, Tony, 37
Schudson, Michael, 54, 86
Schultz, Ida, 31
Schweiger, Wolfgang, 131
scope, 41, 89–90, 144
sense of belonging, 6–7
sense of place, 6–7, 37, 45, 55–7, 180
sharing, 11
Shoemaker, Pamela, 39
Singer, Jane, 138, 178
Sissons, Helen, 99
situational geography, 38
Sjøvaag, Helle, 170
Smith, Adam, 21
Smyrnaios, Nikos, 82
social media, 21
    links with news media, 104–5
    paywalls and, 168–9
social pages, 94
social responsibility model, 10, 14–15,
    17
soft news, 92
solidarity
    mechanical, 52
    organic, 52
Song Yunya, 69
sources, *see* elite sources; news
    sources
space, 40
specificity, 191–3
spot.us, 181
Stamm, Keith, 3–4
Starkey, Guy, 142
state control of media
    China, 5, 24–5, 68
    grey zones, 68
    Vietnam, 5
State of the Media 2014 white paper
    (UK), 163
Steiner, Linda, 120
Strauss, Christine, 180
Strömbäck, Jesper, 145
subsidies, 172–6
    see also government funding for
        media
Sutherland shire, 7–8
symbolic capital, 49, 98–9

Tacchi, Jo, 72
talkback radio, 131
Tate, C. Dow, 130
Taylor, Sherri, 130
technological advances, 59
Television New Zealand, 77
terrorism, 59
Tewksbury, David, 93
third space, 177, 178–9
Thomas, James, 39
Thurman, Neil, 178
Thurman, Neil, 20
Tichenor, Philip, 98
time-space compression, 38
timeliness, 90–1
Townend, Judith, 64, 172
Tribune, 162–3
truth, 6
Tsfati, Yariv, 74
Tuan, Yi-Fu, 45
Tuchman, Gaye, 28
Tucker, Catherine, 166
Tumber, Howard, 144
Twitter, 104, 140, 149–50
  role in disasters, 102

Ukraine plane crash, 90
Ullah, Sahid, 71, 72
unexpected events, 94–5
urban ethnography movement, 3
US Society of Professional Journalists,
  151
user-generated content, 177–8

van Gelder, Tim, 158
van Vuuren, Kitty, 75

Vietnam
  state control of media, 5
Voakes, Paul, 117, 118
Voice Local, 166
Voltmer, Katrin, 82
volunteer news sources, 178

Wahl-Jorgensen, Karin, 64, 193
Warrnambool Standard, 171
Wasko, Janet, 21
Wasserman, Herman, 82
watchdog role, 17–18
Waugh, Evelyn, 190
WBEZ 9.5 Curious City, 20
Webb, Jen, 37
Weber, Patrick, 131
Williams, Andrew, 100
Williams, Ted, 166
Witschge, Tamara, 137–9
WLRNFM radio, 143–4
Wolf, John, 139
work practices, 23
  see also labour conditions
World Association of Newspapers,
  141–2

Xinhua news agency, 68

Yorkshire Evening Post, 141
YouTube, 21

Zahariadis, Nikolaos, 174, 175–6
Zapatista movement, 73;
Zeitlen, Janine, 133
Zelizer, Barbie, 27, 179, 191
Zuckerberg, Mark, 61, 168, 189

CPSIA information can be obtained
at www.ICGtesting.com
Printed in the USA
LVOW04*0014050117

519722LV00012BA/268/P

9 781137 504777